# London Calling New York New York

## By Peter Silverton

TROUSER PRESS
BOOKS

*London Calling New York New York* © 2025 the Estate of Peter Silverton.

All rights reserved. The right of Peter Silverton to be identified as the author of this work has been asserted by them in accordance with the Copyright, Designs and Patents Act 1988. No part of this publication may be reproduced, stored in a retrieval system, or transmitted in any form or by any means, electronic, mechanical, photocopying, recording or otherwise, without the prior permission of both the copyright owner and the publisher of this book.

First published in the United Kingdom in 2025 by Rocket 88,
an imprint of Essential Works Limited, 40 Bowling Green Lane,
London EC1R 0NE

This North American edition published 2025 by Trouser Press Books,
Brooklyn NY

LS261

Cover concept and illustration: Spike Silverton
Design: Kristina Juzaitis

ISBN 979-8-9898283-5-7
Library of Congress Control Number: 2024950478

www.rocket88books.com
www.trouserpressbooks.com
books@trouserpress.com

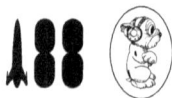

# Contents

Editor's note — 1

Author's note — 7

Introduction — 9

Chapter 1: My London Calling — 17

Chapter 2: "London Calling" — 33

Chapter 3: 1979 and All That — 95

Chapter 4: Frank Sinatra's "New York, New York" — 119

Chapter 5: London Calling New York New York — 193

# Editor's note

This book was in the works for a long time before Pete really got to grips with it. The idea first surfaced around the beginning of the century, when, intrigued by the origins of certain songs — "Staggerlee" being one — and investigating several, he realized that the Clash's "London Calling" and Frank Sinatra's recording of "New York, New York" had occurred at roughly the same time.

Not long after making that connection, he bumped into one of "London Calling"'s co-writers, an old, old friend from school: Joe Strummer. Pete describes that meeting in his introduction to this book, which is where he sets out why that realization was such a strange one for both of them.

That it took the best part of twenty years for Pete to write this book is due to many things, among them the paths that life and experience took him, as it does us all. Other books were published (an update to his *Essential Elvis* as well as *Filthy English: The How, Why, When and What of Everyday Swearing*), several magazine and newspaper features written and the family business was taken in hand in the way that only he could, helping to make Ready Steady Go the early-years school that everyone in Primrose Hill wanted to get their children into.

But the reason that Pete completed *London Calling New York New York* is because on October 10, 2020, life showed him the way along a different path. That Saturday morning, he collapsed at his daughter's home and was rushed to the intensive care unit at

University College Hospital in London. Eight days later, he was home from the hospital; while the medical experts worked out exactly what had happened, Pete wrote. Ever the observant, curious journalist, he wrote about the condition his condition was in — which, two weeks after his seizure, he discovered was a stage 4 glioblastoma. The stark news was that treatment seemed to not be in the cards, although the doctors said, "If he improves and becomes more lucid, then radiotherapy may be an option. The cancer is not, however, curable."

Later that day, his partner Jennifer sent out an e-mail to friends and family scattered around the world. As she wrote, "The consultant says this presentation is highly unusual, but we all know Pete is highly unusual."

That you now hold this book is proof of how unusual, unique and determined he was, because Pete did become lucid — after a few days during which he hallucinated inventively, as Jennifer described in another e-mail. "He talks almost non-stop (not a huge change there, some may say), mostly about the universe, God and infinity. He tells us he sees coloured lights and hears the hum of the universe in his head. That he is rebuilding himself from new, and that every cell in every person and everything is connected. Essentially, he appears to be on a very good acid trip." His neurologist later told Jennifer that Pete's "universe" trip was something called postictal psychosis — and rare in his experience, adding, "This is a fascinating story."

Of course, at the time we were all living a strange, semi-hallucinogenic existence with various Covid lockdowns and a government seemingly straight out of a dystopic novel, so for a few months following his initial seizure, Pete's observations on the state of his world didn't seem that odd. He grew stronger as chemotherapy and radiotherapy did their work, and he began to take slow walks around the neighborhood with family and close friends in attendance to make sure he didn't bump into anyone on his left-hand side — his sight in that eye was severely restricted by the tumor.

As he became used to the condition his condition was in, Pete wrote e-mails to friends and family with exactly that phrase — the parenthetical title to Mickey Newbury's 1967 psychedelic novelty hit for Kenny Rogers' First Edition, "Just Dropped In" — as the subject line. In most of them he let everyone know that he was "writing," alongside whatever new medical development there had been (if any). Mainly though, they were about writing. Not just this book, but also a fascinating series of essays on all manner of songs — from "Happy Birthday" to "YMCA," the Champions League anthem to "You'll Never Walk Alone" and many more. There's another manuscript, too, about funeral songs, which includes those he was contemplating to have played at his own. (That will hopefully be published in the not-too-distant future…)

The final manuscript of this book was completed a few months before Pete left us. During the two and a half years between diagnosis and his passing, he revealed parts of himself, his life and his last wishes in his writing. He did it with almost unbelievable humor at times, and with unbearable sadness at others. Although *London Calling New York New York* seems on the surface to be about two popular songs from two different cultures and with different meanings to each, in Pete's telling there are many more things to consider, among them (and illustrated with episodes from his own life and experience) nostalgia, mythmaking, family, crime, war, art, infidelity and propaganda. The narrative ranges across the Atlantic and over many decades, taking in the almost biological connection between the cities, the songs and their creators.

Not long after Pete let go of the manuscript for the book you now hold, he wondered if perhaps it might be published in New York by Trouser Press Books and in London by Rocket 88 Books. His unspoken reason being (we think) that *Trouser Press*, a music magazine co-founded by Ira Robbins, was the first publication to print Pete's journalism (a profile of pub rockers Ducks Deluxe; a long piece he submitted at the same time about the 101ers, fronted by Pete's old school chum Joe Strummer, was set aside until 2021, when they put it online). Now a flourishing book publisher owned and run by Ira, this publication brings Pete's professional writing career full circle.

And so it was that, on the day of Pete's funeral, May 26, 2023, the first sound heard as his coffin was carried into the chapel was that chopping guitar riff — which we all recognized as his mobile telephone ring, always answered before Joe Strummer's voice declared "London calling to the faraway towns…" Only this time, the song played all the way through. Pete was no longer there to take our call.

**Peter Grant Silverton**
11/18/1952 – 5/15/2023

Peter Silverton, circa 1978

# Author's note

This is a story about two songs and the cities they came to represent, those songs' writers, the two cities' many other emblematic songs (and *their* writers) and the two metropolitan cultures: their differences and their similarities.

It's also a personal story: mine. It reaches back to my decades-long light friendship with Joe Strummer, my presence at several significant early performances of "London Calling" — and at Joe's West London cremation in December 2002.

That story is entangled in "New York, New York," too.

I wasn't born in London, but my life, from childhood to grandparenthood, has almost always been based in the city. I'm definitely not a New Yorker, but my writing was first professionally published there. I'm both a citizen of London and as at home in New York as someone who's spent as much time — work, family, play — there as I have.

Many years ago, there was a TV show called *NY-LON*, and it was my original idea for this book's title, but it turned out to be a clodhopper of a transatlantic rom-com which far from did justice to the musical, personal and cultural dance between the two cities that I was looking to chase down and bring to life.

# Introduction

"No, no, no," said Joe Strummer when I told him that the Clash's "London Calling" and Frank Sinatra's "New York, New York" are the same age. It's a fact that seems impossible to believe, but it's a fact, nonetheless. The two recordings are almost exactly the same age. Their birthdays are mere weeks apart.

Joe and I were in a pub in Primrose Hill sometime in the late 20th century, no more than a fifteen-minute walk from the bench on the Regent's Park boating lake island where his older brother David was found in the summer of 1970 — suicide by a hundred tablets of aspirin. That was around the time Joe and I first met, as wayward teenagers, back when John Mellor (the name on his birth certificate) was known as Woody — after Bob Dylan's mentor, Woody Guthrie — and long before he changed it again, to Joe, in 1976.

Ours was a friendship which persisted, loosely, through the subsequent three decades. We shared psychedelic experiments (one featuring a middle-of-the-night police raid) in the late '60s. In the mid-'70s, I became a devout follower — stalker, almost — of his first notable band, the 101ers, who took their name from the house number of a West London squat. My girlfriend of the time was half in love with him. A poetry lover from rural Essex, she found in him a quintessence of the rough-textured big city glamour she so craved. He had that effect on women right to the end; ask his wives and girlfriends. Little did my partner know that, like her, he was profoundly shaped by the final tremblings of the British Empire.

In his case, a peripatetic childhood of the BBC World Service and second-rank embassies. In hers, a family interned in Japanese camps from 1942 until the end of the war.

In the summer of 1976, Joe and I saw the Sex Pistols *and* the Rolling Stones together. (Joe waved at Bill Wyman, and Bill waved back.) The following year, a word from Joe got me my first proper writing job. In the late '70s, I spent time with him in recording studios in London (though *not* when he was working on "London Calling") and in New York, where he and fellow Clash member Mick Jones passed a long night slowly working out a rhyme for "London town." A few months later, in Paris, we found ourselves in something of a riot at a Clash show organized by the French Communist Party.

Our later meetings were sometimes professional but more often random — like this pub encounter, which was the last time we saw each other before his death in December 2002.

He was looking for a member of Primal Scream who he knew drank in that pub. As ever, Joe wasn't alone. He always had something of an entourage with him. That evening, it was a bristly teenage skinhead, a fan who clearly — in his own mind, anyway — had appointed himself Joe's bodyguard for the night.

Joe had a boombox with him. He'd always compiled and decorated cassettes, for himself and for others; I've still got one somewhere. The cassette in his boombox that night was a collection of his latest passion, 1970s Venezuelan music — the kind of music he played on *Joe Strummer's London Calling,* his BBC World Service radio program, which aired in the three years prior to his death.

The tape played as we sat and talked — loud enough to hear, not quite loud enough to draw complaints. There were no complaints either about the weed Joe was (illegally) smoking. He had that kind of effect on people. A force field of charm which enabled him to — just about — get away with all kinds of bad behavior, as both his wives and most of his work colleagues/comrades would confirm.

When I told Joe about the temporal link between "London

Calling" and Sinatra's "New York, New York," he cradled his head in his hands theatrically, laughingly seriously. "How could that be? How could that be?"

But it is.

Both songs were recorded in the late summer of 1979. As Joe was singing "London Calling" in a North London studio, so more or less was Frank Sinatra singing "New York, New York" in a Los Angeles studio. Even as I type that sentence, even as I know it's true, I'm not sure I believe it. It's not just that they're two very different songs, or even that they present two very different ideas of what constitutes a song, with quite distinct expectations of the listener. It's more than that. The fact is that "London Calling" and "New York, New York" come from different worlds. They belong to different generations — with different views of modern life. Sinatra's is a show tune, rooted in the precision and elegance of mid-20th-century urbanity. "My parents' music," in the words of Barry Myers, who did a two-year stint as DJ for the Clash in their "London Calling" years. (He's just out of the shot on the *London Calling* album cover.) The Clash song is, for want of a better phrase, rock and roll.

Their differences go beyond the simply musical. "New York, New York" is buoyant and striving. "London Calling" is raw and dystopic. The two songs embody and represent notably different ideas of urbanism: about what cities promise and offer their citizens; about their thrills and threats, blandishments and temptations. Frank's is a city of achievement and aspiration, of nightclubs and tuxedos. Joe's is a city of loss and fear, of rising waters, nuclear horror and heroin addiction. "New York, New York" is a hymn to individualism; "London Calling" comes from the other side of the cultural battlefront. It always sounded, however spuriously, ideological, a war chant of democracy and collectivism, of street-level opposition to the ever-rising tide of neoliberalism's global hegemony.

Still, there are also likenesses — maybe even a kind of brotherhood — beneath all that dissimilarity. The two songs came to life at a time when both cities were in particularly bad shape. (The state of late-'70s New York and London — and the general view of them — was caught in a contemporary cartoon. Set in a rural idyll, with a distant view of a metropolis, it featured two rats, with one saying to the other: "I hear the streets are paved with garbage.")

Both songs are as much speeches as they are songs. Both are dramatic and self-dramatizing, which is why they could (and have) become local anthems — "New York, New York" semi-officially, "London Calling" by popular acclamation. And it's why both songs took on lives of their own, beyond their creators' control.

Each became a symbol for its city: easy source material for headline writers and aural equivalents of the visual shorthand of the Manhattan skyscraper and London's red double-decker buses. When the American sitcom *Friends* visited London, the Clash song welcomed them on the soundtrack. When the New York Yankees win a home game, it's Frank's song that plays.

The songs achieved that symbolic status by parallel routes, too, via the political struggles of the 1980s, a time of principles and ideals — or, if you like, of doctrines and ideological theatricality. Both songs became rallying cries of that decade, emblematic anthems for the two opposing armies in its cultural and political battles. Reaganomics vs. anti-capitalism.

In the right corner: Thatcherism, Porsches, striped shirts and "New York, New York." In the left corner: poll tax riots, keffiyehs in Knightsbridge, No Nukes T-shirts and "London Calling." Or, in traditional British political terms: the red of radicalism vs. the blue of conservatism (color-switched in the modern U.S. to the red of Republicanism vs. the blue of the Democrats and progressivism).

Yet the two songs have also had wider, more diffuse impacts — less politicized ones which don't so much forget their parentage as just pay blithe inattention to it. "London Calling" was taken as the title of a quarterly report on British agriculture published by the British branch of the U.S. Department of Agriculture and, in time, used as the soundtrack of a Jaguar car advertisement. "New York, New York" is the name of a small chain of Asian hot dog and burger joints headquartered in Singapore, as well as a hotel–casino in Las Vegas. Things are rarely simple with songs that tunnel their way deep into our emotions.

The affinity — brotherhood, even — between the two songs reflects the actual relationship between the two cities. As the world's financial and trading capitals, they are linked (and sometimes separated) by language and the Atlantic Ocean. As one city breathes in, the other breathes out.

There is kinship in their genesis, too. Both songs were written in anger. "London Calling" is a clear rage against the world and its boss classes. Less obviously, the birth of "New York, New York" was powered by the righteous fury of its writers against *their* bosses — the ones who commissioned the song and rejected their first attempt at it. "London Calling" tells us the world is a bad, bad place. "New York, New York" tells us, "That'll show them, those bastards won't drive us down."

Both the similarities and the differences are there in the titles. Both phrases are as much mythic as actual — and were made even more so by these songs. Both titles are simple, bold statements taken from the fine detail of their city's administrative arrangements. For New York, its postal address. For London, a historic radio call sign.

Yet each song starts from a very different place and looks in a quite different direction. This is clear from the very first notes. Both begin with a simple little musical figure. For "New York, New York," it's an uncertain stumble of a phrase which introduces the song tentatively and gets bigger, bolder, brassier as it goes along. It's a class-of-a-generation intro: once heard, forever remembered, the kind of musical moment that even the best composers write — or find — no more than a few times in their lives.

There's something odd about its initial appearance, though. It questions the very words and emotions of the song it introduces. That hesitancy is pretty much a commentary on what follows — on the singer, too, maybe. It's the worldly grownup in a not entirely grown-up song: a little vamp that questions, enriches and deepens the coarse hunger of the song's ambition. It's the skeptical slave of legend whispering in the ear of a triumphant Roman general, "Are you sure? Do you really believe all that praise the crowd is shouting at you? Do you think you'll be on top of the world forever? Don't you have any self-awareness?"

"London Calling" starts — no, kicks off, that's more like it — with repeated chords, the classic form for a rock riff (and Beethoven's 5th Symphony). In this case, the chords are E minor and F major, in a sequence which repeats over and over. Unrelenting, unforgiving, almost martial. Not so much riff as repetition compulsion. It aches for release — musical or emotional — but that release doesn't come. The guitar-led phrase goes again and again and again until it finally — even later than you expect, maybe even later than the music itself expects — decides to let the song begin. It's an intro that stretches the rules of pop — where you rarely need to wait more than a bar or two before the singer starts singing.

When the words of "London Calling" do finally arrive, though, they are unequivocal, a simple statement of intent: the song title is barked out. So, that longed-for relief at last? No, not really. Which is the point — this is not a song of relief. It's a chant of stoicism.

What is actually going on there, musically? How can something so repetitive also be so unsettling? I asked someone far more knowledgeable than me about such things: Florian Lunaire, a wonderful pianist, arranger and composer.

"The opening chords to 'London Calling,'" he told me, "have the same foreboding quality as 'The Imperial March' in *Star Wars* by John Williams — which, in turn, was heavily 'borrowed' from Gustav Holst's 'Mars.' Mick Jones plays a constant E minor throughout the intro. Strummer's guitar (lower in the mix) plays an E minor at first, then a second, mysterious and much-argued-about-online chord. What's certain is that during the first half of the sequence, the two guitars are in unison. In the second half, we have an E minor in one ear and a C or F or something else in the other — which is super discordant and a central element of the menacing tension that never seems to resolve. Towards the end of the intro, there's also an overdubbed guitar playing a single D that adds to the dissonance and leads us into the first verse." (I've also seen a description of the central chord as Fmaj9#11 — pick the notes out of *that* one if you can.)

Both songs give great prominence to their titles. "London Calling" are the song's first words. "New York, New York" are the last words of five choruses and the first of another. Both titles are four syllables long and both break into a pair of two-syllable halves. One pairing ("New York, New York") is a direct repeat. The other ("London Calling") just sounds like it might be — particularly as formed in the mouth of Joe Strummer, whose dental problems were long-standing and expensive to resolve.

"The very name London has tonnage in it," wrote V.S. Pritchett in *A Cab at the Door*, his luminous 1968 memoir of an early 20th-century Thameside childhood. "The two syllables are two thumps of the steam hammer, the slow clump-clump of a policeman's feet … or the sound of coal thundering down the holes in the pavements of Victorian terraces." Almost exactly the rhythm and sound of the city in the Clash's "London Calling."

But, oh, how differently those two titles are sung. "New York, New York" rises. Duh-dah! Duh-dah! Bullish and sanguine, stepping confidently into the future (even if there is that life-hardened self-doubt tucked away in the stumble of the introductory vamp). "London Calling," by contrast, is flat, barely accented, with just a little rise at the end of the phrase. Duh-duh-duh-dah! Both are shouts, almost. But you try singing (or shouting) either one to the other's rhythm. You can't.

# 1  My London Calling

*"Culture, we all know, is made by its cities."*
—DEREK WALCOTT NOBEL SPEECH (1992)

Both "London Calling" and "New York, New York" are songs set deep in their particular cultures with distinct identities and notions of citizenship. So, what about me? How do I self-identify?

Once upon a bad time, I was woken up in an emergency care ward in a world-renowned central London teaching hospital. I remember being told two things. First, my diagnosis was extremely serious (terminal, in fact — though I'm still here, and writing this, more than two years on). Second, I was "Irish." At least I was according to their records. But I'm not "Oirish." True, I've got Irish DNA heritage, via both parents — unlike, say, President Biden, who once gave the brushoff to a BBC reporter on the grounds that he was Irish. He meant "Irish," of course, that specious admixture of romanticism and self-promoting cynicism that you see in bar signs all over the world, from Thai brothel bars to Manhattan's midtown and London's Camden Town.

That kind of "Irish" I'm not. I have never lived in the country. I didn't even visit the place till I was pushing twenty. Over the decades, I have spoken more Polish and Portuguese than I have "the Gaelic," as I learned to call the Irish language. Any tentative claim to Irish identity would have to rest on just two things: having been raised

Irish Catholic and reading widely and deeply into Ireland's literature. But I greatly doubt that either of those two factors showed up as markers on any of the numerous blood and biochemical tests or brain scans which various hospitals did on me.

So, how do I identify? Of which nation or cultural groupings am I a self-acknowledged member? Now, there's a question. Identity is such a slippery thing. Often, it's an exile looking for a home. Think of James Joyce, an archetypal Dubliner exiled in Trieste, where he created a perfectly shaped and shined dream-memory of the city left behind and which he set on the day he lost his sexual innocence to a country girl. With her uncultured help, he passed joyously (Joyce-fully?) through one of those life-doors you can never walk through twice. Your "identity," however, can be set and reset as often as you like — or can get away with.

In time, Joyce's sensual encounter became not just a central moment in the formation of his novel *Ulysses* and, inevitably, his "identity," both public and private, but also a day of annual celebration, featuring communal commemorative walking, mostly touristically, around Dublin. A hand job in a linen closet from a hotel chambermaid who you will soon marry and love profoundly till your death, twenty-five years later, in the bourgeois stolidity and isolation of Switzerland, neutral in a time of global war? Now there's a moment which a minor metropolis can take and use as a brick for its sense of self, particularly one mythologized as Strumpet City. But not so apt maybe for places that like to boast of themselves as the Big Smoke and the Big Apple.

So, back to my identity: what are the bricks I built it from and what sort of citizen am I?

When asked, by an official form, to state my nationality, ethnicity and/or religious beliefs, I like to write "Jewish-ish (by marriage) Irish Catholic atheist north Londoner." (I also try to add "and typical of the sort," but there's rarely space.) So, I usually settle for "Londoner." Or, if I can get away with it, "North Londoner." If the significance of that compass point adjective eludes you, ask a Londoner, any Londoner — north, south, east, west. Each will have their own view of their city's northern reaches.

What marks out a North Londoner from other kinds of Londoners? How might you spot one at a party or on the street? Well, there's no traditional or folk dress. Citizens of Munich may still express and affirm their provincial urbanity by wearing collarless jackets and peasanty, flowery frocks — *lederhosen*, even. But there's no North Londoner equivalent. A distinct North London accent? Not really. It's mostly just a bog-standard London accent, but perhaps a little less pronounced. Like mine, for example? I guess so. Nor are there any defining foodstuffs or verbal shibboleths I can think of. Though, as a North Londoner — and typical of the sort — I am always open to an argument. Even one proposed by a South Londoner. In fact, I would add that open-mindedness is something of a North London characteristic. But then, as a North Londoner, I would say that, wouldn't I?

In October 2016, British Prime Minister Theresa May made the silliest of many silly speeches made in the run-up to Brexit. The vicar's daughter from Berkshire (yes, I guess that is a typically North London sneer) told the Conservative Party — *her* Conservative Party — that anyone who believed they were a citizen of the world was actually a citizen of nowhere. As a lifelong citizen of North London — and, remember, typical of the sort — I took that personally. I reckon most citizens of North London did. North Londoners are not, by and large, stupid enough to think they are citizens of the world. They also know that all boundaries are always essentially imaginary: fictions, confections, ways of marking out others, separating us from them. The security blanket of anxious — or aggressive — adulthood.

Not that North Londoners don't have a sense of place. But it's a barrier-, toll- and passport-free one which the world is welcome to pop into and stay for a bit. Or, like me, hang around for a lifetime. It looks out — and calls out — to that globe of faraway towns and places. New York. Paris. Addis Ababa. (Berkshire, even.) And it's true that we North Londoners do tend to think the world is our lobster — to steal the comic line written, in North London, for a fictional semi-criminal West Londoner (Arthur Daley, of *Minder*), by someone I was delighted to know fairly well, Leon Griffiths, a Jewish Glaswegian named for a leader of the Russian Revolution who was assassinated in his Mexico City office, which I visited on the way back from my elder son's wedding. (How North London is that associative chain?)

So, is there any distinctive cultural marker of North Londonerdom? Frankly, the only major cultural bind I can think of is Arsenal football club — their stadium was a fifteen-minute walk away from my childhood. On the other hand, if that home had been a little further north, then I'd have grown up in the land of Tottenham Hotspur, "that lot up the road" to Arsenal supporters. Enemy territory, that is. Yes, I do know how silly that sounds. And, yes, I do mean it jokingly — though others wouldn't. Citizenship always has an element of the performative about it.

How did I establish my North London citizenship? By chance and over many years. Not that my story is exceptional or even special. It's just that it's mine. And here's how it began. I think.

I can't prove it — family secrets so often get buried along with the bodies — but my best guess is that I first visited London tucked away in my mother's belly on a southbound train from Liverpool. She was one of that mid-20th-century generation of young women who wanted to dive into life's erotic promises but lacked the technical knowledge needed to prevent the likely outcome — in her case, me. (It was a large cohort. My wife has three cousins with very similar nativity stories.)

On the last leg of the journey, my mother's train would have ducked under Abbey Road (a decade before those other Liverpudlian émigrés, the Beatles, started work in its famous studios) and steamed within 300 feet of the house in which I have lived since my own first child — that elder son who got married in Mexico — was born.

My formal arrival in the city came sometime later, shortly before Christmas 1952. I was six weeks old, and I've never really left the place since, certainly not emotionally. I've moved around and about.

I even lived in South London for a bit. Yet, decades later, I live no more than four miles west along the A502 from the spot where I first glimpsed the city into which I had been adopted — and which I would, in turn, adopt and embrace.

I arrived, cradled in the arms of my new mother, on a number 73 bus. She was Mary Mildred, known as Mickey, an immigrant from the turfy boglands of Ireland's County Laois. Her mother, my grandmother, worked as a servant to nuns. You can't fall much further than that. Little wonder then that the prime focus of her Catholic belief was an oft-repeated faith in the powers of St. Anthony, patron saint of lost things. (At least some of which were then found. Me, for a start.) My new father was Alfred, son of Ettie, a barmaid, and Alfred, son of Alfred, a farrier, and stepson of a third Alfred — who was a coal-heaver, drinker and wife-basher (who, thankfully, I never met). My father was a Bow man, born within the sound of that parish's church bells and therefore a genuine Cockney. Not that he ever made anything of that ancestry.

Yes, I really did arrive in the city of my life on an actual red London Transport double-decker bus. How London is that? Was I on the top deck, with the smokers? Possibly, as both my parents smoked, a lot. More likely, I was in the downstairs cabin, under the care and control of a "clippie" checking tickets and reminding her passengers to "Hold very tight, please."

I had been collected from a nursing home twenty miles to the southwest — well beyond the broadest definition of the city's boundaries. In those days, the 73 bus ran all the way from the leafy, Thameside suburb of Richmond to the bit of London where its east becomes its north, the borderland where [the postal code] E5 abuts and turns into N16. We got off at the route's final stop, on Northwold Road, by Stoke Newington Common.

As a kind of early Christmas present, I was taken to my adoptive father's mother's house to meet my new family. Pretty much all the family — both sets of grandparents, aunts, uncles, cousins, in-laws, the whole lot — lived within a half-mile of the stop. (Not that I knew it for many years, but some of my future wife's cousins — Jewish, secular — lived a short walk away. Not just the odd cousin, either, but two whole families of them, both in the same street.) Within walking distance was the war memorial on which my new father's father's name was inscribed in small gold capital letters. After years in the trenches of WW I, he had died in the flu pandemic, two days after the November 1918 armistice — though I would not learn about that war memorial for half a century, when my younger son discovered it by chance.

My parents had taken a flat — well, a room and a bit — in Stamford Hill. In time, London's mod culture would have its first flowering there, along with the first fully automatic ten-pin bowling alley in Europe. But that was a decade off in the future. When I arrived on that number 73 bus, it was to a bashed-around bit of London, just starting to recover from six years of war. Bomb sites were everywhere, and we children played in them.

It was a neighborhood of immigrants and exiles from, variously, Hitler, Ireland, pogroms and Luftwaffe raids. A home away from home for Jewish socialist tailors and Irish Catholics like my bog-born grandmother — who always had a box of matzo crackers in her kitchen, along with cabbage, potatoes and "a nice bit of (boiled) bacon."

Milk and bread were delivered every morning by horse and cart. We younger children chased after it, trying and failing to haul ourselves up for a short clippety-clop to the end of the road. One older boy scooped the horse droppings into a bucket and sold them to rose gardeners — an early and memorable lesson in economics. (If I were you, I'm not sure I'd believe that story, but it's true. Decades later, I found it confirmed in the actual delivery man's memoir, commissioned and issued by a local community publisher.)

Since the end of the war, native fascist Sir Oswald Mosley and his thugs had launched regular attacks on Jewish stall-holders in nearby Ridley Road market. Yes, that really did happen in the wake of victory over the Nazis and the ever-emerging truths of the Holocaust, as seen by many Londoners in the determinedly graphic newsreels shown at cinemas. By the time of my arrival, however, counterattacks by the 43 Group of ex-servicemen, mostly Jewish, had effectively dealt with the Mosleyites. It was also the time of Israel's struggle to establish itself as a state — in all, 141 British troops were killed and many more injured by Jewish "insurgents" — or, from the other end of the telescope, "terrorists." Which was, of course, one of the justifications the Mosleyites gave for their attacks.

Something else I didn't know for many, many years was that future mischief-maker and Sex Pistols "manager" Malcolm McLaren was growing up nearby, on the western side of the road the Romans called Ermine Street — now the A10 on national maps, Stoke Newington High Street in the *A-Z* and "the high road" to us. (It was at a cinema on that road that I saw Bambi's mother shot and killed. I was shocked but not traumatized. McLaren titled his unfinished 1977 Pistols film *Who Killed Bambi?* Perhaps he saw the film at the same cinema and *was* traumatized.) Also living in the area was the future (male) reggae writer Penny Reel — again, Jewish — who took his pen name from a Jamaican chant. In his memories, recorded for the local museum, Penny remembered our joint-but-separate post-war Stoke Newington as thirty-percent Jewish with the odd Irish Catholic. From my eastside perspective, the demographic balance was pretty much the reverse.

Mine was an Irish and Catholic world with only the occasional romantic nod to Anglicanism. It was never "Oirish," though there was the raucous charm of fiddle, accordion and folk song whenever a Saturday night family gathering came together. For the women, there was gin (mostly diluted with bitter lemon, a sweet fizzy "mixer" then only available in tiny bottles from pubs and liquor stores, not corner shops or their new competitors, supermarkets.) For the men, there were pint bottles of frothy, yellowy-headed Guinness. But there was no Irish dancing or boozy dance halls as there were in other Irish parts of London — Kilburn, say. St. Patrick's Day involved nothing more elaborate than a shamrock from Ireland and my grandmother heading off to early mass.

As a teenager, I gave myself a sense of specialness by identifying as Irish for a while — inspired partly by my grandmother's romantic memories of pre-WW I Dublin and partly by my romantic reveries of James Joyce and my ambition to become, like him, if in the smallest imaginable way, a playboy of the western word. Then a summer in Ireland made me realize just how English I was. How North London, even.

I arrived in London as one more recent-born addition to the city's ever-growing stock of post-WW II Irish immigrants — a Liverpool-Irish bastard conceived, illicitly, in a Dublin flat or perhaps in a Liverpool suburb. Not that I ever felt illegitimate; enough good-enough mothering and fathering, I guess. My adoptive parents were kind, loving and supportive, if flummoxed by a baby who threw up constantly for his first year of life and was a little precious, certainly by Stoke Newington standards of the day.

The name on my birth certificate was Michael Moylan. How Irish is that? Within six months, I had a new name, a reinvention of self for a new life in a new city. How London is that? I now had an apostle's first name — a boy of rock in a city of clay. And, to go with it, a surname that sounded Jewish (to non-Jews anyway) but wasn't.

Neither of my grandmothers, with whom I spent many hours and days as a young child, was fully literate. Both were born, in deep poverty, in the 19th century. My father's mother was as round as a potato and not much bigger. She lived in a tiny house with an outdoor toilet, an Anderson air-raid shelter in the backyard and a bomb site where the house next door used to stand. Rather than the other way around, she loved getting me to read my first storybooks to her. The micro-sentences of Peter and Jane's simple, even simplistic, adventures were enthralling to her — and I was the spell-weaver. She did, however, have me playing a decent game of cribbage with her by the age of six or seven — ha'penny a hand, I think. Maybe a penny.

My parents were smart and energetic people — fluent readers and writers — but unworldly, unacademic and scantily educated. My father left school at fourteen, as you generally did in that part of London back then. My mother, in the depths of the Irish countryside just twenty-five miles west of Dublin (but it might as well have been a million), started work at thirteen. Her stepfather was a Cork man in a flat cap who looked just like Wilfrid Brambell, the actor who played both old man Steptoe in the classic British TV sitcom of the era, *Steptoe and Son* (the template for America's *Sanford and Son*), and Paul McCartney's "very clean old man" of a grandfather in *A Hard Day's Night*. My grandad, a builder, worked on clearing bomb-damaged houses during the Blitz. I was told as a young child, possibly too young, that he never really recovered from the sights he saw. Even now I remember a story about a dead baby alone in a room.

Yet I found myself in a glorious, gritty, hubble-bubble of language, surrounded by the incessantness of what must surely be the two gabbiest cultures in the world, Irish and Jewish: a delicious mixture of Irish garrulousness, with its "Jaysus, Mary and Joseph," of irony-heavy Yiddish inflections and speech rhythms plus a schmuttering of actual Yiddish words, of music hall lyrics and their double entendre as folk song, of *Daily Mirror* headlines on the breakfast table and rhyming slang as standard speech. Not that I knew it was rhyming slang. I was in long trousers (and studying Latin) before I discovered that "butchers" was not just a synonym for "look" but a truncated rhyme ("butcher's hook"). From such stuff are communities made. Or at least imagined into a kind of reality. Of identity, confused, and all the better for it. Mongrel city. And a home, for life.

There were, of course, other things I didn't know — couldn't have known — at the time of my arrival. For example, within steps of that number 73 bus stop, at 25 Stoke Newington Common, lived a five-year-old boy called Mark Feld, Marky to his friends, of which I wasn't one. We never even met but he would become one of the lead instigators of that Stamford Hill mod moment and, like me (if far more spectacularly), make his way into the wider world with a new name — Marc Bolan in his case.

A child's walk away was the real square on which the central focus of the future BBC TV soap *EastEnders* was based. It looks just the same, almost worryingly so, as its fictional self, although there are no shops, no Dot's launderette, no pub at all, let alone the TV show's Queen Vic pub.

My uncle Paul — my mother's half-brother, by her mother's second, bigamous, marriage, to that man from Cork — would, in time, turn a good penny or two building mikvahs (ritual baths for Orthodox Jews), spending a good bit of it on increasingly smart cars, peaking with an Aston Martin whose life ended after a red double-decker bus bashed into it in Trafalgar Square — not a number 73, so far as I recall. Paul's son (also Paul and four years my junior) would grow up to run London's first 24-hour bagel bakery. As a teenager, his best friend was John Beverley — soon to be better known to the world as Sid Vicious. Hence the future Sex Pistols bassist's unexpected arrival at my twenty-first birthday party, three years before he became punk's emblematic figure of self-hatred and replaced my friend Glen Matlock in the band.

In October 1967, infamous East End gangsters Ronnie and Reggie Kray killed Jack "The Hat" McVitie next door to my grandmother's house, in the flat of the woman known to the court as "Blonde Carol." The link to my Nana Hendrick was slender — she was merely a rent-collector for the absentee landlord. Like I said, mongrel city.

In 1971, at the zenith of Marc Bolan's career (*Electric Warrior* was the top-selling UK album of the year), the police raided a flat just down the road and around the corner from my Nana's. They were after the Angry Brigade, a homegrown anarcho-leftist grouplet which had been running a small-scale terrorist campaign for several years, sending letter bombs to Tory politicians, mostly — twenty-five in all, but no deaths and just one minor injury. Publicity-savvy, the Angries (as they were known in countercultural circles) issued communiques, which were duly published in the alternative press. Communique #8 unwittingly presaged the Clash's conviction that boredom was a driver of revolution: "Life is so boring there is nothing to do except spend all our wages on the latest skirt or shirt," it pronounced. "You can't reform profit capitalism. Just kick it till it breaks."

The police found three guns, several dozen rounds of ammunition, thirty-three sticks of gelignite and a list of home addresses for Members of Parliament in the cell's top-floor flat — which was merely minutes' walk from both Bolan's childhood home and the then-residence of the fourteen-year-old who would, all too soon, become Sid Vicious. (My grandmother collected the rent from Sid's mum Anne Beverley, too.) Ah, pop music.

The year of that raid was also the summer that the British government introduced internment in Northern Ireland. Not that the Stoke Newington Irish seemed to care much, if at all. There were certainly no riots, marches, demonstrations or even posters.

I knew nothing of this at the time. I was away, in southern Europe. Briefly, I stayed in the Athens apartment of a woman who had been interned — and maybe tortured — by Greece's neo-fascist regime of "the Colonels." There was an episodic police watch on the apartment. So, I was not blind or unsympathetic to the Angry Brigade's politics and passions. And, in retrospect, the decade had clearly started as it meant to continue, plotting a clear, if tangled, line which led from Stoke Newington's Angries to the Clash's "London Calling."

In all, eight of those arrested at Amhurst Road and other addresses went to trial, which became one of the longest in British legal history. Mostly, they were recent university graduates, swept along by the *jouissance*, to use a contemporarily fashionable Lacanian term, of post-1968 radical politics, as was Malcolm McLaren (soon to be a legendary recent alumnus known as "Red Malcolm" at my South London college). In the radical, grandiloquent argot of the day, the accused self-identified as the Stoke Newington Eight. Their defense was, essentially, that it was a politically motivated trial — a police frame (far from rare at the time) and that the munitions had been planted (again, a not uncommon police tactic of the day). Four were given ten-year prison sentences. Others were acquitted, including a woman who later became a lecturer at the London School of Economics, a leading figure in the New Labour administration, deputy leader of Camden Council and long-time director of the LGBTQ pressure group Stonewall. In 2007, she was made a Commander of the British Empire — an award she would have accepted from the Queen at Buckingham Palace. For more than a decade now, she has been a local councillor close to where I live. We may even be members of the same constituency party. Oh, politics. (It seems unfair — judgmental even — but I do find myself thinking of some lines from "Death or Glory," a track on the *London Calling* album, reckoning, metaphorically, that a man who has sex with nuns will eventually embrace religion.) Some years ago, I found myself in the building which was home to the Angries. By then, it was an African club. We drank Nigerian Guinness, a super-strength "export" version of the Irish original loved by my grandfather and his friends. In summer 2022, flats in Amhurst Road were fetching an average of £555,330. Oh, fifty years.

In the December of my arrival in London, the city had been visited by the most epically dense fog — or smog, rather, as such pollution-driven weather events came to be known. The pea-souper of all pea-soupers, it crept in yellowy billowings along roads and into buildings — onto buses, even. The whole of inner London disappeared into it. The city that has called itself — not without a little boasting — "the big smoke" was unable to see itself. Yet London, always a rough old place, could have recognized itself in the dense, sooty fog's yellow clouds, seeing a painfully true reflection of its own ills and evils in the industrialized perversion of the once innocent but long-ago poisoned early morning river basin mists that crept up from the Thames.

It was the worst air pollution episode in London's history. Thousands died. An initial government estimate of 4,000 deaths was later raised to 10–12,000. In time, that murderous December fog would prompt the Clean Air Act of 1956, one of the first major moments of environmental awareness and action.

Coincidentally, my family left London for the countryside that year and I wouldn't return to London — except for visits, regular ones, to grandparents, Arsenal and other metropolitan delights — till I started university, in the city's southeast. Since then, I've never stopped living in London — currently, and for many years, in a house scarred by the shock wave from a V-I "flying bomb," one of the last to land on the city, in late 1944. (Not that it's easy to spot the damage. Even war's deep wounds eventually heal.)

No irony then — well, only a little — that my best-beloved token of London is a terra cotta roof tile, blackened with smoke on one side. It's the object I would take with me if — irony again — my home was on fire. It's the size of a large playing card and as thick — or, rather, as thin — as a 1970s London sandwich. It's made of clay — the wet, sticky stuff beneath London's feet and streets which was dug up, pressed into shape, baked hard and used to build the city. London clay is a seabed deposit from a time that predates humanity. It contains the remains of tropical plants and creatures that were swept out to sea. (You'll find the odd bit of prehistoric crocodile in there if you look hard.)

As long as it remains underground, London clay is blue. Only after firing does it turn into its distinctive self — the defining mottled biscuity yellow of the city's housing stock. Associating terra cotta with the Mediterranean, I long thought my tile was some kind of import. But, no, I'm assured that it's a genuine local, from a terra cotta layer beneath Londoners' feet. I was assured of that by my friend Duncan Hooson, born and raised in the Potteries town of Stoke and now a senior lecturer in ceramics at Central St. Martins of London's University of the Arts.

The smoke on the tile is old, very old. Hundreds of years old. I know the location of the house it roofed, and I know the day — the hour, even — that its oh-so-London layer of black soot was laid down. It was September 2, 1666, a Sunday. At some time after 2:00 a.m. that night, the Great Fire of London swept through, in the wake of a lengthy drought. (It was not a good time for London. England was at war with the Dutch; damaged ships were still making their way back from an indecisive naval engagement the previous day. Tall tales of a Messiah from the east were sweeping through the city, along with the gale from Kent which turbo-powered the Great Fire.)

On Monday morning, Samuel Pepys, the now-famous diarist, inspected his city, then on the brink of becoming the richest and most powerful place in the world. He found that 300 houses had burned away to nothing, along with half of London Bridge. (The accepted final total of houses lost to the Great Fire is now 13,200.) He also noted the departure of the plague which had eaten away at the city and its citizens for the previous two years, killing 50,000. Pepys himself was beset by nightmares, and his wife fell victim to what would now be diagnosed as PTSD because of it. Though only six people seem to have died in the Great Fire, foreigners were beaten up in the street, falsely accused of starting it.

My tile is from the last house on Botolph Street, which runs down to the River Thames. The fire melted the nails which held the roof tiles in place, and they shot into the river. For centuries, the tiles stayed in place on the river's edge, pulled back and forth by the tides, but always returning home. I found my tile in the early 21st century, at the point where it would have dropped into the Thames in September 1666. I was guided to it by Mike Webber, a freelance community archaeologist with links to the Museum of London. He's the world expert on the Thames foreshore. I wouldn't have dared pick it up and take it home without his express permission.

A small slab of clay, cooked and hardened, battered and pitted, a beaten-up tile with a layer of soot on it. How downbeat is that as a personal treasure of your home city? And how so very London. Others, even non-Londoners, understand my attachment to a smoky old domestic roof tile. (Which is why I've had to persuade some of them not to steal it.)

"Bad weather, coal fires and good society in a crowded city." These were the reasons given by Sydney Smith, an 18th-century Anglican cleric, for preferring London to his Hampshire parish. In death and eternity, he got his wish. He was buried in Kensal Green cemetery — where he was later joined by, among many others, the South London playwright Sir Terence Rattigan, the Nobel Prize-winning East London writer Harold Pinter and "London Calling" composer Joe Strummer.

# 2 "London Calling"

*"When eight million men and women decide to live together on the same spot, things are bound to happen."*

—H.V. MORTON (1951)

"London Calling" was conceived in that most London of spots, the back seat of a black cab, and born, suitably, in a place called World's End. The cab was heading west along Cheyne Walk, the riverside stretch of Chelsea on which both Mick Jagger and Keith Richards lived in the 1960s, and to which Jagger returned, with L'Wren Scott, in 2009. Long, long before that, Cheyne Walk was an artistic heart and hub of the city: painters Rossetti, Whistler and Turner and writers George Eliot and Ian Fleming all lived there (though not at the same time). "If a street can possess a dissipated glamour, then Cheyne Walk has it by the gold coke spoon," wrote Adam Edwards in the property pages of the *Daily Telegraph* in 2009. (That newspaper was somewhat less star-struck in 1973 when a police raid on Richards' Cheyne Walk house resulted in serious gun and drug charges — an event depicted, after a fashion, in the guitarist's autobiography, *Life*. The year before, in Whistler's former house, the British government held secret peace talks with IRA leaders, including Gerry Adams and Martin McGuinness, flown in direct from internment in Northern Ireland.)

In the taxi were Joe Strummer and his girlfriend Gaby Salter. Strummer was the second son of a mid-level British diplomat. His childhood and upbringing bounced him around the world, from birth in Ankara, Turkey to Egypt to Mexico to the archaic, stultifying English boarding school he was trapped in when we first met. After all that — and time spent in Wales, studying art, being in bands — London became his home, a resting place for him, his guitar, his imagination and, in time, his bones. City of dreams. Dystopic nightmares, too.

Gaby was younger than Joe, by nearly ten years. Like the girl in the Beatles song, she was just seventeen, a student at then-fashionable Holland Park Comprehensive. Still, the couple would stick together for many years — from 1978 to the early 1990s — and have two children. That late afternoon on the Chelsea Embankment they were on the way home to their flat at the top end of Edith Grove, a car-infested one-way through-route which connects the river with West London's inner suburbs.

Actually, it was Gaby's flat. (Pause for an old music business joke: What do you call a musician without a girlfriend? Homeless.) Even more actually, it was Gaby's *mother*'s flat. Rather than let her teen-aged daughter live in Joe's squat, she invited him to move in, joining mother, daughter and two brothers at the dog-leg end of the King's Road. It's the bit of Chelsea where, a decade earlier, the princes and princesses of pop psychedelia had languished and shopped, beautifully, in Granny Takes a Trip.

It was one of punk's birthplaces, too. John Lydon/Rotten had a flat there. Malcolm McLaren's shop was there — at the time of "London Calling," it was called, suitably, Seditionaries. The following year, the shop would be renamed — and stay renamed — World's End. Even now it's a western outpost in Vivienne Westwood's fashion brand world.

World's End: it seems a suitably apocalyptic punk of a name. But no, it's just what the local area has been called for a very long time. There's been a World's End pub there for a couple of centuries at least. The current iteration, built in 1897, is a Grade II-listed corner of sparkling gin palace glass and stonework. Long fallen on hard times, it was reborn as a modern eating venue.

Junctions and localities all over London have taken their names from big, iconic corner pubs. (Some of them are long gone or transformed. Bye, bye, the Angel of Islington. Wave hello to West London's North Pole — no longer a pub but, for several years, a boutique branch of the Tesco grocery chain.) It's the other way round with the World's End boozer, though. The pub took its name from its neighborhood.

It's said the area has been known as World's End since the late 17th century. The designation, according to this tale, came from a complaint made by Britain's last Catholic monarch, James II — a terrible king but of great, almost heroic help to London in the Great Fire of 1666. Appointed by his brother King Charles II to oversee the firefighting efforts, the future king (1685–1688) rode through the locale most days and would say as he passed, that it was "the end of the world." (The King's Road was originally just that, a private thoroughfare for the monarch which ran from his central London palace to his western riverside estates.)

It is also probable — highly likely, I'd say — that the name had nothing to do with James II or any royalty. It's just a classic metropolitan elite sneer at the world beyond, the kind of dig that locals make about the next village. The clue is in the pub name. There have been — and still are — pubs called World's End all over London, generally on the margins of the city, on the borderline between here and not-here. The world has ended — for drinkers anyway — in Stepney (eastern boundary of the city), Southwark (just over the river), Hendon (across the North Circular Road) and Hampton (well, frankly, that is pretty much the end of civilization).

Gaby, her mother, her brothers and Joe lived at 31 Whistler Walk, so named for the American painter who settled in Cheyne Walk. It was a three-bedroom, third-floor flat in a low section of the recently built World's End estate, designed by Jim Cadbury-Brown and

Eric Lyons: the last large-scale hurrah of high-rise London council estate-ism. Seven towers, linked at low level, clad in that most London of facings, brick — only it was the tough red brick of mid-century architectural fashion rather than the traditional soft and crumbly yellow of London stock bricks. Muscular and elegant, World's End stands out on the skyline and apart from the windy, democratic mess of the streets it replaced. "More than any other London scheme, it demonstrates brutalism's debt to expressionism," wrote Jonathan Meades, architecture critic and onetime flatmate of 1960s pop psychedelicist Syd Barrett.

Joe and Gaby were on their way home from Vanilla Rehearsal Studios, a couple of miles downstream. The Clash was using Vanilla to prepare for recording what would become the *London Calling* album. Tucked round the back of the Tate Gallery, at 36 Causton Street, the Vanilla was a typical example of the ramshackle side-street premises that are the creative and entrepreneurial compost heaps of any great city. Industrial motor salesmen, taxi drivers, hi-fi specialists — they'd all passed through the Vanilla building, made money and moved on. Now it was the Clash's turn.

Gaby and Joe were talking about the Three Mile Island meltdown — the near-disaster at a Pennsylvania nuclear power plant which had happened just a few months earlier. "There was a lot of Cold War nonsense going on," Strummer told his biographer Chris Salewicz. "We already knew London was susceptible to flooding. Gaby told me to write something about that."

Apocalyptically paranoid as it might sound, catastrophic flooding really was a real threat to London at the time. It was the urgent reason behind the defining major public building project of the period: the Thames Barrier. Designed to protect London from high tides and storm surges, the movable flood protector was being built a dozen or so miles downstream on the far side of the city. Construction began in 1974 and would take ten years.

Finished, it would become a separation line, a marker of another world's end, the point where London finishes and everything else begins. In a very real way, the Thames Barrier became a new eastern gate to the city. That wouldn't be until 1984, though. In 1979, the waters could still keep rising.

Back home in the World's End flat, Joe considered how to write a song about those rising waters and imminent apocalypse. "I sat in the front room, looking out at Edith Grove. Years later, I found out I was looking right on to the flat where the Stones lived when they started out, which seemed appropriate."

**Murder and bombings**

The song that would become "London Calling" took shape slowly. Several sets of lyrics were rejected — "We've had a little murder and bombings of late" was one line thankfully lost. Also dumped was the one in which London was calling out not to faraway towns, but to "the fools and the clowns." (Other early versions included lines about going to a football match and sections of what would become another song entirely, the *London Calling* track "Lover's Rock.") The title changed, too. For a long time, it was called "News of Clock Nine," a rhyme-driven mangling of *Nine O'Clock News* — BBC One's prime-time TV news show, nightly chronicler of murder, death and treason.

Those apocalyptic horsemen were not just something on news shows. They rode closer to home than that. Closer to Joe Strummer. At a London show, he'd worn an H-block T-shirt, a protest against the British government's prison regimen for the IRA. He had also announced, in the nation's leading pop music weekly, the *New Musical Express*, that British troops should be withdrawn from Northern Ireland. Musicians made those kinds of statements then — particularly punk bands, particularly the Clash, particularly Joe Strummer.

His words didn't go down well with Protestant paramilitaries, though. The Red Hand Commando sent Joe a death threat via the *NME* letters section — the nearest thing they could find to a home address for him, I guess. The letter was brought to editor Neil Spencer. "I sensed it was trouble," Neil told me in 2022. "It was scrawled in ink. We called in the cops, and they corroborated it was the real thing. Special Branch dropped into Vanilla and told Joe."

Nothing more came of the threat — though Neil says Joe could never go to Belfast again. But it colored the air: another tone of the wild and whirling times in which "London Calling" crystallized — and which, in turn, it helped crystallize.

Things happened in 1979 which resonate even now. The year began with Britain's "winter of discontent." Rubbish piled up in Leicester Square — barely 300 feet from the side-street hall in which "London Calling" would have its UK premiere. Gravediggers went on strike in Liverpool. Prime minister Jim Callaghan came close to declaring a state of emergency. *The Times* went unpublished for most of the year, silenced by a labor conflict. At the end of March, in a significant foretaste of the UK's constitutional future, the Scottish National Party forced a vote of no confidence in parliament. A general election was called. And, on Friday, May 4, Margaret Thatcher became prime minister.

Straight away, decisions were taken which would shape the country's future. The first cabinet meeting agreed to spending cuts of £4 billion and set in motion the sale of nationalized industries. Income tax was reduced by three pence. Council house sales began. Like many seemingly pivotal moments, particularly in tumultuous times, this policy switch was also part of wider and deeper tectonic shifts and changes. (Two years earlier, London's local authority, the GLC, had launched its Homesteading Scheme, putting thousands of council houses up for sale. Not that it was a local innovation. It was a London adaptation of a successful project developed and pioneered on the far side of the Atlantic from 1973, by future U.S. president Joe Biden, then a thirty-one-year-old senator from Delaware.)

Murder, death and treason stalked the land. Two days after the general election was called, the Irish National Liberation Army (INLA) — the IRA's revolutionary socialist counterpart — assassinated Airey Neave, a central figure of the Thatcherite ascendancy. His Vauxhall Cavalier was blown up on the ramp from parliament's underground car park — almost literally the soft underbelly of the state. INLA's press release called it "the operation of the decade." Not unusually for the times, it was made possible by treachery — an informant from inside the Palace of Westminster. And there was more. The assassination was masterminded by the son of a retired British army major — and former right-hand man of Ian Paisley, the ranting reverend of Ulster Protestant revanchism. Hubble, bubble, gunpowder, treason and plot. Some even thought, despite that press release, that it wasn't the INLA who killed Neave. Ulster Unionist MP Enoch Powell believed it was an inside job, carried out by MI6 on behalf of — who else? — "the Americans."

Two days after Neave's killing, ten people died in a fire in the central Manchester branch of Woolworths. On August 27, the IRA struck deep and hard, killing the Queen's cousin Earl Mountbatten on his boat in Sligo and eighteen British soldiers in an ambush in County Down.

Wild and whirling times. The Yorkshire Ripper murdered twice. (It would be two years before he was caught. In that time, he attacked five more women, killing two — both while out on bail for drunk driving.) Jeremy Thorpe, former leader of the Liberal Party, was tried for conspiracy to murder — hiring a hitman to shoot his former (male) lover. (He was acquitted, despite being quite evidently guilty — a perverse example of the decade's many and varied miscarriages of justice.) Sir Anthony Blunt, keeper of the Queen's pictures, was exposed as a Russian spy, outed in the House of Commons by Margaret Thatcher. On television, Alec Guinness (as George Smiley) teased out betrayal in *Tinker Tailor Soldier Spy*, John Le Carré's fictional version of the British espionage game.

It was around this time that a work colleague told me that BBC DJ Jimmy Savile liked to have sex with corpses in the mortuaries of the hospitals in which he volunteered. I knew Savile was a wrong 'un. You could smell the immorality of him through a TV screen. He was widely distrusted in the music business circles I moved in, as were fellow DJs Jonathan King and John Peel. But necrophilia?

Surely not. Particularly when the story came to me from someone who once swore blind to me that the government would introduce conscription the next day. He was wrong about that, but he was right about Savile. Those were the times we were living in.

It was also a time when racism and brutal class hatred dared show their ugly mugs — all too often soured to the point of derangement, a self-bittering fury which still infests and infects the country a half-century later. As the nationally revered alcoholic librarian poet Philip Larkin wrote to his old and like-minded friend Kingsley Amis, widely disregarded alcoholic poet and author of one excellent novel twenty-five years earlier (*Lucky Jim*, 1954), "The lower-class bastards can no more stop going on strike now than a laboratory rat with an electrode in its brain can stop jumping on a switch to give itself an orgasm."

On Monday, April 23 (St. George's Day, Shakespeare's birthday), at an Anti-Nazi League demonstration in Southall (West London suburb, capital of South Asian Europe), Blair Peach (New Zealander, Trotskyist, National Union of Teachers activist) died from blows inflicted by the SPG, the Metropolitan Police's Special Patrol Group (neo-military, armed — informally — with baseball bats, crowbars and sledgehammers). Peach was laid out "in state" at Southall Dominion, a central location in the British Asian community which showed Bollywood movies and hosted boxing, wrestling and cultural events. Eight-thousand filed past Peach's body, including many Bengali women who addressed him as *badu* (son).

On September 11, one of Thatcher's senior ministers, Jim Prior, told journalist Hugo Young, "We are sober people who can see real collapse staring this country in the face." Apocalypse was in the air. (And Francis Ford Coppola's ridiculous, ravishing Vietnam movie *Apocalypse Now* was in the cinemas.)

In June, Joe Strummer told the *NME*: "There's only 10,000 days of oil left. It's finite." That's roughly twenty-seven years and four months. Say, mid-to-late November 2006. So, Strummer was wrong, says the present, completely wrong. But all too believable in the wild and whirling times of late-1970s London.

**The call goes out**

His song finished, Joe played it to the band, and they banged down a demo of it at their rehearsal studio. Mick Jones took home a cassette of that first recording. At the time, the Clash guitarist was living on Portobello Road, in a flat he shared with Tony James, an old friend who was the bass player/leader of the band Generation X. He played the demo to Tony. "Listen to what we did today," he said. Tony was the first outsider to hear the song that would become an anthem of sorts for its city. "I was floored by its genius," he said, many years later.

With that demo as a basis, "London Calling" was "properly" recorded in Wessex Studios, a small complex in the former church hall of St. Augustine's, an almost clichéd piece of Victorian neo-gothic ecclesiastical, set back from a wide tree-lined side road in Highbury New Park, a mid-19th-century upper-middle-class housing development. Roughly midway between the antique arcades of Islington Upper Street and the art deco facades of Arsenal FC's Highbury Stadium, the building had previously been home to the Rank film company's "charm school" — nurturer of a generation of British movie stars, including Diana Dors and Christopher Lee. In 1975, it was bought by Chrysalis Records. By the time of "London Calling," Wessex was a well-used and well-loved studio. Queen worked on "Bohemian Rhapsody" there in the summer of 1975. The Sex Pistols recorded *Never Mind the Bollocks* there in spring 1977. The Pretenders and the Tom Robinson Band both used it to cut their debut albums.

It was a two-studio set-up. The Clash sessions in Studio One went on for a month or so. They probably started on Monday, July 30, 1979, and ran right through August. (No one knows for certain, as the only session log was stolen not long after recording finished.) The Damned were next door in Studio Two, overdubbing and mixing their own third album, *Machine Gun Etiquette*. Both Strummer and Jones helped out on backing vocals. That album's co-producer, Roger Armstrong, was one of the owners of the Damned's label, Chiswick. Three years earlier, Roger had produced and put out Joe Strummer's first record, "Keys to Your Heart" by the 101ers. The band broke up the day that single (their only one) came out, so that Joe could head off to join/form the Clash. "Wessex was one of the best-run studios in London, fronted by the wonderful Joyce, ably backed by Betty the cleaning lady," Roger told me. "But the real attraction was Studio One, a large and airy space that allowed a band to have distance but with eye contact, and to play at reasonable volume without too much spill across mics." A room is also only as good as the engineer using it, however, "and, in house engineer Bill Price, Wessex had one of the finest ever to come out of the UK."

Price was an established — if eccentric — engineer who had been based at Wessex since 1975. Early in his career, at Decca's West Hampstead studios — where the Rolling Stones cut demos — he'd worked on hits for the great hairy-chested 1960s belters Tom Jones and Engelbert Humperdinck. He also did Tim Rice and Andrew Lloyd Webber's *Joseph and the Amazing Technicolor Dreamcoat* album, with Roger Daltrey of the Who as Joseph. At Wessex, he worked on almost everything that came through the door, including the Sex Pistols.

At the time of *London Calling*, Chris Briggs worked for Chrysalis — "half A&R, half PR." We became friends, and Chris became something of a legend in the English music business game — not least for crafting Robbie Williams' recovery and solo career. In 2022, I asked Chris about Bill Price. "A very clever, lateral-thinking engineer," said Chris. "He knew things, chain-smoked Dunhill menthol cigarettes and always explained what he was doing and why. He was generous with his knowledge and collaborative with artists."

The nominal producer of *London Calling* was Guy Stevens. A great London "face" of the 1960s, Stevens ran the Sue label, which brought all kinds of American rhythm and blues and soul music across the Atlantic — Bob and Earl's "Harlem Shuffle," Donnie Elbert's "Little Piece of Leather," Inez and Charlie Foxx's "Mockingbird." He was the Monday night DJ at the Scene Club, a sordid little Soho cellar which — because of Stevens' musical taste, knowledge and passion — became the prime mod hangout. Rohan O'Rahilly ran the club, as well as the boat-based pirate station Radio Caroline. "Everyone came to hear Guy," O'Rahilly told *Mojo* magazine; "The Stones, the Beatles, Eric Clapton."

Young bands also played the Scene, among them the High Numbers. In July 1964, Stevens introduced their manager to a couple of R&B tunes — Slim Harpo's "Got Love If You Want It" and the Dynamics' "Misery." The manager took tape copies away and wrote new lyrics for the tunes; a week later, the High Numbers recorded them as "I'm the Face" and "Zoot Suit." Three months later, the band changed its name to the Who. Two years after that, on a winter Friday afternoon in Wembley, Stevens was introduced to amphetamine by Who drummer Keith Moon. Within a couple of years, Stevens had been to jail twice for drug offenses, the second time for eight months.

Stevens was also the man who came up with the phrase "whiter shade of pale." Around 4:00 a.m. on a winter 1967 night in his flat at 23c Gloucester Avenue, Primrose Hill, he told his friend Gary Brooker — singer in the band Procol Harum — that was how he looked. The band's lyricist Keith Reid was there, too, in that pre-dawn North London hour. Within weeks, Reid and Brooker had used Stevens' phrase for the title and emotional heart of Procol Harum's debut single, "A Whiter Shade of Pale." Set to a Bach-ish melody, it went on to sell ten-million copies worldwide. Stevens didn't get a credit of any kind — and therefore not a penny of the royalties.

A couple of years later, working as an A&R man at Island Records, Stevens created and produced Mott the Hoople — which is how he came to work on *London Calling*. Mick Jones *loved* Mott the Hoople — so much so that he insisted Stevens produce the first Clash demos in 1976. It was, as it often can be when you work with your heroes, an unhappy, unproductive and unsatisfying experience.

For long-term Clash associate Kosmo Vinyl, Stevens was "shamanic." Kosmo (né Mark Dunk, of Bow) joined the Clash crew in the middle of the *London Calling* sessions, as some kind of mix-and-mash of PR man and personal manager. In time, his official(ish) title would become consigliere — the band flirting immaturely, as they so often did, with the language of bad men and their violences. Kosmo and his toilet-brush of a haircut stayed pretty much right through to the end of the Clash. For this story, the important thing about Kosmo is that he would become the main conduit between the band and Martin Scorsese. He was a direct link between "London Calling" and "New York, New York" — and he was as surprised as Joe when I told him how the two records pretty much share a birthdate. (For decades now, Kosmo has lived in New York — the actual city, that is, not the one of Scorsese's dreams or Sinatra's "New York, New York.")

By the time of *London Calling*, Guy Stevens was a rabid Arsenal fan — he wore a red-and-white team scarf to every recording session — and a chaotic, sometimes nasty drunk. Using him again wasn't Mick Jones' idea; he was still sadly disappointed by those early demos. It was Joe who wanted Stevens, in part at least because Mick didn't, such was the band's fraternal dynamic. Joe also welcomed Stevens' angry craziness, although he'd call it passion.

It hadn't been that long since the Clash had parted company with another passionate man: their first manager, Bernard Rhodes, who Joe loved and hated and missed the way you love and hate and miss a father. A tiny, tight-trousered motor-mouthed North London hustler, Rhodes talked such convincingly improbable gibberish that he spieled the Clash into a contract with the giant label CBS, proclaiming it as a great victory over corporate capitalism. In fact, its savagely label-biased terms were a major factor in the band's collapse in 1985.

Stevens was Joe's way of recreating the manic edge that Rhodes had brought to the group gestalt. Where Rhodes used language, Stevens used his body. To convey his desires and dreams, Rhodes would spew inspiring — if hermetically impenetrable — spirals of words. Stevens threw chairs and hit people. "Direct psychic injection," he called it. (Some have suggested that bringing in Stevens was actually Rhodes' notion.)

"It was very tense," said Sumi Jenner, wife and colleague of Peter Jenner — who, with Andrew King, took over as the Clash's management not long before the *London Calling* sessions. Jenner and King, who traded as Blackhill Enterprises, were major figures in the London music business world. They put the Stones on, free, in Hyde Park in 1969.They were Pink Floyd's first managers. They managed T. Rex (for a while) and Ian Dury. They were introduced to the Clash by another of their charges, Philip Rambow (Canadian-born singer-songwriter, friend of Mick Jones and co-writer of Kirsty MacColl's 1981 hit "There's a Guy Works Down the Chip Shop Swears He's Elvis").

"We were Mick's boys, never Joe's boys," King told me. That was not entirely true. Jenner told me that he and Joe "bonded" over their shared taste for "exotic cheroots." But the perception alone that they were "Mick's boys" added a certain extra twist on the corkscrew of the band's social and emotional partnership. And it's the kind of interpersonal twist Jenner and King came to know even more about, via firsthand experience. After the Clash, Jenner went on to look after Billy Bragg while King ran Mute publishing (Depeche Mode, etc.). For many years, the two former partners worked right near each other on either side of the Harrow Road, but their contact was minimal. Their fallout was in good part the result of the Clash tipping their partnership into bankruptcy.

This brought a certain dispassion to King's reflections on his time spent managing the Clash. Or, at least trying to. "Because of their experience with Bernie, they thought the manager's job was to fuck it up," he told me in his office on the south side of Harrow Road. "They believed a manager's role was to create mayhem." Hence Guy Stevens. During the *London Calling* sessions, he attacked Mick Jones with a ladder and threatened to pour booze into the piano if he had to wait any longer for his taxi to arrive. "He did a lot," Jenner told me, in his office just north of the Harrow Road. "But it wasn't about twiddling knobs. He wound the Clash up into a vision they hadn't had before, but they actually made the record on their own, with Bill Price."

As the man who had to bring the music together, what did Bill think of Guy Stevens? "A very unusual record producer," Price has said. "He would challenge the artist verbally and physically, tackle him and bring him to the ground and punch him and stuff, in order to get more emotion out of him when he performed. Funnily enough, this worked better on some people than others. It worked very well with Joe, actually." Stevens died, two years after *London Calling,* in his mother's house in Forest Hill, still dreaming of the next great record.

**"We worked till we dropped"**
The Clash sessions were grueling, beginning with ten-hour days and rising to sixteen-hour ones. "We worked till we dropped every day," Kosmo told me. Thanks to Bill Price and www.digitalprosound.com, we now know all kinds of stuff about how *London Calling* was recorded — probably more than the band ever did. Probably more than anyone other than Bill would ever care to. Stuff like the fact that the studio's ambient sound — one of the main reasons people chose Wessex — was recorded straight to tracks 17 and 18 of *London Calling*'s 24-track master and also to "tracks 7 and 8 but gated through Kepex gates and triggered by the snare mike." That was Bill's way of controlling the crunching snare drum sound which drives the rhythm. "It works very well," he wrote. To mike up Topper Headon's drum kit, Bill used a Shure SM57, a Neumann KM86, two Sennheiser 421s and … enough, enough, I know. But there is some significant stuff in those notes, too.

One is that detail above about the triggering of the sound of the studio — the room, in engineer-ish — by the snare drum. On a music recording, the sound of the room is the world — or, at least, a version of the world — intruding into the technicalities of musical instruments. In a way, the sound of the room on a recording is a stand-in for us, the listeners. It represents the relationship between the player, the played and the listeners. The sound of the room is very often what studio music makers would refer to when trying to explain the emotional tug and tussle of a particular recording. It's where the heart hangs its hat. On "London Calling" that hat is hung on Topper's snare drum and hi-hats, the crisp, snappy percussive sound that marks every beat of the track. "We were at our absolute peak," Topper told me in 2022. "We rehearsed, then recorded. So, in the studio, we were right on it. We had the wonderful Bill Price taking care of the technical side. The wild and exciting bit came from Guy Stevens — a special, mad talent. His input was incredible."

It's sometimes said that "London Calling" is in 12/8. Which is an uncommon (but not unknown) time signature in pop. Tears for Fears' "Everybody Wants to Rule the World" and Stevie Wonder's "Higher Ground" are both in 12/8. In fact, "London Calling" is in pop music's eternal 4/4. The reason for thinking that its basic rhythm is something more complex is down to the extraordinary skill and rhythmic fluency of Topper's drumming. For a start, his playing always swung — as they put it, oh so indelicately, in the jazz world — like a motherfucker. Plus, here he added a clever and technically challenging flourish to that basic, hard-pounding 4/4, playing three different patterns on two hi-hats — with one hand. "While the vocals come in sixteens," he told me, "my hi-hats are in fours, eights and sixteens. So, each chorus and verse is slightly different. That's what gives its distinct sound." Things stay the same, that is, but are also ever-changing, unstable even. A rhythmic echo of the song's lyrics and narrative. "I'm proud of it," said Topper. "It's a nice, clever bit of drumming."

Chris Briggs: "Topper is a proper musician. He could play anything, really. Bands are only as good as their drummers. A great band has a balance of charisma, technique, studio nerdiness, imaginative writing, a decent lyricist, maybe a luxury player, an art student with mad ideas unrestricted by technical knowledge and, of course, some solid players." Plus, in Topper's case, a drummer who would write the music for their biggest hit, "Rock the Casbah" (the lyrics are Joe's).

Another informative piece of stuff is Bill's note that the bass intro was played by bassist Paul Simonon rather than, as was often assumed, the more musically articulate Mick Jones — though he did overdub it later, perhaps on guitar. Mick's flatmate Tony James: "The bass countermelody makes it sound like there's a lot more chords than there are. It uses what Mick calls the West London Scale."

Bill revelation three: There are six guitars on the track. One was

Joe's. The other five were layered on by Mick. Briggs: "Mick was the other proper musician in the Clash."

Bill detail four: The weird guitar sound on "London Calling" was achieved with a Roland Space Echo — to which Bill added a backwards overdub.

And number five: The apocalyptic urgency of Joe's vocal was at least partly thanks to his famously bad teeth. "Joe has a very bassy voice," noted Bill. "And at that time, he was undergoing a lot of dental work."

When it came time to mix the track, Joe told Bill how he wanted it to sound — "like London." The image he had in mind, he explained, was the fog swirling on the Thames, with seagulls all around. That's the whooping sound in Joe's vocal — he's imitating seagulls. Joe's description of the sound he was after, explained Bill, "suggested the echoes for the mix, particularly the slow repeats in the instrumental."

P.S. The building that housed Wessex was torn down in 2003 and redeveloped as eight flats and a "townhouse." In a nod to the site's history, it was named The Recording Studio. The Wessex mixing board is now in a studio in South Wales.

**"London Calling" goes public**

The first time the Clash played "London Calling" publicly was in a draft version on July 5, 1979, more than a month before they recorded it. It was at a secret show in London, in the Notre Dame Hall, just off Leicester Square. (The Sex Pistols' first TV appearance was filmed there three years earlier.) It was the first time Joe's father, Ron Mellor, saw him perform. English fans wouldn't hear the song again till the end of the year.

This most London of songs ironically had its first widespread exposure in the U.S. Having recorded the track in late August, the Clash played a series of dates in the U.S., starting with the *Tribal Stomp II* festival, in Monterey, California on September 8. "We're gonna play a new one now," Joe shouted from the stage. "For the journalist in the back, that one is called 'London Calling.'"

I first heard it four days later, at the Civic Arena in St. Paul, Minnesota. It was the first date on *The Clash Take the Fifth* tour, referencing the McCarthyite anti-Communist witch hunts and trials with typical rhetorical nostalgia. I was there as a writer for the English music weekly *Sounds*. My relationship with the band was close, even intimate, and barely professional. The first thing Joe said when we met up in the hotel bar was, "You've put on weight." We had known each other for more than ten years by then. In my *Sounds* piece, I described their new songs — badly, emptily even — as "a bridging link between the histrionics of the past and the more measured pacings of the moment." I didn't even mention "London Calling" in the article. I was not alone. No one else remarked on it in their reviews either.

Nor did I notice that Bob Dylan was at the Civic Arena that night. It was more or less a hometown show for him — he grew up on the other side of Minnesota. He apparently also brought forty members of his family along with him; I didn't notice them, either. Nor that, as Kosmo Vinyl insisted to me, Dylan signed Strummer's copy of *The Music of American Folk Song* (with foreword by Pete Seeger). Nor that Dylan suggested to the Clash that they cover a song of the Abraham Lincoln Brigade, the group of American volunteers who fought in the Spanish Civil War (not that the Clash took up his idea). I do wonder if they mentioned to Dylan that they had recently recorded a version of his 1970 song "Man in Me" at their Vanilla Studios sessions — though it wouldn't be released for twenty-five years. Maybe others really did see Dylan and family that night. I didn't see him or them, but I did see the stage setup for ABBA, the next act in the Civic Arena, later that week. It was several times the size of the Clash's.

The tour, which ran through mid-October, was ostensibly to support the belated U.S. release of their first album, but it was as much an excuse for the band to explore their love of Americana, giving them new and multiple opportunities to pick up old guitars and the kind of clothing and accessories needed to look like what have since been called "rogue heroes" — acted out by rock musicians and styled by the fine talents of British art school graduates. Around this time, for a photo shoot in London, I took the whole band to theatrical outfitters Berman's, which was then buried away in a wind-torn council estate arcade, not far from the Clash's first HQ in a Camden Town warehouse. They all headed to the militaria section and got themselves dressed up as their fantasies. Combat rock, perhaps.

From Minneapolis–Saint Paul, the tour bus made the daylong journey to Chicago, where the Clash played the Avalon Ballroom on September 14, supported by Bo Diddley. The dressing room looked out on El trains as they rattled past, creaking with age and neglect. It felt like being in an Edward Hopper painting. More so when I noticed the holes in the fishnet tights (or stockings?) of the two overweight, life-worn and short, short leather mini-skirted women on the far side of the room. They were, I was told, prostitutes — supplied, gratis, by the show's old-style promoter. He'd heard that punk was a rough old thing, so he'd graciously made sure that the backstage provisions included a matched pair of aging, drugged-up, cheap street workers. I wish I could say I made that story up, but unfortunately, it's true. (And then? They were paid up and invited to leave. They offered to stay anyway, but the band said their goodbyes and left, in pursuit of their own idea of midnight hour adventurings.) On my lift back to the hotel with someone I knew from London, I drank a beer and threw the empty bottle into a curbside rubbish bin — sorry, trash can. Cue the whoop-whoop-whine of a police car — the full "blues and twos" as we Londoners know it. The driver — i.e., not me — was charged with having an open bottle in the car. We followed the police to the station. I paid the fine. A hundred dollars, I think. Most expensive beer I ever drank, but I probably squeezed it onto my expenses somehow.

Also traveling with the Clash was cartoonist Ray Lowry, a whippet-thin manic Mancunian cartoonist who was ten years older than the band and liked a drink. He was sketching anything and everything that caught his eye, sending weekly dispatches back to the *NME* in London, describing himself as a "war artist" who was "covering the battle" — the kind of rhetoric that hung, comfortably, around that

Clash tour. While in Chicago, he took a cab out to 2449 North Lincoln Avenue, the location of Wax Trax, the city's hippest record store, and bought a record. Not a new record but an old one, two decades old — Elvis Presley's first album, the one with a wild cover picture of the singer onstage, rocking his microphone stand. His name is in giant capital letters: ELVIS down the left, in pink, PRESLEY along the bottom, in green. Lowry paid six dollars for it. (I certainly spent a couple of hundred dollars at Wax Trax that day. Among my pile of albums and 45s was a complete set of the *Pebbles* compilations of 1960s U.S. punk obscurities.)

Five days later, on September 19, the Clash were in Boston, appearing at the Orpheum — the same day Frank Sinatra recorded "(Theme From) New York, New York" in Los Angeles. Their next two shows were in New York, at the Palladium, a (now-demolished) concert hall on East 14th Street. They took the stage to the sound of Sinatra's "High Hopes." "London Calling" was the fourth song in their set, as it was on most dates of that tour. Ira Robbins reviewed the night in *Trouser Press* magazine and called it "a sloppy mess of a wonderful show." It was there, at the Palladium, that Pennie Smith took the photograph used for the album cover, an image of Paul Simonon smashing his bass down onto the stage, at 10:50 p.m.

The whole *London Calling* package was designed by Lowry — he placed Pennie's blurry black-and-white photo within his reinterpretation of the cover of that six-dollar Elvis record. On the inner sleeve were lyrics in Lowry's hand with funny little Lowry sketches dotted between them. Kosmo Vinyl: "Everything about the *London Calling* album was planned during that U.S. tour."

Lowry's original cover artwork sold at Bonhams in London in 2009 for £72,000. The following year, his *London Calling* cover design was used for a UK Post Office first-class stamp, one of a set featuring classic album covers. Lowry's life had a less happy ending. He died a year before the Bonhams sale, consumed by booze and himself. (P.S. He was not related to a fellow Mancunian artist, the painter L.S. Lowry.)

The band first heard an almost complete version of the *London Calling* album backstage after one of those Palladium shows. Bill Price had flown over to play them rough mixes. Kosmo Vinyl was there and listening. "It was the bomb," he told me decades later. "Huge as fucking huge. My hair stands on end, anyway. But even if it didn't, *London Calling* would have made it."

From the rehearsal sessions at Vanilla and for a long time after that, the album's working title was *The Last Testament*. The notion behind that hubristic title, Kosmo told me, was equally hubristic. The idea was that it was "the last rock and roll record" — a closing bracket to the opening one of the Elvis debut referenced in Lowry's cover design, "the first rock and roll album."

**Armagideon times**

As on all band tour buses, a main focus of the day was the choice of soundtrack for the journey. On the *Clash Take the Fifth* tour, the favorite sound was an apocalyptic reggae single, Willie Williams' "Armagideon Time." Although recorded two years earlier by producer Coxsone Dodd in his Studio One base at 13 Brentford Road in Kingston, Jamaica, it had only just been released.

The Clash were so taken with Williams' single that, tour over and back in London, they made their own version of the song — and named their fanzine/tour programme *Armagideon Times*. The original idea was for the Clash to record in Kingston, using the Williams backing track, but they couldn't get rights clearance. So, they cut it in London, at Wessex, using Mickey Gallagher of Ian Dury's band, the Blockheads, to recreate (and refashion) the organ part, played on the original by Jackie Mittoo, the tune's co-writer.

They decided it should be their next single — i.e., not just *not* issue "London Calling" as the single, but not even another track from the album. As ever, the band's enthusiasm swamped its scanty (at the best of times) business sense. "They felt 'London Calling' was a bit old by then," said Kosmo. So, they decided to relegate it to the B-side of the "Armagideon Time" single. Kosmo knew this was a deeply incorrect decision. Determined to retain "London Calling" as an A-side, he came up with a sneaky argument which won the band over. "As a Faces fan, I remembered that 'Maggie May' was actually a double A-side. That convinced the band and kept the record company happy." (That's a memory malfunction: "Maggie May" was not a Faces single. Originally a track on Rod Stewart's third solo album, *Every Picture Tells a Story*, it was issued, in July 1971, as the B-side of Rod's version of Tim Hardin's "Reason to Believe.")

When the test pressing of "London Calling" arrived, there was a gathering for a collective first listen to it at Mick's place. Or, rather, his grandmother's place, a council flat overlooking the Westway, the elevated urban motorway that was such a central element in the Clash's early public image. The band's name was sprayed on the motorway in 1976 in giant letters (probably by them) and stayed there for many years. When the time came, as it does, to celebrate themselves — and turn a little coin — with a historical documentary, it was titled *Westway to the World*.

There is a photograph (also by Pennie Smith) of the band in Mick's grandmother's sitting room, on the eighteenth floor of Wilmcote House on the Warwick Estate. Mick is wearing a bow tie. In the corner of the picture is a cheap and not-new stereo, with a smoked glass lid. That's what the band played the "London Calling" single on for the first time.

Kosmo Vinyl told me, in the 21st century, that he knew it was "anthemic" right away. "It was always fucking monumental. It's got the apocalypse. Everything. All in a song. There aren't a lot of records where you couldn't change anything. Junior Murvin's 'Police and Thieves.' Marvin Gaye's 'Inner City Blues.' And the Clash's 'London Calling.' It's their great one. The one that they will be remembered for."

The Clash 45 was released just in time for Christmas. Reviewing it in the *NME*, Charles Shaar Murray noted that it reflected the year's anxieties and hyperboles in equal measure, describing it as "a call for solidarity and trust in the face of impending disaster." In *Sounds*,

Garry Bushell described it, probably tongue-in-cheek, as "a fine irrepressibly melodic groover."

Claire Skinner, a young fan, was excited, very excited, about this new Clash single. Fourteen years old, she was in her third year at Cavendish, the first "comprehensive" school in Hemel Hempstead, a "new town" twenty-five miles north of London, in Hertfordshire. "It was my big brother's copy of 'London Calling,'" Claire told me in a 2022 e-mail. "Possibly, he went up to London to get it. I wasn't as cool."

I lived in Hemel, too, for ten years — though more than a decade earlier than Claire. Even before that, I would have passed through the town's railway station on my first journey to London, in my Liverpudlian mother's womb (remember?). I loved Hemel and was bereft when my parents moved us to a village in Sussex. I was thirteen at the time and, as I later learned, Hemel then had more teenagers per capita than anywhere else in the country. Culturally, we ruled the town — boys and girls both, in Ben Sherman button-down shirts and navy or burgundy V-neck sweaters — cheap market-stall nylon knockoffs of the American originals. For me, by the time of "London Calling," Hemel was a paradise lost.

Claire lived in a different town. By her time, Margaret Thatcher was in power, with one of her closest associates, the sleazy Cecil Parkinson, as MP for the Hemel area.

Claire just wanted out of the place. And the Clash symbolized that out-ness for her. In 2009, she was asked by the *Guardian* what one song would feature on the soundtrack to her life. She said: "'London Calling' by the Clash."

In that 2022 e-mail, she wrote, "When I hear 'London Calling' now, it takes me right back to a specific time and attitude. It's very immediate and clear, very dramatic and energizing. I have it on my show reel. Joe Strummer, I bloody loved him!" (As did many women, despite his grubbiness, inconstancy, terrible teeth, drink and drug intake and episodic unreliability.)

Claire eventually got out of Hemel, of course. She studied acting at LAMDA, the West London drama school that's a short walk from the dance hall in which Joe Strummer attended the "UK pop reggae" all-nighter immortalized on the 1978 Clash single "(White Man) in Hammersmith Palais." She then joined the Royal Shakespeare Company and became a well-known actor, most famous in the UK for playing the dippy, ineffectual mother in the long-running family sitcom *Outnumbered*. She was more recently a dentist in the hit U.S. show *Ted Lasso*. She lives in Muswell Hill, an inner North London suburb which sits above Alexandra Palace, the big white building from which the BBC broadcast its signals to faraway towns beginning in 1936; "This is London calling."

I lived in the same area for several years, in a flat where Joe and I partied in the long summer of 1976. And it was from there, on Christmas Day 1979, shortly after *London Calling*'s release, I set out on my third (fourth?) trip to New York. It was my first or second holiday with the glamorous bass-playing woman who would, in time, become my wife. (She still is.) We spent a week in a deep-frozen Manhattan, at her father's apartment on East 49th Street, near the United Nations building, while he spent the festive season at his London flat, in Soho.

Not everyone was as keen on the new Clash music as Claire. Paul Weller, then of the Jam, was interviewed by Dave Schulps of *Trouser Press*. "*London Calling*'s a cop-out," said Weller. "It is for British people anyway. It's alright for Americans; I suppose you're getting a decent blast of music, but it's a cop-out as far as we're concerned." (That's "we," I guess, in its secondary — but not uncommon — meaning of "I.")

**Down by the river**

By 1979, every single in want of a high chart placing had started to need a video to promote it — particularly if you were the Clash and had established a one-band boycott of *Top of the Pops*, the weekly TV show which powered the UK music business for decades.

The video for "London Calling" was shot at the start of December and directed by Don Letts — who told me, in the 21st century,

"To this day, I don't know the words of 'London Calling.'" A dreadlocked South Londoner, Letts was the DJ at punk's first temple, the Roxy club in Covent Garden. A friend and close associate of the band, he became a film director via his work with them. "I'd just got into making videos, inspired by punk. The stages were full, so I picked up a Super 8 camera."

"London Calling" was only his second video. "I didn't know what the fuck I was doing. The cameraman, John Metcalfe, had to talk me through it." In fact, Don wasn't even the official director. A Wardour Street hack was. At the time, unions ruled the British film industry. You could only work if you had a union card, and you could only get a union card by working. As ever, restrictive practices led to corrupt practices. Would-be directors without a union card like Don employed ghosts, who, for a fee, would allow their name to be put on someone else's work. Leftists and unionists abhorred this, of course. The irony doesn't need much chasing, does it? The video for the Clash's most anthemic rebel song involved a touch of scabbing.

Inevitably, given the song's lyrics, the video was shot down by the river. It has been claimed, online, that it was filmed on Cadogan Pier, on the north side of the Thames. In fact, as Topper confirmed to me, the location was on the south side of the river, at the now-gone Festival Pier, between Albert and Chelsea Bridge — a little downriver and on the opposite bank from Cheyne Walk where the song had first been conceived. (In the booklet for the twenty-fifth anniversary edition of *London Calling*, there is a contact sheet of location shots taken by anarchist activist Tom Vague. They are clearly marked "Festival Pier. Vid Dec 79" in china marker the color of Lowry's pink lettering on the *London Calling* album cover.) Vague lived in Frestonia, a West London squat which, in 1977, declared itself the Free and Independent Republic of Frestonia (taking its name from the road it was on) and applied to join the United Nations. Over the years, I met both Frestonia's Foreign Minister, actor David Rappaport, and its Ambassador to the United Kingdom, playwright Heathcote Williams. A picture Vague took of the Clash posing outside the Frestonia building was used for a *ZigZag* magazine story on the band.

Unknowingly, Don had chosen a location redolent with dashed hope, political conflict, structural decay and violent death — also privatization and shopping. Long ago, the flat, soggy riverine area had been a place of duels — the Duke of Wellington fought one there. Its river frontage had then become home to smelly, messy, water-hungry industries and rough old boozers — the Red House was a favorite pub of Charles Dickens. In the mid-19th century, its immediate swampy hinterland was transformed into Battersea Park — created by tipping on to the watery surface earth that had been dug out to create the Victoria Docks, nine miles or so downriver.

Festival Pier was the landing point for the park. It was a relatively new facility, built for the 1951 Festival of Britain, a celebration of all things bright, modern and beautifully British, dreamed up and brought to life under the post-WW II Labour government. The festival's main site was in central London, on the south bank of the Thames, diagonally opposite parliament.

In October of the festival year, Sir Winston Churchill led the Conservative Party back to power. One of his first acts was to order that the festival be closed down and its main site cleared. He left only two things of the Labour government's moment of post-war joy and celebration: the Royal Festival Hall and the Pleasure Gardens in Battersea Park. While the central London buildings emphasized science, progress, state investment and modern design, the Battersea Gardens were completed with private rather than public funds and offered the kind of commercial opportunities traditionally beloved by city-dwellers of all classes, ages and education, etc. — bars, restaurants, shops and an amusement park. I visited the Gardens many times as a child, eating cotton candy, riding the water splash, trying — and failing — to catch plastic ducks with a plastic fishing rod while also getting a basic education in economics — or, at least, a lesson in how carnival folk separate punters from their pounds, shillings and pence.

The pier was erected so visitors could travel directly to the Pleasure Gardens by river from the main festival site in central London. There's another fabulous irony — one of the most notable visual moments of one of the most revolution-inclined pop groups was filmed on a structure designed and built for conveying the general public to shops and pubs. Ah, pop music. (A well-worn and ironic left-wing call-and-response chant comes to mind: "What do we want? Revolution. When do we want it? As soon as the pubs close.")

In 1961, Battersea Park — particularly its Pleasure Gardens — was used as the main location for *The Day the Earth Caught Fire*, an apocalypse fantasy movie directed by Val Guest who, two years earlier, had made *Expresso Bongo*, the first great British pop film. In *The Day the Earth Caught Fire*, a nuclear accident has triggered violent climate change. Globally, the temperature has risen by eleven degrees. Britain is enveloped by the resultant mists. Cities empty. How so very "London Calling."

From there on, things could only get worse for Battersea's Pleasure Gardens — and they did. In 1970, the carnival's main ride, the Big Dipper, burned down. In 1972, repaired and reopened, it crashed, killing five children — still one of the worst accidents in amusement park history. (Fifty years later, plans for a memorial of some kind were finally mooted.) In 1974, the Pleasure Gardens packed away its bent air rifle ranges and cotton candy stalls, shutting for good.

The mid-1970s were, however, also the heyday of the Chelsea Cruise, a post-teenage Friday evening car rally which started and ended in Battersea Park. Once a month, inspired by the movie *American Graffiti* (1973) and a general London love for 1950s U.S. music and stuff, owners of classic American cars, Jeeps, U.S. Army trucks and motorbikes drove their vehicles out of Battersea Park, very slowly and with suitable music rocking and rolling out of their speakers, across Chelsea Bridge, then up and down the King's Road, then finally back over the bridge to Battersea. The Cruise was very much a link between the area's two separate but linked moments as an epicenter of British youth cult culture, the 1960s' beautiful people and 1970s punkdom — maybe the Clash's embrace of U.S. militaria in their *Combat Rock* era, too.

By the time of the video, Battersea Park and its riverside walk were slowly and damply sinking back into their marshy, muddy origins. As much of London did in 1979, it looked like something you'd leave on the side of your plate after a particularly indifferent dinner. Yet it was also a harbinger of a new future, one in which "London Calling" itself would play a leading role.

In September 1978, the park hosted something of a proto anti-Thatcher music event. The headliners were the Stranglers, whose stage set-up included both a pair of strippers and a full-size replica of a tank. Their most London song was "Dagenham Dave," the story of a fervid fan. Support acts included Peter Gabriel, future inspirer of *Glastonbury* as a major annual outdoor countercultural festival — and home turf, literally, of Joe's *Strummerville* gathering round a campfire, as recreated in *The Future Is Unwritten*, the posthumous (2007) film biography of Strummer made by his friend and neighbor Julien Temple.

By pop video standards, the "London Calling" clip is almost puritanically simple. Band plays song at dusk in rain. That's pretty much it. There is no narrative. It's sensibility, not sense. Most people will tell you it's in black and white. It's not. It was shot in color, but the day's gathering, crepuscular gloom and misty rain wash it almost into monochrome.

It begins with Joe walking up the pier, a singer making his way to perform in front of an audience that isn't there. White lights flash into the camera. The band is alone, as if they are the last people left alive in a post-apocalyptic nightmare. The video grabbed — and amplified — feelings that were in the air. "Miserable grey old place, London is," Mick Jones had told *Rolling Stone* earlier that year, on the eve of Thatcher's election. "Very oppressive. Things are going very badly there."

The look and feel of the video — dark, anxious, noirish — were a fusion of the Clash's own ideas and Letts's beginner's incompetence and/or luck. Darkness falls early in midwinter London. What was meant to be a daylight shoot was taken to dusk and beyond by unexpected — though not unpredictable — complications. The start was delayed by Mick Jones' usual lateness. "Mick was famously, incredibly late for everything," said Letts. "But he always turned up with a smile — which made it impossible for you to do what you wanted to do, which was smack him, either physically or mentally."

In conventional directorial terms, Letts was an innocent ignoramus. A more experienced (or competent) director might, for example, have looked up the Thames tide timetable. "I arranged for a boat to shoot from. Being a totally inexperienced landlubber and a typical Londoner, I didn't know about tides or currents. My understanding of water came from having baths. I can't even swim. I always say, have you ever seen a fish walk?"

The tide was out when Don first set up. So, the camera on the boat was too low, fifteen feet too low. From that angle, he would have been filming up Joe's trouser leg. Which meant they had to wait — all day — for the tide to rise. Then it started to rain.

"I couldn't believe my luck: what else could go wrong? But now I can say it wouldn't have been a shit video if it hadn't rained but the rain certainly made it. It's the whole punk thing: I made my problem my asset." (The rain did not rain its benefits on the Clash's amps and speakers, however. It filled them with rainwater. So, at the end of the shoot, and full of Remy Martin brandy, tour manager Johnny Green tipped the waterlogged equipment — all hired — into the Thames. "The band thought it was hilarious to watch it floating down the river," Letts wrote in his autobiography. "It didn't seem so funny when they got the bill, though."

In the video, the camera tracks along the river, giving the feeling that it had haphazardly stumbled across the band on its seabound journey. "A complete accident," said Letts. "I was desperately trying to stay lined up with the pier, but the boat kept drifting off because of the current." He was on the boat, the band was on the pier; he communicated with them like a silent movie director, via a megaphone.

Right through the video, there's a post in the way, blocking the camera's view of the band. "Fucking post," said Letts, who failed to spot it in advance of the shoot. "Couldn't do anything about it." But it gives that air of happenstance, of (fake, of course) verité, of a camera (and crew) chancing on a performance by the band. Letts' amateurism was also responsible for a pair of errors noted by bandspotter fans: Joe's guitar lead is not connected to his amp, and Topper's drumming is out of synch with the soundtrack.

The band is dressed almost all in black, with the merest flashes of color. The low light level bleaches all skin to junkie pallor — both an echo of the line in the song about "nodding out" and a sadly true reflection of the heroin problem then engulfing Topper and others in the band's inner circle. In a black Crombie coat with matching (red) tie and handkerchief, Mick Jones plays a white guitar. Joe wears a black-and-white spotted bandana. Paul has a gun in his waistband. "The folly of youth," said Letts, shaking his dreadlocks, remembering just how deeply he and the band were then obsessed with *Taxi Driver* (1976) and *Apocalypse Now* (1979). Kosmo: "We certainly egged each other on with the sartorials."

Letts again: "The band were so powerful that if I could have used five cameras, I could have got it all in one take. They were like four sticks of dynamite. You'd have to be a complete dickhead not to get something great out of them. It was a case of light the blue touchpaper and retire."

Even Letts' directorial ghost caught a whiff of that dynamite. While the union card holder didn't bother to turn up for the wintry riverside shoot, he arrived, unexpected and unannounced, for the edit. And there, in a Wardour Street post-production studio, some long-buried professional pride welled up in this ghost of a man. He decided he should do the edit in deed as well as in name. "He wanted to take over," said Letts. "He was trying to tell me what to do and poked me with a finger." Letts was not pleased. The ghost poked him again. Letts hit the ghost and threw him out of the editing room.

The video certainly did the trick in the U.S. "It was all over MTV and felt properly apocalyptic," Ira Robbins told me. (The channel didn't launch until August 1981, eighteen months after the video was made and released.)

The pier? Long gone. Its usefulness past, its timbers rotted and returned to the river. It was finally torn down in the 1990s when the whole riverbank was rebuilt. For many years, at low tide, you could just about see the late pier's struts rising out of the river's clay bottom. They looked — dare I write it, even though I know it's true — like Joe Strummer's teeth before he had them fixed. Now, even those remnants have sunk away.

**Christmas parties**
The ascendance of "London Calling" to unofficial city anthem began within weeks of the song's release. The process started just off the Portobello Road. On Christmas Day and Boxing Day, when the whole city was more or less shut, the Clash played a pair of shows at Acklam Hall, small, unannounced seasonal parties for those in the know — friends and friends of friends, mostly. Admission was 50 pence — cheap as chips even then. (I wasn't there. I was in New York, half-frozen to death with my new girlfriend.)

The shows were warm-ups for the band's two-month-long *Sixteen Tons* UK tour, which would start on January 5 in Aylesbury — a Buckinghamshire market town whose prime place on the touring circuit was directly linked to it being home to the rock magazine *ZigZag*. The Acklam Hall shows were a homecoming of sorts — less than a mile from where the band first came together, according to their own mythology, anyway. The hall was (and is) a tiny community venue underneath — literally, physically — the Westway.

Played live in the UK for the first time since they'd recorded it, "London Calling" was the last song in the Acklam Hall sets. From then on, it was almost invariably the set opener — placed there because, as Kosmo Vinyl put it, "it's phenomenally dramatic."

The day after those under-the-Westway shows, December 27, the band played "London Calling" to a (slightly) wider British public, a couple of miles down the road at the Hammersmith Odeon — not far from one of the River Thames' wide, slurry bends. It was at a benefit concert for the people of Kampuchea, as Cambodia was known during Pol Pot's murderous regime, which had been brought to an end by an invasion of Vietnamese soldiers, which had begun on the previous year's Christmas Day.

On the day of the Kampuchea benefit, there was another invasion in a different part of Asia: 3,500 or so miles to the east of Hammersmith. It was a cold snowy morning in Kabul when Zenith Group — a small unit under the direction of the KGB — led Operation Storm-333, the start of the Soviet Union's benighted attempt to subdue and conquer Afghanistan. At 4:15 p.m. GMT, dressed in Afghan army uniforms, the unit led a takeover of governmental and military buildings. They poisoned the central committee and attacked the Tajbeg Palace, killing President (of 104 days) Hafizullah Amin and 200 of his guards. It was nearly a decade later, in 1988, when the Soviet forces finally gave up and went home, having suffered 70,000 casualties. They left behind some two million dead Afghans, as many as five million refugees and the seeds of the regional conflict which has bubbled along, murderously, ever since.

Six or so hours after Zenith Group went to work in Kabul, the Clash played "London Calling" at the Hammersmith Odeon. Reaching out to the faraway towns. War is declared, etc., etc. And so, right from those first live performances, the song started accruing an anthemic sense of self.

**Hitsville UK**
"London Calling" was the biggest British hit of the Clash's real-time career — despite only reaching number-eleven in the UK. (It didn't chart at all in the U.S., where the band's greatest single success was "Rock the Casbah" — number-eight in 1982.) "We didn't feel 'London Calling' was going to be a huge hit," said Andrew King, their co-manager at the time. "And it wasn't, in conventional terms. But, in those days, it was possible for tracks to have a career."

He then quoted a dictum of another of his charges, Ian Dury, a songwriter and performer who, like the Clash, rhapsodized London in song and had a fine, worldly eye for the songwriting and pop games. If you've cut a good track, Dury told King, you don't have to do anything. It will just run off to *Top of the Pops* by itself and "do the bollocks." And "London Calling" did just that, said King. Why? I asked him. And how? What gave it that capacity? "There is a tension in it between the solid rhythm and its tremendous feeling of impermanence," King told me. "It's about modernity. In it, uncontrollable forces of change are sweeping across society — and that's what modernity's all about."

Prior to his arrival in London, the young Suffolk lad David Copperfield drew a word-picture of the city he was headed to. He imagined it to be "an amazing place … fuller of wonders and wickedness than all the cities of the earth." At least that's what Charles Dickens imagined in his 1850 biography of Copperfield.

The phrase "London Calling" predates the Clash by nearly six decades. It began its long life in the heart of the city on May 11, 1922, in the Marconi Building, 335 Strand. That's just north of Waterloo Bridge, just south of Covent Garden, just east of the Savoy hotel, just west of St. Clement Danes, the Wren church whose bells ring out that early London anthem "Oranges and Lemons" — and just across the road from Somerset House (which was then, and for many more years, home to the tax people). The kind of spot from which London really does call out to the faraway towns.

That day, on the seventh floor of the stone-faced Edwardian office block, 2LO radio announced its presence to the world with the words "London calling." Arriving two years after commercial broadcasting had started in the U.S., 2LO was the second radio station in Britain. Both were run by a private business with American roots, Marconi's Wireless Telegraph Company.

The first station was 2MT, which broadcast from an army hut near the company's labs in rural Essex. The second, 2LO, reached out to the world with a 100-watt transmitter — which gives a range of roughly thirty miles. So, no actual reaching out to faraway towns just yet. Still, such were the worries about this newfangled public-facing soundwave thingy that the station was restricted to one hour of broadcasting a day.

Later that year, 2LO was transferred to the British Broadcasting Company, a new and commercial Anglo-American set-up. Four years later, the business was de-privatized and became what is still the BBC — effectively state-owned but independently run. (2LO? While the LO most likely stands for London, I like to think it might also stand for a London-accented 'ello.) John Charles Walsham Reith, the BBC's giant (nearly six-and-a-half feet tall) Scotsman of a first general manager, would describe its mission as "a return to the city state of old." London as the Athens of the modern era, calling out to those faraway towns.

In 1994, BBC Radio launched a sitcom about its early years. It was called — of course it was — *London Calling*. (I wonder how many listeners wondered why it took its name from a Clash song.)

When "London Calling" first made its way onto the airwaves, it was a phrase of modernity and the march of technology. Noël Coward adopted it as the title of a 1923 revue. Coward being Coward, and musical revues being musical revues, an exclamation mark was added: *London Calling!* The show featured Coward's first hit song, "Parisian Pierrot." In his autobiography, Coward recalled, "For the first time, I had experienced the thrill of hearing my own music played in restaurants." The show moved to Broadway the following year: London and New York were already kind of show business twins.

I have a record called *Noel Coward in New York*, a gift from a New York cousin. It's a vinyl album, a Columbia Masterworks reissue of recordings made in the city in late 1956. I don't care for the music much at all — nor did the cousin, I think, hence the gifting of it. But the cover image, my oh my. It's a black-and-white daylight photo of the great man with the Manhattan skyline behind him. He's standing erect but casual, in evening dress, with a white handkerchief in his top pocket, drinking tea from a white china cup and saucer, a smoldering cigarette clutched between the second and third fingers of his left hand.

His gaze is lightly sardonic, but there's a camera-welcoming smile, too. Because of optical foreshortening, he's a giant of a figure, standing head and shoulders above the city's skyscrapers. As the Colossus was to Rhodes, so a real-life version of this Cowardly image could replace the Statue of Liberty: a first Noël for the Port of New York. The highest priest of camp as frontman for the city where camp was invented, in 1964 — or, at least, first publicized, by Susan Sontag. I encountered her essays three or four years later — a little Londoner's introduction to modern, even post-modern, New York intellectual trends and trendiness. London–New York. As one city drinks its cup of coffee, so the other sips its cuppa tea. As the Clash, in their "London Calling" video, stand with their backs to a decaying Thameside park in driving, squally rain, so Coward stands elegantly by New York's East River, on a lightly breezy afternoon, with his back to the United Nations building (and 42nd Street).

The picture is credited to Bernard Cole (presumably the London-born photographer of that name). The image is a direct, conscious echo of an earlier shot made by *LIFE* magazine photographer Loomis Dean in the Nevada desert for Coward's *At Las Vegas* live album in 1955. The image of Manhattan's East Side is the view out of the left-hand window as you make the final descent into LaGuardia Airport, finishing your drink as you pass the UN. The picture looks like it was taken on the waterfront of Long Island City — pretty much the spot where, the last time I was in New York, I had breakfast with an old friend from London — a journalist who had made the transatlantic crossing decades earlier and has, for many years, self-identified as her new city's "professor of punk and reggae."

**World at war**
It was World War II that made the phrase "London Calling" widely famous. Announced in the most BBC of voices, "This is London calling…" was the introductory announcement for the BBC broadcasts

which really did reach out to faraway towns in occupied countries, to resistance movements and anti-Nazis everywhere.

The phrase was an element of conscious pre-war preparations for the inevitable conflict. The BBC had begun international broadcasting, in English, in 1932, with the launch of the Empire Service. A global listings pamphlet followed, along with foreign-language programming: Arabic in January 1938, German in March; loud heralds of where the Empire Service thought the coming war would be fought. On July 14, 1939, it was decided to expand the listings magazine from twelve to sixteen pages and change its name from *BBC Empire Broadcasting* to *London Calling*.

The first issue of *London Calling* was published three months later, three weeks after England and France declared war on Germany. The earliest copy I've seen is number 37, from 1940. On its cover is an image of ships in heavy seas. The final issue was in October 1992. Its cover star was Slash, Stoke-born guitarist for Guns n' Roses. (The magazine didn't actually disappear, just its name did. It was changed to the truly uninspiring *BBC Worldwide*, then the even duller *BBC on Air* and finally closed in 2004.)

The decision to call the listing magazine *London Calling* was a political one, taken at a meeting of ten people in the Overseas Intelligence Department. (BBC's international radio stations were directly funded by the Foreign Office until 2014.) In November 1939, again with an obvious eye on the gathering clouds of war, the Empire Service was renamed the Overseas Service — to reflect a new wider remit, perhaps, or to deflect the growing pressures for independence across the empire, from India to Egypt.

Great Britain might not have had enough tanks or fighter planes, but it did have a global radio station and a magazine to go to war with, a rebranded one at that.

Britain (London, really) was playing to its strengths. If Hitler was to be defeated, it was time to gather and galvanize — not single spies, but battalions of words and pop music, of George Orwell's chatty broadcasts and stirring brassy tunes.

The end of the war began to seem possible in 1942. America joined in, the Russian army defeated the German invaders at Stalingrad and the World Service commissioned its own theme tune, a march entitled "London Calling." Written by Eric Coates, "the uncrowned king of light music," it was originally the signature tune for what was then known as the BBC's *Overseas Children's Programme*. Coates finished writing it on December 11, 1941.

The introduction to the tune is a musical "verbalization" of the phrase "This is London calling." The first "on-air" appearance of Coates' theme came on March 22, 1942, played by an orchestra on the BBC's Latin American service. Though Coates was a Nottinghamshire lad, he had a deep and romantic musical attachment to the metropolis. In 1932, he had written a three-part "London Suite," inspired, it is said, by the view from his flat in Chiltern Court. Music about London was notably popular then: Albert William Ketèlbey's "Cockney Suite," Haydn Wood's "London Cameos," John Ireland's "London Overture" all appeared around the time.

Chiltern Court itself was a most London of residential locations. It was — and is — a block of 200 apartments sitting on top of Baker Street station, i.e., just around the corner from Sherlock Holmes' bachelor rooms. Built as an eleven-story top piece to the Metropolitan Railway's new headquarters, the apartment block had opened only three years before Coates wrote his suite there. It was a modern vision of urbanity and urban home life, with full central heating and each flat cabled-up for both phone and radio. H.G. Wells lived there.

In 1942, the Special Operations Executive (SOE), which ran Britain's secret behind-enemy-lines espionage and sabotage, was founded at a meeting there. The SOE called out "This is London calling" to a continent of young men and women — too many of whom would be killed, tortured, shipped to camps or executed in police cells.

Later, and for many years, it was a home-sour-home for Hughie Green, the extreme right-wing alcoholic host of the TV talent show

*Opportunity Knocks*. (Catchphrase: "I mean that most sincerely, folks." Yes, it did always sound like a creepy lie.)

It's unlikely — very unlikely, even for a man of his musical hungers — that Joe Strummer would have known the story behind Coates' "London Calling." But, as a diplobrat, he would certainly have known the tune. He was a child of the post-imperial British diaspora. (His father was from Lucknow, born to an English father and an Indian mother.) As a child, Joe lived in a succession of faraway towns: Cairo, Bonn and many others. The tune and the World Service call sign were part of him and part of his childhood's dreams of a capital life. "This is London calling…"

**A visit from the boss**
Chaos was a familiar, if unsafe, haven for the Clash. One evening during the *London Calling* sessions, their record label boss, Maurice Oberstein, paid a visit to the studio. He arrived, as ever, in his Rolls-Royce, driven, as ever, by his uniformed chauffeuse, and accompanied, as ever, by his small dog. A louche, fifty-year-old gay American, Oberstein had signed the Clash to CBS Records. He had witnessed such early adventures as the band's fans rioting in the Rainbow Theatre and the band's members projecting war movies on the studio wall as a way of avoiding work on their second album, *Give 'Em Enough Rope*. He saw the Clash as beloved charges whose American success would transform him into a world player in the music business.

"He loved the Clash, absolutely loved them," said Muff Winwood, elder brother of Steve, and then head of A&R at CBS UK. Mostly, the feeling was reciprocated. "They loved him to bits," said photographer Pennie Smith. Yet, encouraged by former manager Bernard Rhodes' wild words, the band also often saw Oberstein as an enemy. So did others. "One of the world's greatest snakes," in the estimation of Clash co-manager Peter Jenner, who blamed Oberstein for the collapse and dissolution of his relationship with the band.

The night that Obie — as most everyone called him — visited Wessex Studios, the Clash told him they wanted to make *London Calling* a double album. When he demurred, chaos-loving producer Guy Stevens started a fight that ended with Stevens lying flat out on the road in front of the waiting Rolls-Royce — not because of anything prosaic like being hit by Obie or having been knocked down, but simply because he chose to. Stevens turned himself into a road hump — a sleeping producer, if you like — in a one-man passive-aggressive, almost Ghandi-like, protest against the tyrannical enemy. Well, against a dog-carrying record company executive who didn't agree that the best way to consolidate and build the band's place in the U.S. market was via a double album. *Take that*, fascist music business…

"At the time," engineer Bill Price has said, "this did not appear to me to achieve much at all. But thinking about it a little more over the years, I think it was probably quite a contribution in influencing CBS to allow the Clash to do what they wanted, to give 'em enough rope. I think it made a big difference. There had been endless arguments about musicality, about profit, about how much the sleeve cost, about the songs of their lives. There had been absolutely no meeting point. But the fact that Guy Stevens lay down in front of the limo and had to be carried back to the studio by myself and Johnny Green — when he [Stevens] finally stopped fighting us — I think made a big impression on Maurice."

The band got their way, but it was a pyrrhic victory. "The Clash see the merits of reaching a wider audience," said Sandy Pearlman, American producer of their second album, the perhaps aptly named *Give 'Em Enough Rope*. "But they also like the idea of grand suicidal gesture."

The *London Calling* album came out, as the band wished, as a double, yet priced as a single. Normally, this wouldn't have been a problem. But there was a problem, a big problem — not for the record company, for the band. The original deal that Rhodes had struck was a standard one. It committed the band to deliver a given number of records over a stated number of years. But, like most record contracts at the time, it defined a double album as one record, not two. So, *London Calling* only counted as one album. By making it a single-priced double, the Clash had effectively added a year to a contract that was already chafing them. Not only that, they also effectively halved their royalty rate. The following year's decision to make *Sandinista!* a triple album compounded the problem, hooking the band into almost Dickensian servitude to the record company. The contract grew longer and longer and longer. In getting their own way, they had turned themselves into indentured laborers. They became, financially, sharecroppers on the CBS plantation.

"It was a classic piece of Clash double-thinking," Jenner told me. "A good idea not thought through — and therefore having the opposite effect." Nor was this an exactly out-of-character or isolated event. The band, he said, set its management "impossible tasks." For example? "They wanted to perform in the Gun Court in Jamaica." The Gun Court was the popular name for the South Camp Rehabilitation Centre, a high-security Kingston jail. Various reggae stars, including the late Jacob Miller and Bob Marley's widow Rita, performed there for the inmates — though no white rock bands from far, far away in their safe European homes.

Also, Jenner and King's management style was itself — let's be polite — not unchaotic. I saw this for myself on that *Clash Take the Fifth* tour of the U.S. that the band made between starting and finishing the *London Calling* album. Arriving for a show at Chicago's Aragon Ballroom, the bus pulled up outside the downtown Holiday Inn, just beyond the Loop. Tour manager Johnny Green went into the hotel. After a while, Strummer followed him. The rest of us waited on the bus. And waited and waited. Eventually, Strummer returned, made his way to my seat and asked if I had a credit card with me. The band had plenty of cash, but the hotel wouldn't let us check in without a credit card as surety. I offered up my Visa and prayed — successfully — that it could withstand the impact of twenty rooms plus extras for two nights. Why didn't they have a credit card?

Because Jenner didn't believe in them. Decades later, he laughed. "I thought they were the devil's work."

Neither Jenner nor King was with the band on that tour. Jenner was running things back in London, while King was in New York, concentrating on building relationships with the band's U.S. record company, Epic. "I virtually lived in Black Rock [the building at 51 West 52nd Street, where CBS had its headquarters]." King's major project was to fix the Clash's contract — the one they'd signed in London with Oberstein included the U.S. "It was effectively a twelve-year deal. We could have got them out of it. That was why Obie fucked us." That is, King believes that Oberstein finessed a situation which he reckoned, correctly, would bump the Clash out of their relationship with the honest — if chaotic and hippyish — Jenner/King Blackhill partnership and back into the hands of Bernie Rhodes. A man, that is, whose thoughts, opinions and use of English are like well-oiled spaghetti. If you aren't completely confused by everything he says, you clearly aren't paying attention.

Record royalties take some time to come through. By Christmas, the Clash was still a long way from seeing any of the *London Calling* monies. The usual practice would be for the record company to give the band an advance via their management. Oberstein refused to do that. Instead, Jenner told me, "He personally insisted on giving each [member] of the band a check for £1,000. It was a great way of undermining us." It worked, too. The band cut their ties with Blackhill at the very moment they were starting to gain their first substantial (i.e., lucrative) international success.

The split with Blackhill was also hastened, according to Jenner, by the band's refusal to acknowledge Topper Headon's escalating heroin addiction — he overdosed after a show at the Rox Club in Lubbock, Texas on October 7, 1979. "Topper was the best musician in the band and such a nice geezer," said Jenner. "But whenever I raised the subject of his drug abuse, I was told, 'Fuck off, old man.'"

By the spring of 1980, Bernard Rhodes was back as manager. "Some strange Faustian deal was struck there," said Jenner. In 1982, "they [went] on tour with the Who. In a way, they lost their souls. Something happened to them when they went back with Bernie and threw Topper out."

Jenner had never signed a formal contract with the Clash. "I had no contract because I thought they were nice guys. Classic error. They never paid us back the money we spent on them. We never got a penny out of it. Do I still feel sore about it? I do. *London Calling* is a great record, but they were real arseholes. It bankrupted Blackhill. I'm very ambivalent. I like them as people, and I like their music. But I was really hurt by them — and what they did to Topper. Professional musicians but amateur human beings. They were so mixed up. It was such a shame. If only they could have sat down and taken a sensible pill."

In later years, Jenner would bump into Joe on the streets of West London. It was always "cordial," said Jenner. Joe was forever embarrassed by what he and his band had done to Blackhill Enterprises. "We all do stupid things. But I'm proud to have worked with them."

**In tune with London**
Right from the start, the Clash made a big thing about being a London band. They were photographed by the Westway. They were interviewed on a tube train. They consciously, even self-consciously, wrote songs about the city, their city: not just "London Calling" but also "London's Burning," "(White Man) in Hammersmith Palais," "The Guns of Brixton," "Clash City Rockers," "Capital Radio" (a full-frontal attack on the city's first commercial station — "in tune with nothing," in Strummer's satirical reconfiguring of a Capital jingle). Songs that took a poetic stance towards inner urban decline, that simultaneously bemoaned and celebrated the sweet smell of decay. Works of the imagination which described a landscape every bit as mythical as the one Scorsese dreamed up for *New York, New York*. Clashworld was more of a nightmare, though. Or, in the words of that other poet of urban collapse, Alex the Droog of *A Clockwork Orange*, more horrorshow.

"We were all about London, ultimately," said Strummer. "And I've always thought London is a very poetic city. It certainly inspired me." French poets Rimbaud and Verlaine thought the same way. They and their illicit love fled Paris for London, taking up romantic residence a mile or so south of the Clash's future base in Camden Town and just north of St. Pancras — a century and a half before that railway station became the London terminus for the direct *sous-Manche* train to Paris and Brussels, to which the poetic pair moved next and where Verlaine shot his Rimbaud, twice (but didn't kill him). A third great 19th-century French poet, Mallarmé, fell in love with London's "perpetually grey sky," justifying his ardor in an 1862 letter to a friend with the idiosyncratic explication that "God cannot see you."

"London's Burning" (1977) was one of the Clash's first angry anthems. It references two old children's rhymes. The title echoes the rhyme about a fire on London Bridge, while the lyrics echo the 19th-century children's rhyme "Pop Goes the Weasel," which tells the tale of an impoverished tailor reduced to pawning the tools of his trade. (Pop = pawn. The Eagle = the City Road pub in which the tailor drank away his income. Weasel = tailor's iron.) Or rather, that's what I've always known it to be about. My father gave me that story and explanation when I was young, and it seemed to make sense of words that had previously bordered on nonsense for me.

From then on, I experienced it as something of a local folk tale, set in the topography of my childhood. We lived not far from the City Road, and there were many, many tailors in our part of East London back then. We didn't live in the rhyming tailor's world of pub, pint and pawn (pop), but it was one I knew from my parents' recollections of their own poverty-wracked early years. My father's stepfather drank away his week's wages on the day he got paid and regularly used pawn shops to manage and regularize the family economy.

The Eagle was a real pub, a glass-fronted Victorian glory on the junction with Shepherdess Walk. It's still there, too. And that personal link is, I think, why I was so drawn to the rhyme. It made "art" — or, at least, anthropology — out of my life. I was deeply touched by the way its tale gave meaning so lightly yet sharply to my world, its streets, its trades and traditions. It was East End without being in any way "cor blimey." Nor was there anything Eliza Doolittle or Cockney performative about it. Not even a single piece of rhyming slang. For me, it did a moving but dry-eyed job of "representing" my home patch and its ancestral citizens.

More recently, I learned that it ain't necessarily so. My father's tale of a tailor's tale is, it seems, just that: not fact, but a tale and not the only possible explanation for the rhyme or even the most likely or favored one. Its musical roots are not in London, but in mid-19th-century America, perhaps on fairground hurdy-gurdy machines. As to the words, in the current running, the favorite definition for weasel is a weaver's shuttle part, the bit that makes a "pop" sound.

In fact, my childhood rhyme has become quite a matter of cultural studies debate. With my many years of professional writing and academic study (though in quite different fields), that makes me feel even more appropriately represented by the rhyme. And I still prefer my story about it. While there were plenty of tailor shops in the City Road area, I never saw a weavers — though I did have a horrid summer job in a small factory nearby, doing final assembly on fashionable children's slippers. When it comes to manufacturing, London's choice has long been either small-scale or very upscale, too. That's where all the money is. Up and down the City Road. Now as then. Probably more so. Just stay out of the pub.

In the Clash's "London's Burning," we are taken up and down not the City Road but the Westway. (It was written in Mick Jones' grandmother's flat, with its view of inner West London's road network — something of a nightly light show in the hours of darkness.)

Yet, despite its title, "London's Burning" is not that incendiary a lyric. What is the capital city burning with? Rage, rebellion, revolution? No, London is burning with boredom. The evidence for that statement? People are watching too much television — which does rhyme nicely with religion.

Still, the song's attack on boredom was launched with such passion and brio that it achieved a paradox: it made boredom exciting, something to be sought out and achieved. A mainstay of teenage self-explanation — "I'm bored" — was justified and lionized. Punks everywhere told anyone who'd listen that they were bored. How thrilling was that. How very revolutionary.

"London's Burning" also, perhaps, provided the title for a black comedy TV film about the city's firemen — written by the great Jack Rosenthal, a Mancunian who lived a quiet, settled family life in a quiet, settled, red-brick Edwardian street in North London's Muswell Hill. When the one-off was being turned into a long-running TV series, Strummer turned down an offer to write the theme tune.

The Clash's urge to write hometown anthems outlived the group and persisted into their subsequent endeavors. Big Audio Dynamite was a joint Mick Jones–Don Letts project. "With B.A.D.," said Letts, "me and Mick were always trying to write the great London song. Never managed it." Among their attempts were "Harrow Road," "Stone Thames," "The Battle of All Saints Road" and "London Bridge" on *Megatop Phoenix* — which Letts reckoned was the closest they got to success. Too wordy to my mind, it's a list song which, like "London's Burning," echoes the children's rhyme about the bridge which has symbolized the city for many centuries (about which there will be more soon). Eric Coates also composed a "London Bridge" tune, by the way, in the same Baker Street apartment as he wrote his own "London Calling" theme — as well as melodies about Knightsbridge, Holborn, etc., etc.

Better, far better, than the B.A.D. songs was Strummer's post-Clash hymning of the unconsidered parts of northwest London in the Mescaleros' "From Willesden to Cricklewood," a track on 1999's *Rock Art and the X-Ray Style*. Almost an answer record to "London Calling," it's the narrative of a walk across the city's inner suburbs north of the Westway. It's also strikingly optimistic in a middle-aged-man kind of way. "The town looked good," Strummer reported. It was one of the first tracks he recorded after getting free from the sharecropper-like contract he'd signed back in 1977.

*"London is the only real place in the world.
The heart of the world is in London."*
—RICHARD JEFFRIES (1892)

It's not only Strummer, Jones and Letts who have tried to write the great London song, of course. Lots of people have had a go. The first London "song" I've found is, give or take, a thousand-year-old piece of verse. Fittingly for a city so dependent on the talents and efforts of incomers, it was written by a non-local, a man from the freezing north named Óttarr svarti (Óttarr the Black). An 11th-century Icelander, Óttarr worked as a court poet: first in Sweden, then Norway, back to Sweden and finally as poet-in-residence to Cnut, "King of all England and Denmark and the Norwegians and of some of the Swedes," as he described himself. (Others refer to him as ruler of the North Sea Empire.) Óttarr's verses were a celebration of the 1014 destruction and incineration of London Bridge by Norse invaders, led by Cnut's father, Sweyn Forkbeard: "London bridge is broken down. Gold is won and bright renown."

Money, fame, violence: all there. The eternal attractions of a great metropolis in two short lines. (When Cnut finally took London a couple of years later, he had the nerve to charge the city for his incursion — £10,500 to pay off his troops. How London is that? Adjusting for inflation over the thousand years since, that's northwards of £20 million. "Sounds doable," I imagine 11th-century London replying to the invaders from across the North Sea. "Ask Cnut if he'll take a check. We'll put it in the mail. Honest.") In his 2008 stage show, (then) cross-dressing comic Eddie Izzard had a riff about how the U.S. has city anthems — he namechecked "New York, New York" and "Chicago" (a.k.a. "My Kinda Town") — while London doesn't. If it did, said Eddie, it would be something like "London Fuck Off, Come Back (And Give Us Your Money)." Exactly.

The other, far better-known London Bridge song, the children's rhyme "London Bridge Is Falling Down," is far younger. Its words were first published in 1744 — by which time there had been four completely new actual London Bridges and any number of refurbishments since Cnut's men torched it. (The fact that the first two lines of the children's rhyme are so similar to Óttarr svarti's is happenstance. The Norse poet wrote in Old Norse, not English, and his verses remained untranslated till very recently.) The rhyme's tune is even more recent. Far more recent. Not at all London either. It first appeared in print in Philadelphia, in 1879 — a mere (and exact) century before "London Calling." It was published in A.H. Rosewig's *Illustrated National Songs and Games*. Not a local song, then, but one of the wider world. How very London.

In early 19th-century London, pioneer journalist Pierce Egan wrote chronicles of adventures and journeys, not always legal or moral, on the big city's streets — an English Regency predecessor of Manhattan's poet of Broadway, Damon Runyon. In his collection, *Life in London*, there are the lyrics to a contemporary song, popular in the bars and funhouses favored by his semi-fictional alter-egos.

*Such prime joking. Lots of smoking.*
*Here all dash on in the fashion!*
*Dancing. Singing. Full of glee.*
*O, London. London town for me.*

I asked around about more modern London songs. What are the good ones? Why so many truly bad ones? How do they compare with the ones about New York? I started with Kirsty MacColl. (We talked long ago, a year or so before she was killed, in 2000, swimming with her children in Mexico.) She wrote songs about London and New York. She didn't write the Pogues' "Fairytale of New York," but she did sing on it, and it was her choir of voices that made it a hit, an anthem and, in the mind of a *New York Daily News* piece, the ninth best song about the city. Sung by an English-born Irishman and a girl from Croydon, daughter of a Scottish-Mancunian communist folksinger.

MacColl did write her own anthemic, gritty, song about New York — "Walking Down Madison." One of her most strikingly London songs was "England 2, Colombia 0," a sardonic story about football, adultery and the Sir Richard Steele, a pub on Haverstock Hill, halfway between Hampstead and Camden Town.

The smoke-stained bars of the Steeles — as it was known — were home to generations of actors and performers. In the 1990s, when Kirsty's song was written, it was the local for the Jude Law/Kate Moss crowd, Mancunian emigrants Oasis and an Anglo-American movie-making couple, Tim Burton and Helena Bonham-Carter, who lived in the mews behind the pub. England's 2-0 World Cup victory over Colombia was on June 26, 1998. I don't know if Kirsty's song was set on that night. But I do know it was autobiographical, based on her own night of romantic disappointment which began in that pub on a hill.

She also co-wrote "Soho Square," a song about love and loss and an empty bench. Eight months after she was killed, a memorial bench was placed in the southwest corner of Soho Square — 250 feet from Paul McCartney's London headquarters and maybe twice that distance from the former CBS Records building in which the Clash signed their contract. Each October, on Kirsty's birthday, a small and dwindling clutch of people — those who loved her and those who loved her music — gather at her bench. They sing her songs, not that well, but with feeling. The rest of the year, tourists and lunch-breakers sit there, eating and drinking, probably not knowing the bench's history. That's London for you.

So, whose London songs did Kirsty respect and admire? "The Smiths," she told me, without pause. The Smiths of Manchester — creators of one song called "London" and another called "Panic" (the chorus of which adds "in the streets of London"), as well as "Half a Person," which depicts a timid sixteen-year-old's arrival in the capital.

The respect was mutual. Kirsty sang on the Smiths' "Ask," and I remember seeing Smiths singer-songwriter Morrissey dumbstruck with grief at her memorial service in St. Martin-in-the-Fields, the Trafalgar Square church whose bells ring out "you owe me five farthings" in the London children's rhyme "Oranges and Lemons."

Kirsty cited the Pogues, too: "London, You're a Lady" and "A Rainy Night in Soho." And the Kinks, of course — particularly Ray Davies' "Waterloo Sunset," with its Terry and Julie, its innocence and its sadness. "Waterloo Sunset" — like "London Calling" — regularly gets voted the top London anthem on local radio shows. I think it's that sadness that gets the votes in. One of the song's less obvious charms is that it bookends Wordsworth's hymn to the city, his 1802 poem "Upon Westminster Bridge." Both Wordsworth's poem and Davies' song are set on central London bridges across the Thames. They are unshared gazes, though. The beat boom songwriter's is a doleful dusk — a chilly, chilly evening — while the romantic poet sees a hopeful dawn: "This City now doth like a garment wear / The beauty of the morning."

Decades after writing "Waterloo Sunset," Davies made a more self-conscious attempt to write a London anthem. He even called it "London Song." Sadly, it's forced and lumpy. Its list of "great Londoners" features the tourist-guide clichés of Blake and Dickens, but also Arthur Daley, the fictional wide boy of *Minder*, a 1980s TV hit. "And," continues Davies, "don't forget the Kray twins," charmlessly adding the 1960s gangsters to his best of London list.

All kinds have had a go at a London song. Ed Sheeran and Stormzy did "Take Me Back to London" (2019), a title with an air of Edwardian music hall and a track which sounds like a math teacher trying to be hip. Taylor Swift, a country girl from Pennsylvania, wrote and sang "London Boy" (2019), a love list which namechecks Highgate (rhyming it with "best mate"), Camden Market and Shoreditch, pays tribute to a favorite local pastime — drinking in the afternoon — and makes a passable attempt at the local accent. (Her longtime boyfriend at the time grew up in the Highgate area and went to City of London School.)

Cerys Matthews, a woman of Cardiff, Wales, berated the city and its "poison Thames" on Catatonia's "Londinium" (1999): "London never sleeps, it just sucks … the life out of me." Now primarily a BBC Radio DJ, she still lives (and raises her children) in the city.

Decades apart, some quite different people wrote and performed songs which unequivocally asserted emotional ownership of the city. Working backwards in time…

In 2008, grime artist, garage man, producer, label owner and rapper Wiley (a Bow lad of Trinidadian and Antiguan heritage, born Richard Kylea Cowie Jr. in the year of "London Calling") told the world "I Am London." Well, maybe, if that assertion can encompass Wiley's full CV, which includes multiple stab wounds, an MBE "for services to music," a substantial career selling crack and smack, antisemitic rantings and [currently] being on the lam for failing to appear in court. So, yes, Wiley probably does embody the city — one variant of it, anyway.

In 1991, Saint Etienne asserted "London Belongs to Me." An indie dance-pop band from Croydon, the most southern place in the city, they took their name from a French football team. Their London is essentially a pleasant ramble from the Camden Town tube station to the ravishing, willowed flatlands of Regent's Park — ten minutes easy walking in a strong headwind.

If they'd pushed on a few minutes, they'd have found themselves at the Steeles (see above) or on Primrose Hill, where Paul McCartney walked his dog and found a fool, around the same time that singer-songwriter John Martyn watched the sun set there with his wife Beverley, a local girl. Or maybe Saint Etienne passed Paddington Bear (the marmalade-loving Peruvian refugee lived there in both his bio-pics) — or even Fountains of Wayne (from New York, named after a New Jersey lawn ornament store). On the 1997 B-side "Places," they make a journey similar to Saint Etienne's, though in the opposite direction — standing "like statues" on Primrose Hill, then down the Regent's Canal to try on silver shoes and orange plastic jackets in Camden Lock market. (This part of London is to modern songwriters what Mayfair was to their pre-war counterparts.)

In 1948, Lord Kitchener (né Aldwyn Roberts), a post-war Trinidadian calypsonian, came to London on the Empire Windrush, the first of the stream of ships that brought a generation of Caribbean immigrants to the city. Onboard, Kitchener wrote "London Is the Place for Me," a song glorying in the city's possibilities. With the optimistic and excited eye of a new immigrant, he called life in London "comfortable" and the English people "very much sociable." On June 21st, he landed at Tilbury — way to the city's east and nationalistically famed as the location of Queen Elizabeth I's troop-rallying anti-Spanish Armada speech on August 19, 1588. (She was dressed in white velvet and riding a white horse. Now that's a London girl for you.)

A dockside Pathé News crew filmed Kitchener performing the first two verses of his song, which he recorded in full in 1951, for the Melodisc label, with Eddy Grant's Caribbean Rhythm, and "supervision" by Denis Preston, a Stoke Newington boy like me and something of a music business legend, even now. Maybe the session was at EMI's studios in Abbey Road, or perhaps at Melodisc's Covent Garden HQ, no more than a guitar's throw from the office I was based at in 1979. (A new version of "London Is the Place for Me" was used in *Paddington*, the 2014 movie about that other open-hearted, optimistic incomer.)

The self-limited geography of both the Saint Etienne song — and the somewhat overwrought "And God Created Brixton" by the clearly overnamed Carter the Unstoppable Sex Machine — is not untypical of London songs. There is a distinct tendency towards the small and the specific — the local that can echo globally. Ram Jam Holder, of Guyanese origins, wrote "Wimpy Bar Blues" (1969) about hanging out in a low-rent burger joint on Edgware Road — not far from the tunnel which, in 2009, was named the Joe Strummer Subway. On "Brent Cross" (1980), the punk band 999 celebrated, ironically perhaps, a North London shopping center: "Let's all go where the people go." (999 drummer Pablo LaBritain — originally Paul Buck — was Strummer's closest friend at boarding school and, for a while, in line to be the Clash's drummer.)

This localist tendency brought to mind an older song called "There's Ever Such a Lot of London." It had been mentioned to me by Denis Norden, the late television writer and presenter whose early career ran parallel with both music hall and the last pre-rock and roll generation of professional songwriters. We were talking about London songs. How, I'd asked Denis, do New York and London songs compare? "New York songwriters romanticized Broadway in a way we didn't Shaftesbury Avenue."

But a later generation did find its own London streets to romanticize: (Scottish) Donovan's "Sunny Goodge Street," for example; also (Welsh) Duffy's "Warwick Avenue" and (Scottish) Gerry Rafferty's "Baker Street," which was recorded in Oxfordshire with a solo by Raphael Ravenscroft, a saxophonist from Stoke-on-Trent. Or even "African Head Charge in the Hackney Empire" (2018) by reggae producer Lee "Scratch" Perry (Jamaican, longtime resident of Switzerland).

As ever, romance is the province of the outsider, the foreigner, the stranger, not local boys and girls. Distance is the nourishment of enchantment — and the uses to which it's put. Even in Norden's day, there was "A Nightingale Sang in Berkeley Square" (1940) with music by a man from Philadelphia, Manning Sherwin, and words by Eric Maschwitz (Lithuanian-Jewish, from Birmingham). A former editor of *Radio Times* and a British spy, Maschwitz shipped out to New York the year "Nightingale" hit, then moved on to Los Angeles. (There never were nightingales in Berkeley Square, of course, just rich person clubs, private art galleries and expensive car showrooms.)

"New York had its singing mayor, Jimmy Walker," Denis continued. "And there was even a stage show about Mayor La Guardia. We were better at the comic, like 'There's Ever Such a Lot of London' or 'Pretty Polly Perkins of Paddington Green.'" It's true. There are a lot of fine, if now archaic, comic songs about London. A personal favorite is Ella Shields' "Burlington Bertie From Bow," a compression of metropolitan ironies. It's a music hall song, from 1915, supposedly being sung by a poor man (from Bow, East London) pretending to be a rich man (of the Burlington Arcade area in the West End). The singer — her name is the giveaway — was a woman pretending to be a man. Not that Shields was a Londoner. Or even English, though her first husband was — he wrote "Bertie" for her — and she played the opening night of the London Palladium. She was born Ella Buscher in Baltimore. So: an American woman whose act was pretending to be a poor male Londoner pretending to be a rich male Londoner. And making a good shilling out of it. Now, there's London for you. Later, down on her luck, she moved to New York and took a job as a sales assistant at Macy's. As one city casts you out, the other welcomes you in, sort of. After WW II, she returned to England and success, even to the Palladium for a Royal Variety Performance.

Shields died onstage in Lancaster in 1952 while singing "Burlington Bertie," collapsing either at the end of the song or after its first line — sources disagree. Never regaining consciousness, she was cremated in London, in the same chapel that would later commit Amy Winehouse to eternity; Denis Norden and Marc Bolan, too. (By the by: 1952 was the year Joe Strummer was born and Frank Sinatra, at the low point of his career, was dropped by Columbia Records, sister company of the Clash's future label.)

It's also true that there aren't as many funny songs about New York — it takes itself far more seriously than its European comrade in financial and artistic services. There is, of course, Suzanne Vega's "Tom's Diner," with its 1980s dry-as-toast deadpan and, from an earlier era, "Second Hand Rose" ("from Second Avenue"), a cousin-in-alliteration of London's "Pretty Polly Perkins of Paddington Green" and a 1921 smash for Fanny Brice — comic, star and Jewish Hungarian New Yorker.

There was also, unnoticed by Denis, a fine late-20th-century harvest of comic London songs, mostly with Cockneyish accents. While many writers, singers and bands had a go, only three truly succeeded. First came Ian Dury, whose "cor blimey" persona was an art-schooled confection — though his polio-damaged body and children's-home-battered emotions very much weren't an act. The comic vision of his songs was a deeply fictionalized one of London's eastern reaches — the flat, estuarial homeland of "Billericay Dickie," "Plaistow Patricia" and spruced-up Ford Cortinas.

Behind Dury came Squeeze (Difford/Tilbrook) from South London ("Up the Junction" concerns unplanned parenthood with a "girl from Clapham") and Madness from North London. Perhaps you could add West London's Lily Allen to that list, but only one song of hers, "LDN," would be a definitive addition to the modern-ish London comic songbook, primarily thanks to its bouncy Carnival-Caribbean horns and irresistible hook of a chorus: "I wouldn't be anywhere else." (Her father, comic and actor Keith Allen, was a regular companion of Joe Strummer on midnight drink-and-drug-powered explorations of the city and its possibilities. At Joe's funeral, he placed a cowboy hat on the coffin.) "Parklife" by Blur — who are from London's far east — has an equally sardonic and attractive hook of a line, the ultra-London question, "Know what I mean?" (Like Coward's "London Pride," it references and teases "Deutschland Über Alles," with a snatch of the German national anthem played on a plastic saxophone.) Not that any of those writers were London parochialists. Dury's list song "Reasons to Be Cheerful" rhymes "Hammersmith Palais" with "Bolshoi Ballet." Madness wrote "Night Boat to Cairo," though they probably never took one. Blur conjured up "Magic America," and Squeeze's "Up the Junction" was put together in a New Orleans laundromat.

It's also the sad case that there have been some truly terrible songs about London. I'll start with the ones called "London Town." Finish there, too. (Even civic self-harm has its limits.) The title alone should be a giveaway. "London town" as a phrase sounds quite foreign to Londoners. To a pre-war generation, London was "town" — as if there were no other — but never "London town." That has always been an outsider's name for it.

The phrase seems to bring out the worst in songwriters. They particularly have problems with rhyming the title. "Town" is not just an awful word to rhyme, it's a nothing sound, with a final "n" that disappears in the mouths of even the most self-consciously precise enunciators. It's the consonant that isn't there. All that remains of it is a memory. Not a good one, either. Who'd settle for a town when they could have a city?

First up (randomly) is the "London Town" (1966) of Shawn Phillips, a folkie from Fort Worth, Texas, which offers up this terrible line: "I laugh with your ups and cry with your downs." It also claims that Londoners are "warm and friendly." Now, there's disinformation for you.

Others did no better with their "London Town"s and often worse. Guitarist Chris Spedding (from, successively, Derbyshire, Sheffield and Birmingham) and reliably surly 1960s London rockers the Pretty Things rhymed "town" with "down." Light of the World's light funk couldn't even manage a real rhyme — "underground" and "town."

Not that rhyming is the only problem lyricists have had over the years with "London Town" songs. They find all kinds of ways to fail. Mike Read, radio DJ and serial bankrupt (from Walton-on-Thames): "London town, it's got all the latest tunes." Even Paul McCartney (Liverpool) tried a "London Town" song (on the 1978 Wings album of the same name) and failed. That's what London town does to even the best of songwriters, it seems.

I can think of only one exception: the lead track on "nu-folk" singer Laura Marling's *The London Town EP* (2007). She was seventeen at the time. The previous year, as soon as she could, she had moved to the city from the woody hills of Berkshire — physically close but socially and culturally distant. "How's it back in London town where you let me down?" Marling sings. Depressed, betrayed, vengeful even: how London is that? Chris Briggs started working with her on her second studio album, *I Speak Because I Can*. He told me that Marling is "emotionally intelligent beyond her years. Her insight into doomed relationships is borderline uncomfortable." Now that's a talent you can put to good use in a big city, particularly London.

*"The citye of London … is to me so dere and sweete."*
— GEOFFREY CHAUCER

Unlike New York, London has never had an official anthem. That's not the kind of thing Londoners have the inclination — or time — to think about. Certainly not when they (okay, we) could be going about their (our) real business, picking the world's pockets. And getting them to thank you for taking the trouble.

Why, I asked Denis Norden, have there been so few open and joyous celebrations of London in song? He answered my question with a question. "Is flag-waving in the British character?"

In fact, there are evocative, meaningful and well-loved musical tributes to London. Pride-filled ones, even. The most anthemic London song of the early-mid-20th century was "Old Father Thames." Inspired by Jerome Kern's "Ol' Man River" and made famous by an Australian, Peter Pawson, it was written by Raymond Wallace and one Betsy O'Hogan — a nom de copyright of Lawrie Wright, a classic showbiz hustler from Leicester and the man who turned Denmark Street into London's Tin Pan Alley. To publicize a song called "Sahara," he rode a camel round Leicester Square. He founded the *Melody Maker*, a weekly paper (1926–2001) whose first cover featured songwriter Horatio Nicholls — another Wright pseudonym. His company slogan was "You can't go wrong with a Wright song."

The most celebratory of mid-20th-century London songs was "London Pride," written by the *London Calling!* author, Noël Coward — son of a lazy, unsuccessful piano salesman from Teddington. A dozen or so miles upriver from central London, Teddington was (and is) to London much as Sinatra's hometown of Hoboken was to New York — close enough to see the big city and wonder at it but never close enough to touch or devour it.

By the time Coward wrote "London Pride," he had moved deep into the heart of the city, pumping blood, spirit and money into its cultural and emotional life. It was the early summer of 1941, and he was living at the Savoy hotel — safe, with a view of the river and bombs falling. In the depths of the Blitz, he turned a refreshed eye on his native city — his gazings brightened, I should imagine, by the quickness of thought and sharpness of feeling that comes when death rains nightly from the sky.

London, he wrote in his memoirs, had always seemed "a little dull and smug compared with the romantic gaiety of Paris and the sharp vitality of New York. I saw it for the first time as somewhere I belonged." From his base at the Savoy, he ventured forth as a tourist in his own home town, visiting the zoo and the Tower of London.

Everywhere he saw bomb sites. Flower-covered bomb sites. Blitzed rubble was often carpeted with seasonal flowers — in particular, the wild-running rock-hugger commonly known as London Pride. A pink-flowered sweet lavender, now widely used as a garden perennial, London Pride is a charmer. Another of its informal names is None-So-Pretty. It's a city urchin of a flower, with its lineage and qualities indicated by its scientific name, *Saxifraga x urbium*. Suitably for the city it celebrates, it's an immigrant — part-Spanish, part-Irish — and something of a bastard, too. The "x" shows it's a species hybrid — specifically, the genetic meeting of *Saxifraga umbrosa*, a native of the Spanish Pyrenees, and *Saxifraga spathularis*, from the west of Ireland.

Life-hardened in both the high country of northern Spain and the damp-drenched west of Ireland, *Saxifraga x urbium* is true to its binomial name. *Saxifraga* is a compound of *saxum* (rock or stone) and *frangere* (to break). *Urbium* means "of/from the town." So *Saxifraga x urbium*: urban rock-buster. Which is why it grew so well on bomb sites: it spreads fast in late spring on dry ground.

It's also a linguistic usurper. At least two other flowers, both also non-locals, were previously known as London Pride. There was *Dianthus barbatus* — sometimes called Sweet William — which is native to the mountains of southern Europe, from the Pyrenees east to the Carpathians and Balkans. And there was *Lychnis chalcedonica*, also known as the Flower of Constantinople — native to Mongolia, Russia, Kazakhstan and northwest China. So, in the flowery battle for supremacy in London's eyes and slang, a southern European mountain-dweller and a central Asian were trumped by an Irish-Spanish bastard immigrant. How very London.

Coward conceived his "London Pride" on a blitzed railway station platform (Paddington, most probably) as a song of clever, willful defiance. Calling it "London Pride" was a sly, Cowardly joke. The melody is based on a traditional street hawker's song, "Won't You Buy My Sweet Blooming Lavender." Behind that allusion to a flower-seller's street call, another, even slyer, joke is at play. The same tune also became the melody of the German national anthem, "Deutschland Über Alles." With malice and mischief aforethought, Coward took the enemy's best tune and turned it, like a double agent. According to biographer Stephen Citron, Coward "considered that the time had come for us to have it back in London where it belonged."

Well, kind of. It's hardly just a German anthem of a tune. It's also the tune to "America (My Country 'Tis of Thee)" and the hymn "Glorious Things of Thee Are Spoken." Anthemic qualities are precious and temptingly recyclable.

Nor does the tune's ancestry stop there. The melody's first (known) appearance was in Vienna in 1797, as Haydn's "Gott erhalte Franz den Kaiser." A stirring anthem for the Habsburg Empire, that tune was, in turn, inspired by the composer's 1794 visit to England, when he was impressed by the strength and succor he saw its citizens draw from singing "God Save the King." He decided that his empire needed a similarly rousing and inspiring anthem to fortify its populace in the ongoing wars with Napoleon's French Empire. So, he wrote a stirring tribute to his dynastic overlord, the man known to us as Francis II, the last Holy Roman Emperor, ruler of lands and peoples stretching from the Adriatic to the Baltic, from the North Sea to the Russian border. Lyrics were commissioned from poet Lorenz Haschka, and it was first performed on Francis II's 29th birthday.

Not that it had much effect. Despite Haydn's best efforts, the Habsburg forces were consistently defeated by Napoleon's. In October of the year "Gott erhalte Franz den Kaiser" debuted, the Empire lost its Netherlands territories. Nine years later, in the wake of defeat at

Austerlitz, the Holy Roman Empire finally expired — after 963 years of life. (Or 843 years, depending on whether you date its birth to the crowning of Charlemagne or of Otto I. Whichever it was, Haydn's anthem couldn't keep the Empire together.) Not that its failure weakened Haydn's admiration for his tune. He reused and played around with its theme in the second movement of his String Quartet in C Major, known as the Emperor Quartet. And he played it at home, three times a day. His final performance was at 12:30 p.m. on May 26, 1809. At 5:00 p.m., he told his children he felt ill. He died three days later.

Unlike Haydn's song, "London Pride" *was* successful at rousing its audience to self-belief and victory. That success lay in it being an answer to an unspoken prayer, offering a promise of resoluteness at a time of terror. Coward biographer Philip Hoare: "'London Pride' was the soundtrack for Coward's simplified war: banal but touching; an evocation of emotion, an emblem of resistance."

Theatre critic John Lahr — son of Bert, who played the cowardly lion in *The Wizard of Oz* to Judy Garland's Dorothy — wrote that Coward "put himself into the narrative the English tell themselves about their struggles, their suffering, their triumphs." (Echoes of which are, of course, in "London Calling." Also, in a way, in "New York, New York"'s narrative of the singer's struggles, ambition and — dreamed-of — triumphs.)

Coward had (as would have been said in the 1950s) "a good war." Before hostilities commenced, he was an arch, if very successful, outsider. Dropping irony and camp for the duration, he became a mainstream, even emblematic figure, producing three of his best-known (and best) works — "London Pride" and the films *In Which We Serve* and *Brief Encounter*. All three are unabashedly emotional and unironic. That the emotion is expressed in a particularly pinched tone and manner only makes them truer: to their author, their subject and their meaning. All three are not so much general hymns to British resilience ("the Blitz spirit") as rallying cries for a particular kind of British middle-classdom. Coward's war was not about democracy or fascism. Decency, restraint, well-tended gardens and church fêtes — that's what Coward was defending from Hitler and his cronies.

Coward wrote a lyric using the simplest of words to express the deepest of emotions. There is no rhetoric, no bloviation, no nonsense about glory or victory or foreigners' knavish tricks — in short, none of the rubbish that clutters up "God Save the Queen." No word is longer than two syllables. Most are only one. This is Orwellian language in its very best sense — plain, clear, calm, direct. God, thank god, doesn't get so much as a look-in. The simple lyrics hymn not kings or queens or battles or empires, but freedom and a wildflower borne to the city on the winds of both south and west. And all sung to the tune of the German national anthem.

Lord Mountbatten — the man the IRA would murder in 1979, "Dickie" to his good friend Coward — gave a copy of "London Pride" to President Roosevelt. It was the final song played at Coward's memorial service, held on Empire Day, May 24, 1973, at that most London of London churches, St. Martin-in-the-Fields.

"London Pride" wasn't the only great mid-century London anthem. There was also "Maybe It's Because I'm a Londoner," which is often wrongly acclaimed as an ancient musical hall standard. *Time* magazine once wrote "this old song has echoed down the alleys of history." No, it didn't. As with "New York, New York," people generally assume it is older than it is. In truth, it only came to fame in the post-war era and is, in fact, younger than "London Pride" by a couple of years.

It was written in 1944, by Hubert Gregg of Islington. A pre-war BBC radio announcer, Gregg played a pilot in Coward's sea-war picture, *In Which We Serve*, and was (baddie) Prince John in both the 1952 Disney movie *The Story of Robin Hood* and the later British TV series about the English robber woodsman. He also wrote "Je Ne Sais Pais," which Brigitte Bardot sang in her only British double entendre comedy, *Doctor at Sea*. His third child arrived when he was sixty-eight — he credited ginseng and his (third) wife's cooking. He chaired the long-running BBC show *The Brains Trust* and hosted his own weekly BBC Radio 2 old-style pop show, *Thanks for the Memory*, till shortly before his death in 2004 in Eastbourne, Sussex, at the age of eighty-nine.

"Maybe It's Because I'm a Londoner" was his second song about the city. He had a wartime hit with "I'm Going to Get Lit Up When the Lights Go Up in London." ("Lit up" being mid-century slang for "drunk.") There were complaints about the song in parliament. Lady Astor MP (American, from Virginia) asked if this was "the disgraceful way Britons were going to behave" when victory finally came. Prime Minister Winston Churchill (half-American, his mother a Brooklyn native) replied, "We shall celebrate a victorious peace in a way worthy of the British nation."

Gregg described "Maybe It's Because I'm a Londoner" as "a love song to my city." Like Coward, he was inspired by German aerial attacks. He wrote the song a few days after he had seen — on leave in the city from the Lincolnshire regiment — one of the first V1 flying bombs cross "the night sky through my bedroom window." As he was mostly away in the army, however, it was three years before his song was first performed in public.

Its stage debut only came in 1947, at the Victoria Palace theatre. It was sung by comedian Bud Flanagan in *Together Again*, the first season of a long-running comedy revue by the Crazy Gang — the most Londonish of mid-century comic groupings. It soon became an anthem for the city — and a particular favorite of George VI, who lived just up the road from the Victoria Palace in a palace of his own, bigger than the Victoria but more socially restrictive. Worse architecture, too, and less fun. Far less.

The song was made even more famous by a pair of New Yorkers, Kirk Douglas and Burt Lancaster, who sang it as a duet at a London Palladium charity show — *Night of 100 Stars*, in 1958 — for which Gregg wrote a new verse. Another New Yorker, Danny Kaye, sang it, too — around the same time he had a hit with "Wonderful, Wonderful Copenhagen."

Gregg's song truly rooted itself in the British self-consciousness in the mid-1950s, primarily because of an early evening TV program. From 1955, it was used as the opening theme of Britain's first TV cop show, *Dixon of Dock Green*. The tune was whistled by the show's lead character, Sergeant George Dixon, who moved with the slow, wallowing gait of a Thames barge. At the end of each episode, he would arrest the villain with a gentle, archaic touch on the shoulder. Then he would tell viewers: "Mind how you go." A lost world, even at the time.

There was a brief period at the end of the century when "Maybe It's Because I'm a Londoner" heaved towards becoming the city's official anthem. It was the time of London's first mayoral election. Yes, there has long been a Lord Mayor of London but his (or her) writ only extends to the City of London's square mile (1.12 sq. mi., to be precise), the financial center whose political structure is little more democratic than, say, Czarist Russia's. But, until the 21st century, there was never an actual mayor of London, all 607 square miles of it. London's first genuinely democratically elected mayor was a creation of Tony Blair's New Labour government, first elected in 1997.

The inaugural London mayoral election was held in 2000. It was notable — suitably notable for such a city, you might say — for its cast of wide boys, liars and performers. London's initial tranche of mayoral candidates featured a punk manager (Malcolm McLaren, whose platform included legalizing brothels and allowing libraries to serve alcohol), a serial adulterer (Conservative politician Steve "Shagger" Norris — some suggested his love-life history would provide excellent experience for the exigencies of running London), a two-time Oscar-winning actress known for getting naked in Ken Russell's *Women in Love* (Glenda Jackson), a bearded northern politician (Frank "Dobbo" Dobson) and the newt-loving eventual winner (Ken Livingstone). There was also, briefly, a contestant whose past prompted the headline "Candidate denies Uncle Little Legs was bag man for the Krays."

Also on the list was writer, politician and soon-to-be jailbird Jeffrey Archer, who chose "Maybe It's Because I'm a Londoner" as a theme song for his amusingly disastrous run at the mayorship — having previously told a magazine that his favorite song was "New York, New York." The litigious lord acted, as ever, in character. First, he used his charm to get Sir George Martin to do a new arrangement of the song. Then he claimed publicly that Gregg had let him use the song for free — not a truth. Gregg, ever protective of his copyright, thundered to the *Daily Telegraph* from his south coast redoubt that he had not "waived all charges" for using it. And so the song disappeared quietly from the Archer campaign.

# 3   1979 and All That

Hindsight can make even the dullest of years seem epochal, but 1979 really was a caution. It was a tipping point in the biography of the modern world, a year which, more than most, marked the end of the post-WW II hangover and the start of both the post-modern headache and the emergence of some of the many wonders of the modern world. It was the year rubbish piled high in Leicester Square and smallpox was finally eradicated. There was the Russian invasion of Afghanistan which, in time and arguably, led to 9/11, the invasion and collapse of Iraq, the Syrian civil war and the fourth Afghan war, more than twenty years long and still struggling through its violent, religio-fascist aftermath.

That was just the start of 1979's geopolitical upheavals. China invaded Vietnam. The Sandinistas took power in Nicaragua. White rule was swept away in Rhodesia. The Camp David peace deal was struck between Israel and Egypt. The U.S. and the People's Republic of China established diplomatic relations. In Pakistan, shariah law was imposed and President Bhutto was hanged — handcuffed and hooded — in secret in a regional jail. In Kabul, the U.S. ambassador was kidnapped and killed. Shi'ite gunmen seized the Grand Mosque in Mecca; false rumors that the attackers were Americans led to assaults on the U.S. embassies in Pakistan and Libya. Saddam Hussein came to power in Iraq.

For technological collapse, there was the nuclear incident which inspired "London Calling": the Three Mile Island power plant on the Susquehanna River in Pennsylvania springing a leak. There was social rupture. In San Francisco, there were the White Night riots, protests against the lenient sentence given to Dan White, assassin of the city's mayor, George Moscone, and Harvey Milk, its first gay supervisor. At Comiskey Park baseball stadium in Chicago, a radio station anti-disco event turned into a riot of sorts — a major moment in legend but, in truth, lots of sounds, bags of fury, few injuries, little damage.

There was a far more serious disturbance in Levittown, Pennsylvania, where 100 were injured and 200 arrested. That one was over not musical styles but the price increase of gas to a dollar a gallon. Oil prices had doubled in the wake of that year's Iranian Revolution — out with the king, in with the supreme leader. Among the decrees issued by Iran's new ruler was one which reduced the age of marriage, to nine for girls and fourteen for boys. (That edict's consequences are still playing out on Iran's streets decades later.) In Tehran, Islamist students and activists took fifty-two Americans from the U.S. embassy, holding most of them captive for more than a year.

On July 29, the Basque separatist movement ETA bombed two train stations and the main airport in Madrid, killing seven. In Vaulx-en-Velin, a suburb of Lyon, on the weekend of September 14–15, "Arab" youths burned cars and fought the police — the first of what would become France's regular *banlieue* riots. On October 16, 185 miles to the south, on the shores of the Mediterranean, a tsunami reared up out of the Baie des Anges and tore into the city of Nice, killing twenty-three.

On November 3, during opposing rallies outside Morningside Homes, a Black housing project (now demolished) in Greensboro, North Carolina, an ad hoc alliance of the Ku Klux Klan and the American Nazi Party shot and killed five members of the Maoist Workers Viewpoint Organization — one Black, one Hispanic, three white.

Later the same month, onstage in Arizona, Bob Dylan — a good few weeks on from his appearance at a Clash show and now brain-deep in Christian fundamentalism — shared with the crowd his prediction that the Battle of Armageddon would come to pass in three to five or "maybe ten" years

Yet, as dystopic and chaotic as 1979 was, it was also a year when the future began to arrive. Of course, that's true for every year, but not every year sees the election of Margaret Thatcher — who was, never forget, the people's choice to lead them into the future. Or of the first papal visits to Poland and Ireland. Pope John Paul II flew into Dublin on a Boeing 747 that had been renamed St. Patrick for the day. He kissed the airport runway and held a mass for 1.25 million Irish men, women and children — a scarcely believable one-third of the country's population.

Perhaps even harder to believe was the recentness of the centenary his visit was marking — the 1879 celestial vision of the Virgin Mary by a peasant girl, in a typically damp August in a County Mayo town called Knock. Generations of Irish had made the pilgrimage there in hope of seeing the statue of Our Lady move. Still, a quasi-medieval apparition in rural Ireland does somehow link to the apocalyptical messianism of the Clash, though not the Italo-Catholic baroque of Scorsese, Minnelli and Sinatra. ("The aunts" — a gathering of my mature God-following but not-unskeptical female relatives, Liverpool and Irish — made a wet summer evening visit to Knock. To the others' hardheaded surprise, one of them announced that she'd seen the statue move. "Ah, now," said the worldly Marjorie, "Perhaps it was the gin.")

That final year of the 1970s was also a year of real future stuff. Walter Carlos, electronic music pioneer, creator of *Switched-On Bach* and composer of the *Clockwork Orange* soundtrack, officially came out as Wendy Carlos, seven years after a sex-change operation.

On October 6, there was an unplanned meeting of the interest-rate-setting committee of the U.S. Federal Reserve — the nation's central bank. Chairman Paul Volcker announced that, because inflation was running at an uncomfortable rate of fourteen percent, the Fed would increase interest rates as a way of tightly regulating bank reserves. "It was the moment when the modern Fed was born," wrote Adam Tooze, setting the scene for the future of finance in *Crashed*, his magisterial account of the 2008 crisis, from its origins in the late 1970s to its still-echoing impact. "The interest rate was its weapon." An act, Tooze added, that sent "a shuddering shock through both the American and the global economies." By 1981, the Federal Reserve interest rate was twenty-one percent — a level not seen, in the words of German chancellor Helmut Schmidt, "since the birth of Christ." Start spreading the spreadsheets...

There's also a good — very good, even — argument that the most important event of 1979 didn't happen in Afghanistan or Iran or the offices of the Federal Reserve or anywhere like that, but in the small Massachusetts town of Bedford. That was where, on October 19 — a month to the day after Sinatra recorded "New York, New York" and the Clash played the Boston Orpheum, fifteen miles south(ish) of Bedford — Marv Goldschmidt's computer store took delivery of a new stock item, a hundred dark-brown vinyl binders. Inside each binder was a manual, a reference card, a registration card and a 5.25-inch floppy disc. On that disc was a computer program — a tiny, tiny, tiny one — that changed the world. Turned it upside down. Not immediately, but pretty soon and consistently — exponentially, even, not to say existentially — from that day till this. Simply, Marv Goldschmidt's Bedford computer store was the Bethlehem stable of the modern world. It was where VisiCalc first went on sale, at $100 a copy.

VisiCalc was the first-ever desktop spreadsheet program, created in a world and time when a spreadsheet was a (large) piece of paper and a desktop was made of wood or linoleum. It was the "killer app" of personal computing. "A new form of computer life," wrote the pseudonymous Robert X. Cringely in *Accidental Empires*, his breathless and breathtaking account of personal computing's early years. (The book's delicious subtitle was *How the Boys of Silicon Valley Make Their Millions, Battle Foreign Competition and Still Can't Get a Date*.) VisiCalc made complex financial planning possible for the first time and put that power not just in the boss's office but on the desktops (in the old sense) of even relatively lowly employees. It facilitated the development of databases — from the simple address book on your phone to the giant ones that governments and corporations use to run your life. It heralded the future of electronic bookkeeping, cash flow, financial projections — even, if you want to think that way, the financial crisis of 2008. Or, more happily, to the complex testing and production schedules essential for developing Covid vaccines — and many another medical intervention, procedure or treatment.

Such was the year into which the Clash's "London Calling" and Sinatra's "New York, New York" were born.

**The London of "London Calling"**

The Clash's "London Calling" fit the tone of its hometown times. It came into a city that felt the same way the song's lyrics did: that things were bad, getting worse and could only end up *really* bad, really soon. It played into, and with a not-untrue picture of, a city in terminal decline. Like New York (not to mention many other big, established Western cities), London was being hollowed out in the 1970s, its center emptying into its suburbs and exurbs. Its population fell steadily from WW II to the mid-1980s. In 1945, there were 8.3 million Londoners. By 1983, there were just 6.75 million. (It took till 2014 to get back to 8.5 million.)

In director Derek Jarman's "punk" film *Jubilee* (1978), the city has turned into a British (and therefore histrionic) version of the South Bronx, a wasteland of bomb sites and emptied buildings where the only street lighting is bonfires lit by rat-like street kids. Buckingham Palace has become a recording studio, Westminster Cathedral a disco.

*The Long Good Friday* was released in 1980 but made in 1979. A tasty geezer of a gangster, name of Harold Shand (played by Bob Hoskins), tries to go straight — well, his idea of straight — by doing a deal with U.S. mafiosi to redevelop East London for the Olympics. He ends up in the hands of the IRA, who have plans to take over his criminal enterprise. In a local radio poll, it was voted the best London film ever. (A vote powered in part, I would guess, by the socio-historical irony of the actual subsequent redevelopment of East London's docklands — a process supercharged by the 2012 Olympics being set there.)

On television, there was the future imperfect of *Quatermass*, the last knocking of a science-fiction franchise which had started in 1953. Set in 2000 but clearly reflecting current anxieties, it showed a London dominated by violent street gangs ranging across a battered wasteland of a metropolis — a bit like the real-life South Bronx, actually. One gang is the Blue Brigade, the other the Badders. Both names were clear echoes of terrorist outfits in 1970s mainland Europe, Italy's Red Brigades and West Germany's Baader–Meinhof Gang. The first episode of this TV dystopia began with a narration. "In that last quarter of the 20th century, the whole world seemed to sicken. Civilized institutions, whether old or new, fell as if some primal disorder was reasserting itself. And men asked themselves: why should this be?"

**Dystopia and smallpox**
The idea of London as chaotic dystopia was not new, of course. Lady Mary Wortley Montagu was the aristocratic wife of the British ambassador to Ottoman Constantinople in the early 18th century. She is known for two things: her waspish letters and introducing to Western medicine a treatment for what she knew as "the speckled monster." Variolation, as the treatment became known, was a precursor to the vaccine that would finally rid the world of smallpox — in December 1979. To Lady Montagu, London was "this Sinful Sea Cole town" and, she added, "May my enemies live here in summer." Her contemporary, Samuel Johnson, shared her doubts. Yes, he did claim that he who is tired of London is tired of life. But he also rhymed of his London: "Here malice, rapine, accident conspire / And now a rabble rages, now a fire…"

If anything, opinions hardened over the next century. In the

1820s, radical writer and ruralist William Cobbett called London "the great wen" — a poisonous cyst on the face of the nation. King George III, like Joe Strummer, became convinced his city was about to flood — though he differed on the reason. While Strummer barked an early warning of global warming, the mad king saw it as a consequence of London's sinfulness.

Yet it is also questionable whether 1970s London was quite as terrible as *Quatermass*, Jarman and Strummer thought it was. Evidence? On "London, London," a song recorded by Caetano Veloso in 1971, the great Brazilian sang: "I cross the streets without fear…" A contemporary critic described it, quite wrongly, as "a sexy calypso." (Trinidadian, Brazilian; whatever.)

Veloso's "London, London" is a serious song, with a lovely melody. It can sound like a dumb, rosy-eyed, archaic view of London, but it isn't. Veloso was in London exile from the Brazilian military dictatorship. He was writing in his stilted, embryonic English because, for him, English was a safe haven of a language, a refuge from the pit of corruption in which neo-fascist generals were drowning his native Portuguese. To write and sing in that language would have been to collaborate with dictators and torturers. He knew what real terror and chaos were like. He knew the difference between secret police and London bobbies. He put this knowledge into his song, calling a policeman "pleased to please" a group that approaches him.

I don't know where he finished writing his London song, but we do know that he started it in Chelsea, where he lived in a four-story stucco house shared with a conspiracy of fellow exiles. It was less than a mile from where the Clash's "London Calling" was born — and just around the corner from Margaret Thatcher's house. Veloso and Thatcher probably passed in the street — he in his Brazilian afro and white fur coat, she in her rigid perm and Tory blue coat. (Those fashion and hairstyle notes are not supposition. Both visions come from actual photographs.)

As ever, the cityscape is as much internal as external. We map ourselves onto the world — the Clash just as much as Caetano Veloso.

For Veloso, a London of pleased and pleasing policemen. For Strummer, a city of chaos and heroin addiction.

There's a paradox here. "London Calling" is a song about foreboding and terror — a not-dishonest reflection of Londoners' romantic attraction to decline and fall. (Like Montagu and Cobbett, Londoners can often seem most at home with the idea of their city in a state of perpetual decay and collapse. It's as if they love it most when it's really, really, really, bad. Which, frankly, isn't a healthy basis for citizenship.)

Yet those concerns can also make London seem a more, not less, attractive place. "London Calling," a picture of nightmare and apocalypse, nevertheless functioned as something of a tourist brochure. Ah, the strange, unpredictable vagaries of soft power. Sometimes bad is exciting. (Ask Lou Reed. If that weren't so, New York's poet of the dark night wouldn't have had a career.) "London Calling" promises a city with the seductive thrill of danger and chaos to the many, many, many well-fed and well-watered European citizens who have been condemned by life's vicissitudes to live in places of quiet contentment where every pedestrian waits, even on dawn-emptied streets, for the little walking man to turn green before crossing to the other side. Unthinkable in London. Praise be, says the hurried and harried Londoner, so pleased to be hurried and harried.

### New York, New York, 1979

New York had its own issues in 1979. Two years earlier, the city had been broke, reduced to begging the federal government for a little something to tide it over. Times Square, famously, was a home away from home for Travis Bickle's people, the ones he fumed about in *Taxi Driver*, the 1976 Scorsese movie which was such a deep favorite of the Clash (for some time, Strummer had a Bickle-style Mohawk haircut) and which crystallized the world's view of 1970s New York. "All the animals come out at night," said the Vietnam vet cabbie in his off-camera narration, which goes on to list the various lowlifes he sees, predicting a Biblical rain to come and cleanse the city of them.

The music beneath his words is an elegant, rhapsodic saxophone leading a languorous, even lazy, string section, punchy brass and a relentless, pulsing, urban beat — romance, nostalgia, modernity, noir, threat, anxiety and sophistication, everything you want in a big city is there in the score. It was the last work of Bernard Herrmann (Benny to friends and colleagues). A New York-born Juilliard graduate of Ukrainian lineage, Herrmann was one of the great Hollywood composers, scoring *Citizen Kane* and many of Hitchcock's films.

Beginning in the early 1960s, Herrmann based himself, on and off, in London. In 1975, he was living just off the east side of Regent's Park in a small mews house purchased from Christine Keeler, prime player in the 1961 Profumo Affair. Maybe that mews — or a calming path through the green, green lawns of Regent's Park — is where the *Taxi Driver* score, so very New York, was dreamed up. While much of Herrmann's film work was recorded in London (some at Abbey Road), *Taxi Driver* was done in a Hollywood studio. Herrmann, who was 64, died in his sleep the night the sessions concluded, on Christmas Eve 1975. The movie was dedicated to him in an end caption, and his score was posthumously nominated for an Academy Award but lost out to *The Omen*, composed by California native Jerry Goldsmith.

Herrmann's mews home was no more than a few minutes' walk from both Guy Stevens' Primrose Hill flat and the white stucco Nash terrace house in which Strummer squatted for a while. (Actually, it was Clash associate Sebastian Conran's family residence. Well, one of the Conran family's several residences — his father founded the furniture and furnishings chain Habitat.) It was from there, in October 1978, that I set off with Joe and the Clash, flying to Paris for the Saturday night show which turned into the adventure I mentioned earlier. The band was headlining the annual "fête" hosted by the Communist newspaper *L'Humanité*, much to the disdain of the folk-favoring Communist Party members, who nonetheless defended the (very low) stage against a full-on, well-organized assault by a phalange of stick-wielding, black-helmeted, leathered-up anarcho-situationists. While Joe was onstage, firing up the cavernous hall, I got trapped in the sour spot between Communist praetorian guardsmen (and women) and the frankly scary autonomes. Tour manager Johnny Green physically picked me up — in those days, I was thin as thin can be — and carried me to backstage safety. The night ended, of course, with a visit to the Parisian nightclub of the moment, le Palais.

In the early years of the 21st century, I was interviewed about that night — the fight, in particular — by a French journalist. Quite by chance, she chose to talk to me on the lawny expanses across the road from both the Herrmann and Conran Regent's Park houses. She wanted to know more about the fight. It was, she told me — assuming I knew far more than I did — that it wasn't just any other pop-show punch-up. Rather, it was an epoch-marking event in French politics, a violent confrontation between the left (Communist Party) and the lefter (anarchists) which led to a long, deep and — being a French thing — philosophical analysis of the state of the left, by the left (and lefter). Who should we be fighting, brothers and sisters, each other or the fascist state? That kind of thing.

**A Londoner dies in New York**
Sid Vicious died of an overdose on Bank Street, in Manhattan's West Village, on February 2, 1979. Two weeks earlier, on January 13, schizophrenic soul legend Donny Hathaway jumped to his death from the Essex House on Central Park South. (I was staying in the hotel at the time but didn't find out about his death till I was back in London. Such is the unremarked privacy and secrecy of the modern international city.)

Manhattan was no longer the undisputed center of the music business — and hadn't been for fifteen years or so, not since the Beatles brought London to the game's forefront. More recently, New York had been eclipsed by Los Angeles. The heart of its old show business district was barely beating. That office on West 42nd Street from which my writing was first published in *Trouser Press* was steps from Times Square. As you walked down 42nd Street, there was a background hum in the air: the rhythmic chant of drug-dealers running their stock line: weed, blow, smack, angel dust, that kind of item. Pimps — or rather their drug-washed representatives — handed out business cards, promoting and displaying their products. The magazine's publisher, Ira Robbins, had a hobby. Collecting hooker cards. It was a big collection. (Decades later, studying for a masters degree at University College London, I emulated him by collecting similar cards from a similarly restricted location — the phone box on the pavement outside the UCL Psychology department. It, too, was a substantial collection, if nowhere as big as Ira's.)

"The New York I lived in was rapidly regressing," wrote Lucy Sante, chronicler of the downtown art scene in 1980s Manhattan. "It was a ruin in the making, and my friends and I were camped out amid its potsherds and tumuli. This did not distress me — quite the contrary. I was enthralled by decay and eager for more."

All decades and cities have their nostalgias, visions of their lost selves. These nostalgias are generally fictions. But 1970s New York's romantic remembrance of its recent past was particular and fervid, shaped by a graphic, frightening sense of what really had been lost and changed.

People, for a start. Like London, New York's five boroughs had been depopulating fairly rapidly from the city's 1950 peak. The city had lost nearly a million citizens over three decades — down from 7.9 million to a low of 7.0 million in 1980. This population loss was citywide, but it was sharpest in Manhattan. The island metropolis experienced a steady drop from its 1910 peak of 2.3 million, when the city's unofficial anthem was the bouncy, celebratory "The Sidewalks of New York." By 1980, it was down to just 1.4 million. That's a forty-percent drop. Every day for seventy years, twenty-seven people or so left Manhattan and didn't come back. Imagine that happening to your town or city. It would feel like a kind of never-ending dying. Ceaseless, unremitting loss that you would sense even if you couldn't actually see it happening. The streets would be just a little emptier every day. A city turning inexorably into a ghost town inhabited by anxious survivors.

The demographic slump happened in two distinct stages. First, Manhattan was depopulated by affluence, as the (mostly white) immigrant ghettos emptied their upwardly mobile strivers into the more spacious suburbs. Then it was emptied by fear, as the city's white middle class fled from riots, crime and the black, brown and beige people they tended to blame for the disorder, violence and robbery.

As it emptied, New York became a distinctly darker city. Its white population fell by 1.2 million between 1970 and 1980: the number of white children halved. It became poorer, too: in 1969, median New York family income was almost exactly the national average; by 1979, it had dropped to eighty-four percent. More than 600,000 jobs left the city between 1970 and 1976, moving west or to the suburbs, creating an unemployment rate of (a then unprecedented) eleven percent, with fourteen percent of the city on welfare.

And New York became dramatically more violent: by the late 1970s, its murder rate was five times what it had been twenty years earlier, when the gangs depicted in *West Side Story* were at their chaotic peak. In round figures, New York's 1979 murder rate was sixty times the 21st-century UK rate. Reported rapes doubled. "City of night like you wouldn't believe," wrote Michael Herr in a 1977 essay, *The Hook*. A former Vietnam war correspondent and author of *Dispatches* (1977), a great account from the U.S. troops' frontline perspective, Herr knew what danger looked like.

By 1979, New York was every bit the city you see in German photographer-artist Thomas Struth's 1970s images of lower Manhattan. Empty streets — or rather, emptied streets — decorated with piles of rats' dreamed-of garbage. The best known of Struth's pictures depicts Crosby Street. In time, this small thoroughfare one block east of Broadway in SoHo would become a sought-after address for artists, bankers and crackheads — though not in that alphabetical order. But, in 1978, the year the picture was taken, the street's tall industrial buildings — with their brick, pale stone banding and webbings of wrought-iron fire-escapery — had become lost versions of their own early 20th-century selves. In Struth's photograph, they have been corroded by a kind of architectural Alzheimer's: forgetting not just their past but their memory of that past.

There is a single lonely car in the foreground: a Dodge sedan, perhaps. The roadway is carpeted with detritus. The paving looks like an esplanade after a storm's giant waves have covered it with seaweed then retreated to their Neptunian home. Even the Stop signs are crooked. They gave up long ago. A theatre of lost dreams — maybe self-consciously, too, in the photographer's viewfinder. There is lyricism in Struth's vision.

Yet there was reality behind his poetic projections. There are, as an old TV crime show had it, eight million stories in the naked city. I'll pick just one of those stories because, well, because it happened in 1979, just around the corner from Struth's picture, on Prince Street — which crosses Crosby Street — and just a few months before Sinatra recorded "New York, New York."

On May 25, 1979, six-year-old Etan Patz, who lived with his parents in comfortable bohemia, went missing. All too soon, he became a symbol for metropolitan decline and anomie. If a child can just disappear like that, in the daylight hours, well… His face appeared on milk cartons and Times Square billboards; May 25 became National Missing Children Day. As the Dreyfus affair was a touchstone for turn-of-the-20th-century Paris, so, in a very different way, Etan's story was for late-1970s New York. An army officer destroyed by antisemitism; a young boy abducted and possibly murdered. Pre-WW I Paris and 1970s New York. What the two stories have in common is this: each city looked itself in the face and found it didn't much like what it saw.

Lucy Sante again: "Most of the city was squalid. If this troubled you, you left, and if you were taken by the romance of it, a long regimen of squalor in everyday life would eventually scrub your illusions grey. At this remove I'm sometimes retrospectively amazed by what I took for granted. Large fires a few blocks away every night for a couple of years would seem conducive to a perpetually troubled state of mind, but they just became weather."

It's hard to exaggerate the state of the city. I remember the emptiness of the streets at night, the constant whoop-whoop of sirens and the almost hyperbolically anxiety-inducing 4:00 a.m. subway journeys. It was the underground hellopolis of *The Warriors*, the subway-set gang movie that also came out in 1979. Subway stations were a set designer's idea of a modern urban Styx. The subway cars were covered with elaborate graffiti. Inside, every surface was spray-canned with young men's tags.

The great Magnum (and Manhattan) photographer Bruce Davidson captured those extraordinary surfaces forever, in rich, deep Kodachrome 64, in his book *Subway*. However horrid, violent and intrusive the graffiti might have been, Davidson found a certain strange beauty in it.

I talked to him about his pictures some thirty years later. "If people asked me what I was doing," he said, "I told them I was recording the state the subway was in. What I didn't tell them was that I saw the subway as both beauty and beast. Some things that were horrible were beautiful and some things that would be thought beautiful were banal."

It was the era of Talking Heads' "Life During Wartime," written by David Byrne in the depths of Lower Manhattan's Alphabet City. The song's title was metaphorical, yes, but only just.

"Crime was at its highest level in the history of the city," said Robert McGuire, New York's police commissioner from 1978 to 1983. "There was a crack-cocaine epidemic, and certain neighborhoods like the Lower East Side and parts of the Bronx had totally deteriorated. We had a city out of control. It was the Wild West."

Below ground, the subway had become dangerous enough that twenty-five-year-old Curtis Sliwa (Polish Catholic from Brooklyn) decided to protect the public by starting a uniformed citizen protection force. He and his volunteers began patrolling the subway in

February 1979, operating under the grandiloquent title the Magnificent Thirteen Subway Safety Patrol. By September, they rebranded themselves as Guardian Angels. As a former McDonald's manager, Sliwa understood branding. His Angels wore red berets and red nylon baseball jackets. And, as the whole world knew, New York was the native home of uniformed citizen crime-busters, in its fictional life, anyway — Batman, Superman, Supergirl, Spiderman, etc.

Things were maybe not quite as they were presented. It is said that the Angels mostly stuck to patrolling "restaurant row," as a central Manhattan section of the subway was known. Scary-looking and feeling it might have been, but it was nowhere near as dangerous as the subway was in the poor and really broken parts of the city.

In 1982, the Clash recorded "Red Angel Dragnet" for the *Combat Rock* album. It was a tribute to one of Sliwa's volunteers, Frank Melvin, who was killed on duty — not by a criminal on the subway in Manhattan but in a New Jersey housing project, by a cop.

In 1992, Sliwa himself was shot, although not fatally. John A. Gotti, a don in the Gambino mob family, was charged but never convicted. Sliwa became a "conservative" radio host. He supported future Trump presidential lawyer Rudolph Giuliani's 1993 run for the city mayoralty. In 2021, Sliwa ran for mayor himself — as the Republican Party candidate. Again, I think of Strummer singing about people who fuck nuns. (Sliwa lost by a landslide.)

Despite spending a good amount of time in New York during its dark years, I never saw much in the way of violence or danger myself. A friend — a female New Yorker — told me that might be because of the way I regularly dressed, in leather jacket, jeans and biker boots. Like a street criminal, my friend said, adding that she'd seen people cross the street to avoid me, worried I might rob them. Later, and more flatteringly, someone else —I can't remember who — told me I looked like the fifth Ramone, the English one with blond hair and a blue, not black, jacket. It was a Lewis Leathers Bronx, named for New York but bought in London, just up the road from the BBC's Broadcasting House. (It disappeared into the undead realm of lost luggage very early one spring morning in the Portland, Oregon airport. I made it across the country in time for dinner on Christopher Street, but my blue leather jacket never joined me. All that remains of it is a photo of me in it.)

I can't be certain, but I should think I was wearing it the one time I did have a brush with violence in 1970s New York. I was witness to a small but determined and messy scuffle one very early morning breakfast in a midtown diner. I was with Strummer and Jones. We'd come from an all-night session at the Record Plant on West 44th Street. With the rest of the band left back in London, they'd been working on finishing off their second album, *Give 'Em Enough Rope*. This night, they were in search of a rhyme — that benighted, elusive rhyme for "London town." They were after a hometown echo of Jamaican toaster Dillinger's New York rhyme on his 1976 hit 45 "Cokane in My Brain," on which the toaster explained how to spell and rhyme New York — with a knife, fork, a bottle and a cork.

It took Mick and Joe pretty much all night to get a chorus overdub right. So, sometime around dawn, there was an after-work diner breakfast — and ringside seats for a fracas by the doorway. There was a lot of shouting and a good bit of argy-bargy. It went on for a few minutes and looked like it might progress into something more serious, more violent. Then a small, wiry, persistent New Yorker joined in — and persuaded the combatants to stop. With well-chosen words, he told them, among other things, that he was a cop and that they were disturbing his coffee break. He also showed them his gun. We Brits were all quite thrilled by this. Cop. Gun. We were all in the movie inside our heads — our transatlantic equivalent of Scorsese's "New York, New York" dream of *New York, New York*.

The coda to this story is that the "London town" rhymes — "a crown" and "half a pint of brown" — appear a half-minute from the end of "All the Young Punks." Both very London and redolent of my Stoke Newington childhood. A crown was an obsolete coin worth one-quarter of a pound, 25 pence in today's money — virtually nothing now but a lot of pocket money back in 1971 when it was last in circulation. Brown ale, a sweet-nosed relation of London's traditional porter, was first brewed in the 1700s, and by the time of "London Calling" was almost exclusively an old man's drink.

### All sorts of termite creativity

New York had its draws, too. "It was the time of broken windows," wrote Louis Menand in the *New Yorker*. "But, in part because of the collapse, the city also felt open, liberated, available." James Wolcott felt similarly, writing in *Vanity Fair*, "For those who migrated to New York and secured a foxhole while the city bled out, terminal conditions weren't all bad ... Having fewer people clogging the scenery aired out the city nicely, opening corner pockets of private and public space where all sorts of termite creativity could take place, and did." (Like — just like — Vanilla Studios on the far side of the Atlantic, where the Clash prepared "London Calling.") And, of course, there was Lucy Sante. "We thought of the place as a free city, like one of those pre-war nests of intrigue and licentiousness where exiles and lamsters and refugees found shelter in a tangle of improbable juxtapositions."

On March 1, 1979, way uptown from Sante's downtown nesting, the latest Stephen Sondheim musical opened at the Uris Theatre on West 51st Street. (Now called the Gershwin, it is home to a bronze statue of Noël Coward. Two cities, one entwined musical culture.) The Sondheim show was a New Yorker's version of an old London story, *Sweeney Todd: The Demon Barber of Fleet Street*. It showcased love, rape, murder and the manufacturing and marketing of pies made from human flesh. With butchering by Todd and baking by Mrs. Lovett — once the maker of "the worst pies in London" — their product became the taste of the town. To some eyes and ears, the show was pretty much a tale of everyday capitalism. It won Best Musical of the Year and seven other Tony awards. The first sung number of the first act is called "No Place Like London." New York. London. London. New York. As one city breathed out, the other breathed in. (The show opened in London nearly a year later, in February 1980.)

**My New York New York**
My New York debut was somewhat different to my London one a quarter of a century earlier. I flew into JFK on a cloudy, windless afternoon in April 1978 on an Air India 747. A daily flight nicknamed the "Curry Clipper," it was an Orient Express of the sky, which linked former British Empire cities to the empire city on the Hudson — jetting from Calcutta to New York via Bombay and London. Then back again. And again. Etc., etc. I was there to interview a poet of the city, Lou Reed.

To my astonishment, as I emerged from immigration, there was a man holding a sign with my surname on it. He told me he was my driver and took me and my bags to a long black limousine. Both he and the car would be mine for the next few days, a perk of being a London punk journalist — and therefore beneficiary of the wondrous largesse of record company promotion departments.

He drove me into Manhattan, via the Queensboro Bridge (with Simon and Garfunkel's "59th Street Bridge Song" playing in my head), to my hotel on Central Park South. Later, as the evening deepened towards midnight, I asked the driver to take me downtown, to CBGB, the already storied punk club at the junction of Bowery and Bleecker. My first night in New York. The door person recognized my name and waved me in along with three European colleagues. Another perk of the job. Before I even got to the bar — ten steps maybe — several people had said hello. We knew each other from London. As one city breathes in, the other breathes out. Another poet of the city, Richard Hell, was playing that night with his band, the Voidoids. I'd seen them in London the previous November supporting the Clash, when they were forced to suffer the spits and gobs of a British punk audience's totemic outrage.

My interview with Lou Reed was a couple of days later, in his hotel room. He was very much the poet of his city, fully, even neurotically, aware of his local stature and status. ("I'm a New York City man," he would write in a song a couple of decades later.) He taught me to drink too many margaritas and locked me in his bathroom, not letting me out till I had read "In Dreams Begin Responsibilities," a story by yet another poet of the city, Reed's mentor Delmore Schwartz. A little over a year later, I read that story out loud deep into the night on my first date with the woman who would become my wife.

I stayed a month. When the record company stopped funding my hotel bills, I sofa-surfed with a friend of a London friend. Her apartment was in a high rise on the East Side, near Bellevue Hospital. Sirens screamed all night. Her flatmate was a tattoo artist. Tattooing was illegal in New York then — from 1961 to 1997, in fact. A parade of clients passed through her informal tattoo parlor day and night. Most were citizens of Lou Reed's city of night. Many had piercings, intimate ones which they regularly invited me to examine. The flatmate offered to tattoo me, for free, but I was too much of a coward to take up her offer.

In that month, I saw the Ramones at CBGB. The Dead Boys (from Cleveland), too. I went to Max's Kansas City and the Bottom Line, among other clubs. Downtown, I spent an evening at the Ocean Club chatting with Brian Eno. It was the launch party for *Grutzi Elvis*, an avant-garde short film by Diego Cortez (né James Allan Curtis, 1946–2021), artist and future co-founder of the Mudd Club. The movie has never come out, but I do still have my copy of the accompanying book we were given that evening. As Eno and I talked, a persistent New Yorker kept trying to join our conversation. Five or so years later in London, I again found myself with Eno. He told me that he had been sent a CV which included "conversations with Eno." It was from that interrupting New Yorker at the Ocean Club.

Uptown, I went to Studio 54. I saw Art Garfunkel and Aretha Franklin (on separate evenings) at Carnegie Hall. My transatlantic love affair had begun.

The following year, I passed a Sunday morning in the lobby of the Chelsea Hotel, waiting for a slack-a-bed musician. I went to a nearby diner for a leisurely New York brunch, then returned to the hotel and made a careful study of the brightly colored, splashy Larry Rivers painting on the east wall of the lobby — the abstract expressionist artist's studio was upstairs. And, yes, of course I thought of Joni Mitchell's "Chelsea Morning" and Bob Dylan's "Sad Eyed Lady of the Lowlands." And of the fact that, just weeks earlier, Nancy Spungen had been killed there, in room 100 — almost certainly by Sid Vicious, my cousin's former best friend. In a way, it was a London domestic, a heroin-driven killing that could have easily happened in the damaged couple's Maida Vale flat but, by the vagaries of fate, was transposed across the Atlantic. While Sid was out on bail, I went to see him play upstairs at Max's Kansas City. I knew it would be a sad occasion, but it was worse than that. I've no idea how I might describe it. Unusually, almost uniquely, I'm lost for words.

Many years later, when his mother Anne Beverley killed herself, I was commissioned to write a piece about her. I found the small house in which she'd died, a lifetime after she'd lived round the corner from my grandmother. It was in a beaten-up Midlands town. I knocked on the door. No one answered. I drove back to London and wrote the piece.

A year after my first trip to New York, I came back from a week in the city to find myself looking into an abyss. I stepped to the edge and didn't like what I saw. I stepped back and away.

The abyss was in me, of course. I was in a bad way. Physically — always bone thin, I was down to less than a hundred pounds. Mentally, I was lost and bereft. I looked to the future and didn't like what I saw there. I talked about it — not to a professional or anything clever like that, just to people — in particular to a lesbian photographer who I regularly worked with. I had a good job and a decent flat and plenty of money but I still felt empty. I remember telling the photographer how I felt on a six-hour train journey back to London from the north in a compartment shared with middle-aged strangers, subdued or embarrassed into silence by my outpourings. Then, back in London, love came along. And hung around. Simply, in the words of Percy Sledge's song, "out of left field love came along." And I never saw the abyss again.

I've never stayed that long in New York since that first visit, but I have visited many, many times. I feel at home there, always have done.

Despite the ocean and 3,000 miles between us, I have had a long, close relationship with New York. I am not a citizen, of course — I am not sure you can ever be a citizen of more than one city. I have never lived there, but I am closer, far closer to New York than I am to any British or European city. My first professional writing was published there, from that office on 42nd Street: rents were low in the area back then. The articles appeared in a music fanzine, started and edited by a young bunch of enthusiastic and knowledgeable New Yorkers, with whom I'm still in touch — there's a picture of us walking together on London's Abbey Road zebra crossing in 2014.

I know New York well — not just the Manhattan tourist and high spots, but all five boroughs and beyond. I've been there in a full-on, knee-deep snowstorm and when it was below zero and windy. I've been there in its scalding, sticky August horridness. I've taken the PATH via New Jersey to get round a subway strike. I've taken the subway alone at 4:00 a.m. in the good old days. Well, the bad and dangerous ones — back when junkies were junkies, and they were everywhere. I used Grand Central Station when it was primarily a betting office. I have suffered Penn Station too many times.

I have taken the Staten Island ferry as well as buses from the Port Authority terminal. I've rat-raced a hire car down the West Side Highway and U-turned it into oncoming midtown traffic. I've walked the High Line — and remember the low life that used to live beneath its rusted steel.

I've had eggs thrown at me by drunk twenty-somethings in the Hamptons and I've done a family yoga session on the beach at Fire Island. For decades, I bought my shirts at Brooks Brothers — until the New York men's shop stopped creating and selling their fantasy version of English gentlemen's outfitting and opted to go all modern and international instead.

I went to night games at both the old Yankee and Shea Stadiums. I ate at the now-gone Carnegie Deli, the Stage Deli and the Russian

Tea Room. I drank an egg cream at the Ritz and ate at downtown kosher delis when they still had little jugs of schmaltz on their Formica-topped tables. (Yes, on my first visit, I did pour the chicken fat into my coffee.)

I have celebrated Paddy's night on 46th Street with the Pogues (I had known the band's guitarist, Philip Chevron, even longer than I had New York), then, later the same evening, I had, not for the first time, been threatened with physical violence in an Irish bar, on account of my English accent. (If only I'd had my birth certificate or DNA records to hand as proof of my actual, rather than romanticized, Irish origins.)

I drank at topless bars — once on a night it was so cold outside that the waitresses were wearing turtleneck sweaters. I've been to apartments with private elevators and two fountains in the lobby. I've taken the elevator to a loft via a shaft hand-painted with a graffiti mural by one of the first generation of hip-hop artists.

I passed through Alphabet City when the pavements crunched as you walked — crackheads' discarded glass vials. I was in Manhattan on the first Independence Day after 9/11. I pretty much had the place to myself. So, I did what I thought was the only right thing to do as a North Londoner in New York at that particular moment: I went shopping.

On my last visit to Manhattan, I stayed not far from the junction where I spent my first night in the city — and just down the block from Katz's Delicatessen, in which Meg Ryan, as Sally, faked that spectacular orgasm for Harry. What was once CBGB is now a men's clothing store — with CBGB memorabilia on its walls — very cleverly displayed, too. My hotel room had a kind of art shrine to the punk club. It was as fake as Sally's orgasm, if far less convincing. I found myself wondering if I was the only person who had both been to the actual fabulous club and seen this fabulated version of it. My disdain for that disjunction made me feel like a real New Yorker; well, an associate one.

An old friend, photographer Janette Beckman, lives close by, in a loft apartment. Janette is a Londoner who I worked with in London, on *Sounds*. She photographed the Clash there and again when she moved to New York in 1983, and famously chronicled the early years of the city's hip-hop world. Decades later, I learned that she is one of my wife's innumerable cousins — not that they knew each other except via me. Trying to think of a New York equivalent of my London-gloomy smoky old tile, I find myself remembering a line in Bronx-born Laura Nyro's "New York Tendaberry," in which she addresses the city as "you," telling it that it feels like a religion to her. And of the boosterish subway token tattoo that former *New York Times* editor Jill Abramson has on her shoulder, which is performative citizenship. The London equivalent would, I guess, be a tube roundel tattoo.

I'm as big a fan of that roundel as any Londoner. I'd even say I'm a connoisseur of it — and the way it is appropriated and repurposed around the world, much as I♥NY is. (A choice example: its use for the sign on a gay sex shop just off Hamburg's Reeperbahn.) But I've never seen a tube roundel tattoo. In fact, I find it hard to imagine a Londoner — true born or just arrived from a faraway town — wearing it on a T-shirt, let alone having it permanently inked into their flesh. But New York, as Nick Paumgarten wrote in his city's house journal, *The New Yorker*, in 2007, has a "cosmopolitanism [which] refracts into a kind of a superheated parochial self-regard."

A second example of that is an old one, and it might have been a knowing one even at the time. But it's a cracker — plus it's impossible, I'd say, to imagine an equivalent London boast, ironic or not. It's a headline from a 1917 edition of the *Bronx Home News* celebrating Leon Trotsky's role in the overthrow of the Czar:

BRONX MAN LEADS RUSSIAN REVOLUTION.

# 4  Frank Sinatra's "New York, New York"

**Frank Sinatra in the Andy Warhol years**
"New York, New York" was the defining song of late-period Sinatra. As "Come Fly With Me" was for the Rat Pack years and "My Way" was for his living-legend era, so "New York, New York" was for his comeback decades. Most people, even those who should know better — Joe Strummer and me, for example — thought it was an old, old song, a show tune from a distant generation, most likely from an era when men wore double-breasted suits and fedoras.

It's not. Sound and timbre to the contrary, it was written not in the heyday of Broadway and Hollywood musicals but long after Fred Astaire had packed away his top hat and white tie. It was, in fact, written in the 1970s, at the zenith of the city's Andy Warhol years, for a movie.

The song's full and proper title is "(Theme From) New York, New York," which distinguishes it from at least eight others called "New York, New York." (About which more, much more, very soon.) It was a movie title tune, composed in a hotel room, by a married couple: jazz saxophonist Jimmy Doyle and singer Francine Evans. That is, its writers were the movie's two stars (Robert De Niro and Liza Minnelli), a couple who can collaborate successfully in work and art but not in life and love.

The lyrics were a tight collaboration. Jimmy offered "vagabond." Francine yoked that word to "shoes." And they were off. The song pretty much wrote itself.

At least, that's the way it happens in Martin Scorsese's sixth feature, *New York, New York*. In real life, it was written by John Kander (music) and Fred Ebb (words). They crafted it to order in 1975 for the film, which was produced by Irwin Winkler, then flying around dreamworld on the success of Sylvester Stallone's *Rocky*, which Winkler had nurtured from idea to Oscar. ("We had a little heat," said Winkler of those glory years.)

*New York, New York* is a love story played out in a 1940s movie world Manhattan — a city of the imagination that Scorsese studied closely as a sickly child enraptured by movies and their dream-like Manhattans. Its loving couple — the ones shown writing the song — are musicians, star-struck stars. Jimmy Doyle is an onscreen version of Scorsese's vision of himself; Minnelli was then Scorsese's real-life lover. The romance in the script intertwined inextricably with the romance behind the camera.

It was Minnelli who suggested hiring Kander and Ebb to write the songs. By the time of "New York, New York," the (actual) songwriting pairing had already made it there. Kander had, as they say, blown in from Kansas City in an era when that really meant something. Born the year Al Jolson brought singing to the movies, Kander was just old enough to have experienced a touch of Kansas City's wild, open, corrupt years, when mayor Tom Pendergast's willingness to take a bribe facilitated the big KC jazz club scene from which Charlie Parker would emerge, blowing flatted fifths on his alto sax. As a child, Kander was taken by his father to see stage shows in New York. He studied music at Oberlin and Columbia. He was the rehearsal pianist for *West Side Story*. The musicals racket, he knew it well.

Ebb was a native New Yorker. Born in the Bronx, he moved to Manhattan as a young man and never left. "I've lived there my whole life," he told me in the late 1990s, when we talked about his lyrics for "New York, New York." He and Kander started working together in

1962. At the time, Ebb's main job was in London — though he never had to leave New York to do it. He was writing lyrics transatlantically for the late-night satirical BBC TV show *That Was the Week That Was*. As London breathed in, New York breathed out.

Kander-Ebb's first success was "My Coloring Book," Barbra Streisand's second single. It didn't chart but it did establish their career. Their first musical was 1965's *Flora the Red Menace*, which featured the Tony-winning Broadway debut of nineteen-year-old Liza Minnelli. "The love of my life," Ebb told me. He also wrote and constructed the show that made Minnelli *really* famous — her nightclub act. It opened on February 9, 1966, in the Persian Room of the Plaza Hotel, which was a kind of a home away from home for her. She'd actually lived in the Plaza as a child. So, in effect, she first came to stardom in the house she grew up in.

The same year, Kander-Ebb created the musical that made them real stars. *Cabaret* originally starred not Minnelli but the now barely remembered English actress Jill Haworth. Minnelli was brought in for the 1972 film version, which won eight Oscars, including one each for her and music supervisor Ralph Burns — but nothing for Kander-Ebb.

I asked Ebb about his "New York, New York" song. "It's a very truthful work about the people who come here to succeed. No one told us how or what to write, just that they wanted a title song." That is, a song called "New York, New York." But it's not exactly true that he and Kander weren't told what to write. "We wrote three or four other songs with the same title that were rejected — for being too light or not as good as our other work. The idea for it was always the same, though: this city is the be-all and end-all, that succeeding in New York is the big thing." Nothing remained of those failed attempts, he told me. Not even memory traces.

How was it having those early versions rejected? "You're a pro. You're just going back to the drawing board. You can't take it seriously. It's not a personal issue. If they don't think it would work, it wouldn't."

Who were "they"? I asked. Who were these judges who rejected

Kander-Ebb's earlier "New York, New York"'s? "Martin Scorsese, Liza Minnelli, Robert De Niro," said Ebb. (Truth be told, there's a name missing from that list: Irwin Winkler, who was also at the meeting. He was the producer, after all.)

Kander was less forgiving about the rejection, as he explained to NPR's Jeff Lunden in 2002. He recalled a "couch meeting" about the song — probably the same one Ebb told me about oh-so-calmly. Kander and Ebb were presenting their latest attempt. Kander was renowned as a song-demonstrator, a master salesman of lyric and music. He played the piano. Ebb sang. There was no round of applause. There were not even any comments. Rather, De Niro called Scorsese over, and the pair of them went out for a walk, leaving Kander and Ebb sitting there, waiting. On their return, actor and director told the pair the song had to be "stronger" and "asked" them to try again.

Kander: "We walked out of there, highly insulted that some actor was going to tell us how to write a song." But the actor turned out to be correct. So, write a new one they did. And nailed it this time, nipping back to Ebb's house and finishing off their new — and final — "New York, New York" in forty-five minutes.

"I think we wrote it in a very short time and with great anger," Kander recalled. Ebb, who instead used the phrase "a kind of rage," kicked off the writing process by offering a possible first line, "Start spreading the news." Kander liked it and played a draft of the opening vamp, dum-dum-da-de-dum — in Ebb's delightful phrasing, "the all-time great killer vamp that's recognized by the world as a kind of five-note abbreviation for the spirit of New York." That vamp is also an expression of rage and anger: the songwriters are casting their not-so-secret suspicions about their song's un-self-knowing singer.

Though Ebb was adamant that no trace remained of the rejected songs, his writing partner later found not only memories of the one that De Niro and the others batted away but a rough version of the final reject. In 2015, he told the *New York Times* that he'd recently had a listen. "It is terrible. De Niro was completely right." Really? It's hard to imagine Kander-Ebb getting it so wrong, but they did.

In a show-off four-part rhyme, they ladle out "do," "Park Avenue," "gnu" and "Central Park Zoo" in two short lines. Charming and witty in a knowingly artful way, it's the kind of uptown fluff you'd hear in a song written in, say, the mid-'40s. Ah, that's the thing, isn't it? I don't know what the music was like but, judging by those lyrics, Kander and Ebb did what all the best musicals writers do. They wrote to plot and character, crafting exactly the kind of song that could have been written, played and sung by Jimmy Doyle and Francine Evans in 1945. It was just what Kander and Ebb thought was needed and were being asked to provide: a song true to its time and its supposed writers in the movie.

But it wasn't what was wanted. That early version of "New York, New York" was distanced, wry. There was no bigness about it. It wore its emotions lightly, even ironically. Which was not what the filmmakers were after. Fuck Park Avenue, they were telling Kander-Ebb, we want Broadway. Get those emotions on your sleeve.

That first "New York, New York" offered up by Kander and Ebb was, in Winkler's words, "a little ditty." What the movie's makers wanted was "a big dramatic song." The songwriters told the movie's supreme court (Scorsese, Minnelli, De Niro, Winkler) that they hadn't written that kind of song because they didn't want to compete with what was then the most famous song called "New York, New York," the one written by Leonard Bernstein (music) and Betty Comden and Adolph Green (lyrics) for the stage musical *On the Town*. That's the one in which the Bronx is up but the Battery's down, and the city is, rhymingly, a "helluva town." Presented with Kander and Ebb's reasoning, the *New York, New York* supreme court told the songwriters, "We don't care about that song. We want you to write a big, big dramatic song, and if you can't write it, we'll get somebody else."

So Kander and Ebb did what was required. They wrote a song that does sound like an old and venerable show tune, only not one from the 1940s. Rather, it sounds like one from, well, maybe the late 1950s or early 1960s.

Comden and Green's "New York, New York" was written in

1944 — i.e., around the time Scorsese's *New York, New York* is set. Kander and Ebb's final (and hit) "New York, New York" theme, that's more like a show tune from fifteen or even twenty years later — big, bold, brassy show-stoppers like "Climb Ev'ry Mountain" (*The Sound of Music*, 1959) and "The Impossible Dream" (*Man of La Mancha*, 1965). The sound of aspiration. Blowsy, overblown, heart on sleeve and up in lights.

Even so, it is far from a standard Broadway belter. Notably, its rhyming scheme is strikingly unusual for a show tune. Most popular songs have either rhyming couplets or quatrains (four-line units). "New York, New York" rhymes across phrases — e.g., that first line "spreading the news" links not to the next line but to "vagabond shoes" in the fifth line. ("London Calling," by contrast, is less adventurous. It's mostly couplets, with some of them near rhymes, particularly in the first verse/quatrain.)

Two weeks after the supreme court meeting, a tape arrived at Winkler's house in Los Angeles. Irwin and his wife Margo were heading out to dinner at the Palm restaurant, so he put the tape in the player in their car. On it was the new "New York, New York," with its killer vamp. "I'll never forget it," he told Marc Maron on the comic's *WTF* podcast in 2019. "I knew we had something."

*"It really is a new world, vast and majestic as the ocean. There is a sense of great human energy being released."*
—HENRI MATISSE

*New York, New York* is Scorsese's movie, but it wasn't his idea. It was producer Irwin Winkler's. A native New Yorker, Winkler was a Coney Islander who'd worked the boardwalk's bumper cars as a teenager. Hustle, hustle, smile, swing from car to car, hanging on to the (insulated) pole which hooked up to the power supply. Flirt, cajole, take the cash (maybe even skim a little). At university, Winkler studied American literature and took it very seriously. Street smarts plus a cultured and trained mind came together to create a movie producer who liked and understood subtlety while also knowing how to pitch it to the bad boys and girls in the back row.

*New York, New York* was based on a true New York story. It was inspired by what Winkler had seen of — and dreamed about — the real-life showbiz partnership of singer Felicia Sanders and her husband, pianist Irving Joseph. Sanders (New York Jewish, née Felice Schwartz) had only one real hit, the theme song of *Moulin Rouge*, John Huston's bio-pic of Toulouse-Lautrec, but she was something of a nightclub star. Her New York haunt was the Blue Angel at 152 East 55th Street, the "quintessential New York supper club." It was an exclusive, tiny boîte. Dorothy Loudon — then a comic, later a Broadway light — said its stage was so small it was like "performing on a cocktail napkin." According to *Billboard*, the club "was so refined and cultivated that … the genteel, reserved crowd … did not dare to respond to the entertainers with unseemly exuberance." Another comic who played it, Lenny Bruce, was less polite about its crowd — "rich hemophiliacs and geriatric Russian princesses." All in all, the kind of place that could spark the dreams of a movie called *New York, New York*.

The Blue Angel was run by Herbert Jacoby — Jewish, tall, thin, gay, English-educated and French-mothered. He'd edited the French Popular Front's newspaper *Le Populaire* before moving to New York in the late 1930s and bringing his liberal European politics to Manhattan nightlife. His club was mixed-race and left-wing-friendly — Pete Seeger and Lotte Lenya played there. Barbra Streisand, too. (The original Blue Angel herself, Marlene Dietrich, didn't play the club it seems, but she is seen leaving it in the 1949 film noir *Jigsaw*.)

Jacoby's joint was also the birthplace of Comden and Green's "New York, New York." That birth moment came one night in early 1944. Comden and Green were playing the club as part of a comedy outfit known as the Revuers. Their friend and sometime piano player Leonard Bernstein wanted to have them write the book and songs for a musical but was struggling to convince his producers. So, he brought them to see a Comden and Green set at the Blue Angel. The producers were convinced. And so, work began on *On the Town* and the first great "New York, New York" song. Like they say, a helluva town. Again, pretty much exactly the kind of showbiz world that Scorsese's movie dreams about.

In Sanders and Joseph, Winkler saw a showbiz story — a tragedy of sorts with an inescapably unhappy ending. In 2019, he talked about Sanders and Joseph on Marc Maron's *WTF* podcast. Sanders was the one who brought in the money, he said, while Joseph, a top-line pianist, "suppressed his talent" for his wife. "I don't know if she ever really appreciated him." When Winkler came up with the idea that became *New York, New York*, Sanders had just died, aged fifty-three. That could well be what prompted the thought to make the movie. Sanders' *Chicago Tribune* obituary quoted her as saying of her singing, "It's not the brains you reach. It's the heart."

For the script, Winkler reached out to Earl Mac Rauch, a virtual unknown. That Rauch's 1969 debut novel, *Dirty Pictures From the Prom*, was even published surprised no one more than Rauch himself. He'd written scripts before the commission from Winkler, but none had been made into films. Which was good for the producer. "I made a cheap deal with him."

Rauch gets sole credit for *New York, New York*'s story, but he shares the screenwriting credit with Mardik Martin, an Armenian born in Iran who grew up in Iraq. Like Scorsese, he had a nose-pressed-at-the-window vision of New York City. As a child, he watched Hollywood musicals — the same films that entranced Scorsese — projected onto giant screens on Baghdad rooftops. He would fall asleep as the films played, dreaming of his favorite movie goddesses. "Baghdad, even then, was filthy, dirty, disgusting, with dust and sand," he told the *L.A. Times* in 2007. "Then you see Betty Grable in unbelievable Technicolor and the beautiful scenery in the background. It's like another dimension, it's like finding paradise."

As a child, he learned English at his British boarding school in Baghdad. As a teenager, he worked for an Iraqi film distributor. He came to New York in 1954, ostensibly to study economics at New York University. He was twenty-one and penniless, according to his own account. He worked as a busboy and a waiter at Toots Shor's restaurant, a Sinatra hangout. He met Scorsese at NYU. They wrote *Mean Streets* together. Martin, no longer poor, researched his dialogue by driving around the city, picking up prostitutes and asking them not for sex but for words. "I would bring a tape recorder and pay them a hundred dollars for their stories," he said in 2007.

Scorsese and Martin last worked together on *Raging Bull*. Then the city bit back. Martin disappeared into a mountain of cocaine, only emerging years later as a respected — and happier, it seems — professor of screenwriting in Los Angeles. "I'm not too crazy about New York, so I don't go there that often," he said. He died, aged eighty-four, in 2019.

Scorsese liked what Martin had done with Rauch's script for *New York, New York*. So did Winkler. Echoing the director's regular description of the movie as "a film noir musical," he said, "He brought the toughness to it."

After the almost documentary quality of *Mean Streets* and *Taxi Driver*, Scorsese wanted *New York, New York* to be a big, glossy commercial picture "in the style of the 1940s films, with all their artifice and the idea of no reality." Fortunately for Scorsese, at the time he was planning *New York, New York* he was at an apex of power and influence, able to recreate the movie dream world of his childhood.

*Taxi Driver* was made on location in Scorsese's city. *New York, New York* wasn't. The Manhattan he put on the screen was not the real one he grew up in but the one he studied, at a remove, in Little Italy cinemas. It was shot not on actual Manhattan streets but on romantically heightened ones on a Hollywood soundstage. When describing how he wanted his movie to look, Scorsese recalled the celluloid city of his cinematic childhood — a place where "curbs were always shown as very high and very clean. When I was a child, I realized this wasn't right, but it was part of a whole mythical city that they had created. Now I wanted to recreate that mythical city."

So, everything in his *New York, New York* is super-real and super-sized. Its curbstones really are far bigger than the real things — also far, far, far cleaner, of course. The clothes, too, were deliberately supersized: De Niro's ties are an inch wider, and Minnelli's shoulder pads an inch bigger than they would actually have been in the mid-1940s. Scorsese described the look he was going for as "totally false, totally '40s Hollywood" — the glossy, garishly emotional world of movie musicals, in particular.

"*The Band Wagon* is, as everyone knows, my favorite musical," Scorsese has said. The 1953 movie is a backstage affair directed by Vincente Minnelli — Scorsese's girlfriend's father. It's about a washed-up Broadway star (Fred Astaire) who makes an (eventual) comeback with help from a long-legged ballerina (Cyd Charisse). What do you mean, do they fall in love and live happily ever after? Have you never sat in a dark and dreamy picture house? Its big number was "That's Entertainment," of which more soon. It was written by ... well, more about that later, too.

The parallels between Minnelli and Scorsese or *The Band Wagon* and *New York, New York* are not hard to chase down. And they multiply. When conceiving Liza's character in the movie, Scorsese surely had in mind his girlfriend's mother, Judy Garland. Hers was a life — and art — of almost willful turbulence. She died, in 1969, aged forty-seven, of barbiturate poisoning, $4 million in debt, in Chelsea. (Not the New York Chelsea, that is, but the London one — the one in which Sally Bowles' friend Elsie lives and dies in "Cabaret," the title song of Kander-Ebb's hit musical — and best known as sung by Liza Minnelli in the film.) Garland's "death bills" were paid by Sinatra.

In his dreams of a movie Manhattan, maybe Scorsese also had in mind the tightly bounded but exceedingly glamorous world of Eloise, the little girl who lived at (and "skibbled" around) the Plaza Hotel. Eloise was based, it's generally said, on Liza Minnelli — who really did live at the Plaza as a child. The Eloise-Liza correlation was disputed, though, by author Kay Thompson, who was also Judy Garland's vocal coach and Liza's godmother. "I am Eloise," Thompson said. And it's true that she did really live at the Plaza for several years. When fans called and asked to speak to Eloise, the operators would put them through to Thompson's room. But she only moved in after the books' success and at the invitation of the management, who saw it as a way of publicizing the hotel. Then, well, she just didn't leave and, in time, just stopped paying her bill, for seven years. When a new owner bought the hotel in 1988, he kicked her out. Time to add another line to Donald Trump's résumé: the man who evicted Eloise.

**Out in Hollywood**
"My concept of the film could never be shot in New York," Scorsese has said. "It had to be shot in the backlots of Hollywood." So, it was — on Soundstage 29 at MGM. Which is the actual place (if anything in the movie business can be thought of as actual) where, thirty years earlier, Liza Minnelli's real-life parents (if movie star parents can ever be described as real-life) had created their own mythical cities. Soundstage 29 was where Judy Garland and Vincente Minnelli began their real-life — that slippery, even useless, phrase again — romance, one that was conducted in the real-time — oh dear, yet another slippery phrase — years in which *New York, New York* is set.

Scorsese hired the actual craftsmen who'd created his childhood dreamworld. His city of dreams was brought to virtual life by one of American cinema's greatest production designers, Boris Leven. An immigrant from Moscow, Leven already had experience in constructing mythical Manhattans. He designed what are probably the most famous and memorable fictional New York streets — the Oscar-winning ones of *West Side Story*. (He also created an Oscar-nominated pre-war Austrian Tyrol for *The Sound of Music* as well as the Oscar-nominated Texas Victorian farmhouse around which the lives of James Dean and Elizabeth Taylor revolve in *Giant*.)

Leven was one of the principal originators of "theatrical realism" in the cinema. That is, art direction and production design which offer "a reconstructed realism which only ostensibly disguises its manufactured qualities." In this case, Scorsese's "mythical city" and "no reality," the heaven-on-Earth he dreamed of.

For a cinematographer, Scorsese hired Hungarian-born László Kovács, best known not for big studio movies but for his poetic view of America in *Easy Rider* (1969) and *Five Easy Pieces* (1970).

To style Minnelli's hair, Scorsese enlisted Hollywood hairdresser Sydney Guilaroff. A London-born Russian Jew raised in Winnipeg, Canada, Guilaroff (pronounced *Gill-er-orf*, with a hard "G") grew up aching with the same kind of New York dreams as Scorsese and Mardik Martin. He went on to tease out many of the century's most defining haircuts, sensual work with scissors and comb that dug deep into all our dreamworlds. Guilaroff did sexy haircuts like no one else before or since. Few people alive haven't had a thrill or more from what he did with female movie stars' hair. It's no mere historical quirk that he was the first hairdresser to get a screen credit, for *On the Town*. He created Claudette Colbert's bangs. He cut Greta Garbo's bob for *Ninotchka* and had a long affair with her — she called him Gilly. He hairstyled Katharine Hepburn — "a wonderful lady and a true friend." He turned Lucille Ball into a redhead, in 1945, for *Ziegfeld Follies*. He did men, too. "My favorites were Clark Gable, Robert Taylor and Tyrone Power."

For his Mexican border noir, *A Touch of Evil*, Orson Welles put Marlene Dietrich in a dark wig. When, in her later years, she returned to cabaret performance, Guilaroff cut and curled her strawberry blonde cascade. "I loved Marlene." He styled Marilyn Monroe's blondeness and was a pallbearer at her funeral. And he did Dorothy's braids for Liza Minnelli's mother in *The Wizard of Oz*.

But even those game-changing haircuts weren't Guilaroff's most influential work. His most extraordinary and innovative haircut was done — as these things so often are — right at the beginning, before his career had really got going. It happened almost by chance — as these things so often do, particularly in the movies. He created it not long after he had run as fast as he could from Winnipeg to New York, a small-town boy with big-city hopes and big-screen dreams fostered by the silent movies of his childhood. In the city that never sleeps, he slept on benches in Central Park. He found work at Antoine's hair salon and, at a mere eighteen years of age, created not just a great haircut but one of the great images of 20th-century womanhood: Louise Brooks' bob.

The story goes that the silent movie actress just happened to walk into the salon, looking for someone to cut her hair. "A lovely, whimsical, feminine creature" in Guilaroff's memory. The teenage hairdresser got the job: he cut it short at the back, angular at the sides and left it black as sin. Brooks took that haircut to Europe and her starring role as Lulu — famous for being the first modern female movie performance, lifelike rather than melodramatic. Yet Brooks is almost outperformed by Guilaroff's brand new hairdo. Its darkness, geometry and masculinity embody the enrapturing possibilities of Lulu's free-flowing, hyper-sexual androgyny. It's short, sharp and not at all feminine. "Almost a man's hairdo," said Guilaroff. It more or less steals the picture.

Photographer Edward Steichen saw that — or something like that, anyway — almost right away. Poet of line and shape, Steichen pictured Brooks, in Hollywood, in August 1928. She's leaning across the back of an armchair, looking down to her left, not so much averting her gaze from the gazer but turning inwards, to study herself. The depths of the picture's meanings are in its surfaces — the straight and curving lines of the actress's face, clothes and *maquillage*. Eyebrows, finely trimmed, darkened with kohl — like two horizontal slashes of a sure-handed artist's charcoal stick. Sharp crease ironed into the arm of her baggy sweater. Lips like New Year's Eve, around 2:00 a.m. And that haircut: black and rich, part simple frame, part warrior queen's helmet. The picture was first published with a short, giddily admiring piece on Brooks in the January 1929 edition of the New York magazine *Vanity Fair*.

It was the haircut of the century — one of them, anyway. It was the modernist moment in women's hairstyling. As Le Corbusier's Villa Jeanneret (1923) was to domestic architecture, so Sydney Guilaroff's Louise Brooks (1928) was to women's hairdressing. Guilaroff originally wanted to be an architect; I really don't think it's stretching things too much to see that young dream and ambition in what he did with Louise Brooks' hair.

Over time, that bob became a symbol for a particular kind of female sexuality — assertive and self-knowing but also inevitably tragic. Far more women have probably had their hair cut to that shape than have seen *Lulu* — or even heard of Louise Brooks. Kenneth Tynan, the English writer who rediscovered Brooks for the world in the late 1970s, would appear at fancy dress parties in a Louise Brooks wig. He'd wear a Louise Brooks dress, too. And he'd get involved in a little spanking. It's that kind of haircut. In *Something Wild*, Melanie Griffith — whose character reflected the film's title — wore a wig of it. And, of course, Liza Minnelli sported a version of Guilaroff's masterpiece as Sally Bowles in *Cabaret*.

"I have a tremendous love and respect for Liza," Guilaroff said in a 1996 interview to promote his autobiography, *Crowning Glory*. "She is a real talent and completely unique. I love Liza. She is like a daughter to me."

**Love stories**
When we think about Scorsese's *New York, New York*, we think about a love affair between a male jazz musician and a female singing star. And when we think about the making of *New York, New York*, we think about an Italian-American movie director in love with his singer star. Or rather we think about two versions of that love story: not just Marty and Liza but also Liza's parents, Vincente and Judy, creators of the movies of Marty's dreams. At which point, the head starts dizzying a little, as present and past, truth and illusion overlap, interweave and merge into one another.

For Scorsese, the movie was a "Valentine to Hollywood." For Liza, it was family, a reliving of her parents' lives — or rather her version of them, plus Marty's dream version of them. No ordinary parents, either. In Vincente Minnelli, there was a father who was quite possibly gay. In Liza, a daughter who has had a habit of marrying gay men. Out of her four husbands, number-one and number-four certainly were gay; number-two probably was. In her mother, Judy, there was a gay icon whose last husband was most certainly gay. And Judy's own father was quite possibly also gay. Life and sexuality, particularly in this family, folds back on itself.

Then there is Guilaroff, the venerable Hollywood hairdresser who did the cuts that made the mother famous and who had now been hired, by the daughter's boyfriend, to create for that daughter a hairstyle from the mother's own heyday. Or rather, to help Scorsese fashion his "no reality" version of that heyday. Fact, fiction, screen-time and real-life: they blur, uncomfortably.

Scorsese even gave Liza her mother's old dressing room on the MGM lot. The room, that is, in which, three decades earlier, her parents had fallen in love and courted. Judy (as star) and Vincente (as director) were making their first film together, *Meet Me in St. Louis* — for which Liza's future godmother (and, even later, roommate) Kay Thompson did the vocal arrangements, notably for the streetcar song, "Zing! Went the Strings of My Heart." Which is what happened to Judy and Vincente (or Frances and Lester, as they were known before they became themselves).

In 1976, Scorsese was falling, too — and not just for Liza. He was tipping into a drug habit. "After winning the Cannes Golden Palm for *Taxi Driver*, we got big heads," he said, twenty years later. "I started playing with drugs when I was doing *New York, New York*. For me it was just the beginning of going into an abyss for about two years and coming out of it just barely alive." Shortly after the film's release, Andy Warhol fell into conversation with Liza and noted what she said in his diary — the great social record of Manhattan's disco years. "Marty has coke problems," Liza told Warhol. "He got blood poisoning, and now he takes medicine to clean himself out." (I've taken cocaine myself, more than once, and it certainly made me carry on a bit like Liza Minnelli and talk with something of Martin Scorsese's pucker-mouthed velocity.)

There were other complications in the Scorsese-Minnelli affair. Marty had just married his second wife, writer Julia Cameron. Their daughter Domenica would be born in late 1976. Liza, meanwhile, was — during her affair with Scorsese — running around with Russian ballet dancer Mikhail Baryshnikov. She was also a couple of years into a five-year marriage to Jack Haley Jr., producer and director of the *That's Entertainment* series of compilation movies. The first of them had come out — so to speak — in 1974, right around the time Jack and Liza wed. *That's Entertainment* celebrated the "MGM Dream Factory" movie musicals, among the best of which were, of course, those directed by Liza's father — including Scorsese's best-beloved backstager *The Band Wagon*. Liza's husband was the son of the Jack Haley who played the Tin Man in *The Wizard of Oz*. The movie, that is, in which Liza's mother played Dorothy. So: Dorothy's daughter and the Tin Man's son got married. Maybe even had sex together. It kind of freezes the brain, doesn't it?

As to Scorsese, what, frankly, did he — a man whose sentimental education came more from movies watched than a life lived — see when he looked at his girlfriend? What did he, through his drug blur, see in the 30-year-old drug-blurred Liza he was cavorting around Manhattan with? Did he see that Liza at all, or did he see her through a scrim of her mother, the Judy Garland of his childhood movie house dreams? Or was his vision colored by her father, Vincente, Technicolor orchestrator of those Scorsesean childhood dreams?

Freud wrote something to the effect that whenever and wherever two people have sex, at least four others are always present — two pairs of parents, he meant. When Marty bedded Liza, there must have been a whole cinema full of people with them, projectionist included. (Particularly the projectionist, probably.) A tin man, too. And maybe a sad sack of a lion. Even his straw man of a pal.

It's a sadly inevitable equation: director sleeping with star plus big heads equals problems. More so when his wife is working on the script, and he is living in the studio. Literally. Scorsese slept there, had his own apartment there. "Our relationships, our marriages, our difficulties, everything that was happening to us during the shoot," he said. "All of that found its way into the film."

Not that the director realized or understood it at the time. It was first pointed out to him some time later, at lunch with Jean-Luc Godard. The legend of a French *nouvelle vague* director told the now-legendary American director how much he liked *New York, New York*. Scorsese: "He said it was basically about the impossibility of two creative people in a relationship — the jealousies, the envy, the temperament. I began to realize that it was so close to home that I wasn't able to articulate it while I was making the film." As ever, we try to smuggle our deepest selves across borders, but the customs officers always open our suitcases and expose the illicit dreams and memories we've tucked away among our clean shirts and freshly laundered underwear.

Then there were the drugs. Even bigger problems. One day on the set of *New York, New York*, Scorsese kept 150 costumed extras waiting while he talked to his shrink. Much later, and much straighter, he remembered, regretfully: "It was a mess, and it's a miracle the film makes any kind of sense. I blame all that on coke."

The first scene of the film, in which De Niro the jazzer picks up Minnelli the singer, was originally an hour long. The first cut of the movie ran four-and-a-half hours. It now runs a little over half that, 164 minutes. In time, Scorsese would come to refer to it as a "$10 million home movie." (Actually, its budget was $14 million — and its gross $13 million.) I asked lyricist Ebb what he thought of the film. "I don't think it's a very good movie, though there are good things in it."

It was edited by Marcia Lucas. She showed a rough cut to her husband George — who had just finished making the first *Star Wars* picture. He offered his opinion to Scorsese, telling him that if he brought Francine and Jimmy together at the end of the picture, it would add $10 million to the box office. Scorsese didn't take his fellow director's advice.

The opening party for *New York, New York* was at Studio 54, playground central of the city's cocaine and disco epoch. I imagine that party through the prism of the 1984 single "A Night in New York" by Elbow Bones and the Racketeers. Not a hit at the time but destined for a long life on late-night dance floors, it was an invention of August Darnell, a.k.a. Kid Creole, a Bronx man with Caribbean, Italian and deep Southern heritage. Or perhaps through the glass of "Westchester Lady," a 1976 jazz-funk eternal by pianist Bob James, which always brings to my mind a dark lady in a white Diane von Furstenberg one-piece wraparound dress. (If in my head only.) I also conjure up a vision of Minnelli making her way through a tray of rum-and-sodas — reportedly, her cocktail of choice in disco's high nights — and making many trips to the bathroom to powder her nose.

The week after Scorsese's picture opened, *Star Wars* rocketed into cinemas. "*New York, New York* looked hopelessly old-fashioned," Scorsese later recalled. Like him, William Friedkin was one of the "New Hollywood" directors. Just years earlier, he had hit big with *The French Connection*, then even bigger with *The Exorcist*. But his 1977 picture *Sorcerer* was also sideswiped by *Star Wars* — which he'd turned down an offer to direct. Forty years on, Friedkin said *Star Wars* marked as big a change in the movie world as the switches from silence to sound and from black and white to color had been decades earlier.

Simply, Scorsese's movie was a flop. The theme tune did no better. Minnelli's soundtrack recording was issued by United Artists, but it didn't make the U.S. Top 100, peaking out at number-four in the "Bubbling Under" sub-chart. Even now, a mint copy will cost you less than a dollar.

Everyone involved in making *New York, New York* was simply astonished by its failure. "We all thought it was going to be a huge hit," said Minnelli in 1998. "But the funny thing is that people still watch it and talk about it and love it." It's the movie that won't die.

Why won't it die? For one thing, it changed the way we dress. Genuinely. Giorgio Armani, who had only been in the womenswear game for a couple of years, was so struck by the outfits in *New York, New York* that he recreated the movie's extra-big shoulders and super-small waists for his next collection. (Not coincidentally perhaps, Italy was the only country in the world where Minnelli's song charted — though even there it topped out at an unexciting number-37.)

So, the film's imaginary 1940s clothing was the real inspiration for an Italian fashion designer's late-1970s vision for a new future — one in which the then-fashionable bright fun-time colors and shapes of Fiorucci etc. made way for proper grown-up clothing like parents used to wear. Suits, ties and lace-up shoes. The kind of stuff Judy Garland and Vincente Minnelli really did dress in (or were dressed in) when they were at their movie peak.

It was the look that made Armani famous, and it became the look of a decade: power-dressing. Armani's (nostalgically) innovative designs were to fashion what the song "New York, New York" was to music: openly ambitious, yearning, striving, in love with a world in which money was the new fun. If something as restless and careless as modern capitalism could be said to have a uniform, 1980s Armani was it. If at first its sharp lines and big shoulders were a little parodic, that didn't last long. It quickly became too mass-market for that. When a fashion is available on every main street in the Western world, irony and allusion have long been left behind.

Five years after *New York, New York*, London's National Theatre revived the classic Broadway musical *Guys and Dolls* (and did it again in 1995). Its design and look were consciously based on Scorsese's movie — super-high curbs and ultra-wide suit shoulders, all that. But it wasn't until 2023 that *Hamilton* creator Lin-Manuel Miranda shepherded a show loosely based on the movie to Broadway. *New York, New York* the musical got nine Tony nominations despite poor reviews and closed after three months.

Mostly, though, Scorsese's *New York, New York* endured because of something that was almost completely overlooked at the time: that title song. "Could you believe the song was never nominated for an Academy Award?" said producer Irwin Winkler, who still owns the song (and its royalties). One reason it was overlooked was its familiarity — or rather, its *seeming* familiarity. It was almost universally assumed to be an old song, one that we all knew but had somehow forgotten, rather than what it was — a new song consciously crafted to sound old, an artistic invocation of an imagined past.

Not that there's anything particularly unusual in a new song sounding old, if rarely one as powerfully imagined and constructed as Kander-Ebb's "New York, New York." Nostalgia is a pop constant. Evocations of lost innocence. Requiems for earlier selves, of worlds before we fell — into marriage, work, children, life. Don McLean's "American Pie." Barry Mann's "Who Put the Bomp." The Kinks' "Where Have All the Good Times Gone." Paul Weller's "Tales From the Riverbank."

That Kander-Ebb's "New York, New York" gets misremembered as an actual 1940s song is, obviously, a tribute to the quality of the job done by the songwriting duo. The song really does reflect and dramatize the textures and emotions of a particular, almost globally shared memory: the mid-20th-century years when midtown Manhattan was the undisputed epicenter of the global entertainment game. Rodgers and Hammerstein musicals. Damon Runyon short stories. Walter Winchell broadcasts. Prizefights at Madison Square Garden. Johnny Mercer lyrics. Nelson Riddle strings. Men in hats, women in strapless evening gowns, cigarette girls, shoeshine boys. Divorcees, rumrunners, press agents. Broadway, 42nd Street, Times Square. Real shows, real people, real places — but also myths, implausibly perfect notions of glossy urbanity. Places to fall in love. Places to fall in love with. Places to fall into. And from.

Tony Bennett talked about this real but also mythical — and self-mythologizing — New York in a 1998 interview; "Anything was possible. Why, just down the street, Yip Harburg wrote 'April in Paris' over cheesecake at Lindy's. And he had never even been to Paris." Harburg's work of the imagination was transatlantically mirrored by Serge Gainsbourg's "New York – U.S.A." (pronounced "yoo-ess-ah"), written and recorded in 1964, before the Parisian had ever visited the city he hymned. As Harburg fell for early 20th century romantic clichés about Paris, so the distinctly French pop chameleon crafted his own, more modern — and sly — New York love affair in song, solemnly chanting a litany of the city's buildings and institutions (Waldorf-Astoria, Time-Life Building, First National City Bank, etc.) along with a blank, repetitive comment on their height — "c'est haut" ("it's tall") — in a chorus performed by French women Gainsbourg told to sing like Africans. Beneath the lugubrious vocals sits a bed of African-ish rhythm "inspired" by Babatunde Olatunji's "Akiwoko," a track on a 1960 compilation album, *Drums of Passion*.

"I was listening all the time to this album of ethnic music," Gainsbourg was quoted as saying in Gilles Verlant's biography of him. "I stole a few ideas from it. 'New York – U.S.A.' is based on a Watusi war chant." (Pause for correction. The Watusi was not a war chant, but a dance craze hit for several artists in 1963. The biggest success went to a Philadelphia R&B quartet, the Orlons, named for the first successful acrylic fiber in a deliberate sneer at their all-natural and upscale high school girl group competitors, the Cashmeres. It was big enough to get namechecked on Chris Kenner's hit "Land of 1000 Dances," a mathematically wrong but rhythmically spot-on identification of the musical source of Gainsbourg's song, which actually refers not to the Watusi but to a chant of the Tutsi, a South African ethnic people who were sometimes, and also wrongly, called the Watusi.)

Gainsbourg's track fully embodies its time: post-imperial but pre-Black Power, almost Warhol-like in its knowing inanity, repetitiveness and unashamed appropriations. It has an artistic cousin in the Afro-European musical mashups made twenty years later by Malcolm McLaren with Adam Ant, Bow Wow Wow and Trevor Horn, producer of the *Duck Rock* album, and it was the subject of a copyright infringement suit by the U.S.-based Olatunji. Ah, pop music. It may just be my favorite New York song of all. (It even namechecks the CBS building on Sixth Avenue in which "London Calling" was prepared for its U.S. release and Andrew King spent many days and hours "vibing up" Epic employees to get them working hard to promote the record.)

**Major chords**

The point of a good show tune — and the best Kander-Ebb ones are eminently among the very, very good — is that they are sung in character. Often, they're monologues, opening up the singer's heart. Character being plot, they also let us peer into the engine of the musical. The song "New York, New York" is the crux of the film. Everything else hangs on and around it. Musically, the song's power is rooted in the directness and certainty of its major chords. The buoyant heart of many big and bigger songs is their major chords. They are, for example, a sound of Christmas — from Mariah Carey's "All I Want for Christmas Is You" to Slade's "Merry Xmas Everybody" to Live Aid's "Do They Know It's Christmas?"

In "New York, New York," major chords are also a conscious — perhaps *self*-conscious — echo of something Jimmy says in the film. Talking about his goals, he describes them, in musicianly terms, as "major chords" — "the woman you want, the music you want and enough money to live comfortably." But Francine wants more, far more than that. She wants to conquer the city that never sleeps. Which is just what she does, starting at a top-dollar nightclub — as Minnelli did in real life.

"New York, New York" came to Sinatra via music publisher Frank Military, his right-hand man right through the 1950s. They remained in touch long after Military quit Sinatra's employ, when the singer left Capitol Records at the end of that decade. Sometime after the Scorsese movie came out, Military sent Sinatra a copy of Minnelli's recording, with the suggestion that he cover it. When there was no response, Military — a man with the organizational inclinations of his surname — followed up his suggestion with regular calls to Sinatra's secretary, Dorothy Uhlemann. "It's on the turntable," she'd tell Military. "He's getting to it."

And eventually Sinatra did. And he liked what he heard, enough to include it in his shows, long before he recorded it. Not that he liked it enough to give it its own spot in his act — not to start with, anyway. At first, he didn't even sing it — not so much as a word.

Just Kander's dum-dum-da-de-dum vamp, used as the soundtrack to Sinatra's arrival onstage. Those few notes were not just instantly recognizable — even then, when the song was no more than the theme of a flop movie — they were already gathering meaning. In those few notes, audiences had begun to sense that they were hearing the whole song in miniature: its driving emotions, dreams, blind ambitions. Songwriters are often asked which came first, the music or the lyrics? "The check," said long-time Sinatra lyricist Sammy Cahn. "The intro," said Kander of "New York, New York." "When you find something like that, it tells you about the direction you want to go in," he said of that little vamp of his.

Sinatra's audience took to this tiny fragment of "New York, New York." They so took to it that, gradually but inexorably, it made its way up to star status in Sinatra's show. In its move from walk-on music to top billing, the song's progress replicated the dream of its lyrics, achieving king-of-the-hill-dom in Sinatra's world. Or top-of-the-heap-dom — that worldly little phrase whose sly sardonicism so many singers miss, particularly Sinatra. A heap is not a hill. You can have a heap of all kinds of things. Generally, in fact, a heap does contain all kinds of things — multitudes, even. Here, though, it can only be a heap of people. The triumph that "New York, New York" dreams about is one that comes at the expense of others. It's a zero-sum game. Not standing on the shoulders of giants but on the faces of rivals.

**Start spreading the news**
"New York, New York" first appeared in Sinatra's show as a song rather than a walk-on fragment on October 14, 1978, during a residency at Manhattan's Radio City Music Hall. Jonathan Schwartz, New York radio man and Sinatra expert (maybe *the* Sinatra expert), was there that night. He told the *New York Times* that the singer looked over to Vincent Falcone — Sinatra's musical director and conductor of many years, as well as pianist on the singer's first attempt at recording "New York, New York," a year later. "What's the first line?" Sinatra asked

Falcone, across the giant stage that early autumn night on Sixth Avenue. "Start spreading the news," Falcone replied from behind his piano. Sinatra turned to his band and said, simply and Sinatra-like, "Shoot."

Falcone himself tells a different story about Sinatra's journey to "New York, New York." The singer, Falcone said, "had gone to see the movie with Robert De Niro and Liza Minnelli. He brought me the sheet music and said, 'Play this for me.' We were in rehearsal at NBC, and I played it. I believe the very first time he sang 'New York, New York' was at the Waldorf-Astoria on October 13, 1978, at a benefit for the Mercy Hospital."

A few days before that, Sinatra led New York's Columbus Day parade. His dream of being king of the hill was coming to life. (In November, he started campaigning for Ronald Reagan.) All too soon, "New York, New York" would make him and the city pretty much synonymous.

Even then, the Kander-Ebb song didn't stand alone: it was in a trilogy of New York tunes stitched together by Sinatra's long-time arranger Don Costa. The other two were songs the singer had first recorded in 1949. One was the 1934 ballad, "Autumn in New York." The other was that other song called "New York, New York," which Sinatra had first sung as the opener for the movie version of the musical *On the Town* — in which he danced and sang with Gene Kelly and the always-forgotten third sailor-on-shore, Jules Munshin (an actual, real-life Jewish New Yorker).

The original stage show of *On the Town* was pulled together by Broadway director and producer George Abbott — whose reach, power and range were such that his nickname was Mister Abbott. Stephen Sondheim called him "the grandmaster of Broadway comedy, musical and otherwise." A few years before his death, in 1995, aged 107, Mister Abbott talked about that earlier "New York, New York" tune. "I always thought that was the best New York song," he told Mark Steyn in his book *Broadway Babies Say Goodnight*. "But the new one's better." New one? Kander and Ebb's "New York, New

York." Better? Mister Abbott must have meant something like deeper, more profound. Comden and Green's song for *On the Town* is bright, peppy, likable. It's wonderful, a showstopper — and a complete and utter fantasy, a tourist brochure for the city and mid-20th-century urbanity. Ultimately, it's childish. Not shallow, it's too much fun, the lyrics too well-turned, for that. But childish in the very best way — simple, gleeful, innocent. Its New York is a city for visitors: trips to museums and the top of the Empire State Building, the yellow of the cabs and steam billowing up from cracks in the sidewalk. There's none of the striving, struggling, yearning that real cities are built on, feed on, flourish on.

The New York of the Kander-Ebb song, now that's a city a couple of country rats could dream about, its streets paved with rubbish and its merchant houses aflutter with junk bonds. Kings of the hill. Tops of the heap. It's a place where the empty — and bottomless — hole of desire can be filled, at least partly anyway. As its singer sings, the listener hears — and responds to — its gross, unsatisfiable hunger. To want everything is a deep human wish. Stupid and mad, but human.

The charm of Kander and Ebb's "New York, New York" is almost brutal. As listeners, we are either swept up and away by its impossible dream — impossible because, in life, unlike musicals, there is always another hill to climb, another heap to top. Or we are outsiders looking in, distanced observers calmly noting how manic, mad even, the singer's impossible dream is — a festival of narcissism. Even more likely, we swing back and forth between the two feelings. From: Oh, what a dream! To: Crazy or what? To: My dream, too! To: Are you mad? To: For the moment, yes, please! To: That song really is a smart portrait of crazed, narcissistic ambition! That, I reckon, is what Mister Abbott meant when he said Kander-Ebb's "New York, New York" was "better."

It's certainly what Sinatra found in the song, even more so than Minnelli. He knew and began to grasp what he had in the song: what he could do for it, what it could do for him. It began to upstage the rest of the singer's Manhattan medley. "Man, this thing is getting big,"

Sinatra told Falcone. "We have to take it out of the overture." So, he started singing it on its own. Then he moved it up and away from the start of the show, putting it later and later in his set list — which at that time ended with "My Way." "But it just kept getting bigger," said Falcone.

As the song moved towards prime position in the set, so it changed. Falcone: "All during that year, he started to grow with the song, and he started to put it into the shape that it eventually took. It didn't start out being as dramatic at the end as it is now, with a much, much slower tempo. That's why he likes to do a song on stage for several months before he records it; he feels that he develops the song. And he doesn't want to record it too early, because then he figures he'll change it."

A couple of onstage recordings were made, but what entranced a live audience just didn't work for an electronic one. In the moment, in Sinatra's presence, you could forget his voice was shot. Beyond that moment, you couldn't. So, at some point, it was decided to record it properly, in a studio.

The first attempt was made, with Falcone at piano, in Manhattan on July 20, 1979. (More or less the same time the Clash were settling in to record *London Calling*.) It didn't work. It was Sinatra's first session in two years. He knew what had happened to his voice. Audience rapture couldn't blind even him to the truth.

"New York, New York" wasn't the only song that didn't work. None of the others he sang in the studio that day worked, either. In a changed world, he was no longer sure where his music fit in. So, he tried all kinds — Elvis songs, Stevie Wonder's "Isn't She Lovely," Billy Joel's "Just the Way You Are" and Neil Diamond's "Song Sung Blue." He kept trying, too. Weeks of this stuff was recorded in New York and Los Angeles, but it didn't really lead anywhere, certainly nowhere worth going. It was painful, but no surprise really, that when Sinatra took the finished recordings to Reprise, the label didn't want to release them. Just to add to his humiliation, he was being rejected by the company he'd helped create, just a decade and a half earlier — though its low revenues had forced him to sell it to Warner Bros. in 1963.

Still, out of all that mush and mess, Sinatra finally got a good recording of "New York, New York." The version we all know was cut in Hollywood as summer turned towards autumn, on September 19, 1979 — nearly a year since he'd first sung it onstage and the same day the Clash played "London Calling" in Boston. The music was by Falcone and his orchestra, in a loud, brassy, almost old-fashioned big band arrangement by Don Costa. This time, instead of Falcone on piano, it was veteran West Coast session man Pete Jolly playing Kander's distinctive, indecisive, stumbling riff at the start of the song.

By the time of the recording, Sinatra was losing command of the only part of himself that he'd ever had under full control — his singing voice, an extraordinary thing. Maybe part of our delight in his singing sits in the space shaped by the contrast, between grown-up voice and infantile vocalist. When he sings, he makes it sound as easy as ABC. And, of course, achieving such childlike simplicity is never simple. And rarely a task for children.

One of Sinatra's sharpest biographers, John Lahr, described Frank's "New York, New York" as "the last big notes he hit." An echo, conscious or not, of Jimmy's "major chords" in the movie. Ebb, Scorsese and Minnelli had crafted it as a song of youthful striving. Sinatra ground it into the world's minds — and hearts — as a titan's swan song, a raging against the dying of the light.

Five days after recording "New York, New York," Sinatra sang it for Egypt's President Anwar Sadat at the Great Pyramid. By the time he played Carnegie Hall in June 1980, the Kander-Ebb song had taken the place of "My Way" as his show closer. And it stayed there for the rest of his career, only being usurped once, at Reagan's inaugural ball in 1981, when Sinatra finished his set with "America the Beautiful."

## Other "New York, New Yorks"

Kander and Ebb's "New York, New York" might have become the best-known and best-loved song with that title, but it was neither the first nor the last. There are at least twenty other songs called "New York, New York," nine of them notable — if for reasons more varied than merit or success. Plus, there are two you can be forgiven thinking are called "New York, New York" but aren't: Jay-Z's "Empire State of Mind" (which depends on a considerable contribution from London) and Paloma Faith's "New York," a 2009 hit in which the singer loses her lover not to another woman but to the city on the Hudson which "stood so tall and never slept." (Its chorus might be "New York, New York" but the title's not. And the backing vocals are by London's Souls of Prophecy Gospel Choir). There is also a triple: "New York, New York, New York" by Martha Wainwright, a Canadian who moved to the city at the age of sixteen, in 1976.

Here, in chronological order, are those nine other words-and-music "New York, New York"s. Each presents a different (if not always fresh) view of the city, its citizens and its possibilities.

One. The 1940s show tune. That's the Comden-Green-Bernstein song from their *On the Town* musical in which Manhattan women are dressed in silk and satin. (Or so the fellas say.) Sinatra wasn't the first to sing it. Its debut was in the original Broadway show, which opened at the Adelphi Theatre on West 45th Street just after Christmas 1944. Which meant it arrived right in the middle of the Battle of the Bulge, the bloodiest battle of the entire Western Front campaign — nearly 20,000 U.S. troops died in three weeks — and the last moment of doubt about who would win the war. What better time to debut a musical rom-com about a trio of dancing, singing seamen on leave in New York City?

*On the Town* started out as a wordless ballet called *Fancy Free*, with choreography by Jerome Robbins and music by Leonard Bernstein. It was then molded and shaped into a musical by the reinventive hands of George Abbott — Mister Abbott, if you remember. Under Abbott's guidance, Bernstein brought in a couple of old friends to write the book and perform in it — Betty Comden and Adolph Green. (See above. And below.)

A pair of native New Yorkers, Comden and Green also wrote the screenplay for that archetypally Hollywood musical *Singin' in the Rain* and the script for Scorsese's favorite musical, *The Band Wagon*.

Essentially, though, for Comden and Green, home was always where their hearts were. Which wasn't out west. As the *Grove Dictionary of Music* puts it, "With few exceptions, the subject matter of their shows is their native New York, which they examine sardonically but lovingly." To them, it was always a helluva town.

Well, almost always. When time came to make the *On the Town* movie, they were hired to write the screenplay — but major changes were forced on the original team. Bernstein's score was dumped — too high-toned for the average moviegoer, said the studio. "New York, New York" was one of the few things left in from the original stage show music. Even then, to placate real or imagined religious sensitivities, Comden and Green were prevailed upon to alter their best-known lyric. So, "a helluva town" was changed to "a wonderful town." Movie aside, no-one else ever sung it that way. Even Sinatra. Particularly Sinatra.

"New York, New York" number two: a proto-rap from 1970. It's on the debut album by the Last Poets, a fractious and fractured gathering of Black Power-inspired poets who informed their listeners that the "Statue of Liberty is a prostitute" and the city has an "exploited colony" or three (Brownsville, Bedford-Stuyvesant and Harlem are named) where "tiny, fat Jews are holding the fiery hoop and watching you burn your ass jumping through it." Yes, you did just read that. (You do have to dig a little to find those antisemitic lines, though. They are generally — and invisibly — trimmed these days. The Last Poets' second album was advertised in *Rolling Stone* with this blurb: "If you're white, this record will scare the shit out of you. If you're black, this record will scare the nigger out of you." Yes, you did just read that. As ever, the past is a foreign country.)

"New York, New York" number three: the 1970s jazz tune. This is a Duke Ellington oddity, composed for a summer festival in the city that the great big-band leader hosted in 1972. It celebrates New York's charms, excitedly. The city, its lyrics proclaim with almost childish naïveté, is the glitter, the glamour, the sunswept, starlit, moonshined supergrandslammer. No inkling, then, of the Last Poets' bitter vision or of the city's forthcoming direction of travel in that worrisome decade. Very much, in truth, a view from 333 Riverside Drive, the Beaux Arts building in which Ellington lived from 1961 till his death in 1974, two years after he wrote his "New York, New York." In 1977, the city renamed nearby West 106th Street Duke Ellington Boulevard. As Ellington told his songwriting partner Billy Strayhorn, take the A train and get off at 125th Street — travel instructions that, in 1939, Strayhorn turned into the Ellington band's signature tune.

The fourth "New York, New York," a 1970s pop hit, was written and recorded in London in 1978 by a Long Islander, Gerard Kenny. It's the one that riffs on the empire city's postal address, the place that's so good "they named it twice" — a line which offered its writer an irresistible rhyme: "vice."

The following year, Kenny wrote "I Could Be So Good for You," the oh-so-London-y theme tune of *Minder*. A giant of 1980s UK primetime TV, *Minder* was a comic series of almost-criminality set in the same parts of West London that the Clash wrote so much about — and something of an English parallel to Damon Runyon's tales of Broadway's sporting life. Kenny also co-wrote something of an (unsuccessful) anthem for his adopted city, Shirley Bassey's "There's No Place Like London" (1986). His writing partner on that song was an actual Londoner, Lynsey de Paul (née Lynsey Monckton Rubin, of Cricklewood), who later crafted the 1983 Conservative party anthem: "Vote Tory, Tory, Tory / For election glory." (The Tories won, by a landslide, despite de Paul's song.)

Kenny wasn't the first to make song-play with New York's postal address. Chuck Jackson's 1963 uptown soul love song, "Big New York," featured the line "Your town's so great that they named you twice." (Jackson was from North Carolina. The song's writer was Ed Townsend from Memphis: an ex-Marine, son of a preacher man and co-author of Marvin Gaye's "Let's Get It On," Townsend rhymed "twice" with "price" — possibly an even more New York noun than Kenny's "vice.")

Four years prior to Jackson's soul single, jazz singer Jon Hendricks used the rhyme "the city so nice they named it twice" in a spoken narrative on George Russell's 1959 album *New York, N.Y*, which featured John Coltrane on tenor sax and Bill Evans on piano.

The fifth "New York, New York" is a 1981 proto-punk roar by the Dictators, all local boys. Their singer was Handsome Dick Manitoba — Bronx-born (as Richard Blum), given a professional wrestler's name and described on the band's debut album sleeve as its "secret weapon."

In the spring of 1978, Handsome Dick took me on a guided tour of his childhood turf, the South Bronx. Not the kind of tour you'd find in a travel agent's brochure, particularly then. I took the bus up from Manhattan, across 110th Street and through the almost picturesque poverty of Harlem. A TV news cameraman's clichéd view of Black inner-city despair — raggedy residents drinking their brunch (cheap wine, beer or malt liquor) while flopped on raggedy sofas in front of battered brownstones.

The South Bronx was nothing like that. In fact, there was pretty much nothing there, just lots of rubble and burned-out block after burned-out block — torched, variously, I learned, by gangs, careless residents and landlords in search of an insurance payout. It looked like it had been carpet-bombed by B-52s, a Luftwaffe-battered landscape of my childhood, only more so. Far more so. There was no-one in sight. Little did we know that behind that post-apocalyptic facade, profound innovation was going on. This was where and when hip-hop, easily the most important artistic revolution of the late 20th century, was being born and taking shape. We were just too blind to see.

Handsome Dick suggested burgers. We walked what felt like — but probably wasn't — miles on streets which weren't there and through rubble which was. He took us to a White Castle, his favorite burger joint. "Best in the city," he said and ordered. I took a bite. It tasted … greasy. To me, that is. To Handsome Dick, I should think it tasted of his past, the long-lost middle-class Bronx-Jewish world of Richard Blum's childhood. His beef patty-in-a-roll to Proust's little biscuit dunked in a floral tisane.

The Dictators' "New York, New York" is very much of its time, featuring a cast of junkies, creeps, b-boys, "fags" (later replaced by "queens"). It first appeared on a live cassette called *Fuck 'Em If They Can't Take a Joke* and then on the lone album by the spinoff band Manitoba's Wild Kingdom. (For twenty years, Handsome Dick ran a bar, Manitoba's, in the East Village. It closed in 2019.)

Six is a 1983 post-punk scowl. This "New York, New York" (a.k.a. "New York/N.Y.") is by red-haired East Berliner Nina Hagen. It's a celebration of Manhattan's early 1980s downtown club scene. It namechecks clubs: AM/PM, the Pyramid, the Roxy, the Mudd Club, Danceteria. And it promises that David Bowie will be there tonight. It made number-nine on *Billboard*'s *Hot Dance Club Songs* chart.

Seven is a minor rap hit, released by Grand Master [*sic*] Flash & The Furious Five in 1983. It's every bit as dystopic as the Clash's "London Calling" but somewhat less articulate. "Big city of dreams / But everything ain't what it seems." Tha Dogg Pound covered it — and developed it — in 1995. The video shoot for their version certainly reflected the song's terror-struck vision of the city. During filming, there was a drive-by assassination attempt on the group's leader, Snoop Dogg.

In the 1990 movie *The Freshman*, you hear the original on the soundtrack as Clark Kellogg (the young man of the title, played by Matthew Broderick) arrives in Manhattan. It's an indication — somewhat labored — of what the city will soon present to him: an entanglement with the Mafia, as represented by Carmine Sabatini, a mobster who is both played by Marlon Brando and meant to be the real-life basis for his portrayal of Don Corleone in *The Godfather*. So … Brando is playing a fictional character who is the "real-life" inspiration for another fictional character — who Brando also played.

Eight is from 2006 — and a nonentity, despite being a collaboration between two local stars, mixing Debbie Harry's singing with a hi-energy dance track by Moby. New York, asks the Blondie vocalist, do you even know my name? A flop in the U.S. but a success in Greece and Italy.

Number-nine jumps us back five years to the days of the most significant moment in the city's modern history — though its connection with that event is merely happenstance. This 2001 "New

York, New York" was written and sung by a man from North Carolina, Ryan Adams. It's about lost love and coming to terms with that loss — if only in the (willed) imagination. A public holiday of a song, set partly on Independence Day and partly at Christmas, it's a reflection on Adams' failed relationship with Amy Lombardi. To the world, she was a music business publicist. To Adams, she was "my Anita Pallenberg, the coolest and most beautiful woman I've ever met." They lived together on East 10th Street and Avenue A, one of downtown Manhattan's several beating hearts.

Failed relationship? Well, sort of. Though Lombardi has remained silent, time has uncovered things about Adams' relationships with women (and girls). Unpleasant, uncomfortable things. So how do you listen to a love song written and sung by a grown man who you know has been investigated by the FBI (but not charged with any crime) for texting and sexting a fifteen-year-old fan? Song and singer: can one ever be separated from another? No. Yes. No. Yes. Etc.

The chorus to Adams' Manhattan love ballad runs: "Hell, I still love you, New York, New York." With a line like that, you'd think it inevitable that it would become an anthem of sorts. And it did, despite the best efforts of both Adams — a persistent career self-sabotager — and the world. The track was released in the second week of September 2001. The video, which was shot on September 7, celebrated the Manhattan skyline. By the time it was edited and ready, that world was gone, forever. Adams gave the profits from the track — most likely, by far the most successful of his many, many, many recordings — to a 9/11 charity.

Three years later, the same skyline — now apocalyptically different — featured in the video for the Beastie Boys' "Open Letter to NYC," which includes a sample from Robert Goulet's version of "New York's My Home." That song was written by Gordon Jenkins, a Missouri-born figure in the 1940s and 1950s music business game. Among many other adventures, Jenkins worked with Peggy Lee, Sinatra (in Los Angeles) and Judy Garland (in London). He also gave the world the original "Wimoweh" and *A Little Touch of Schmilsson in the Night*.

**Bob Dylan's New York**

Adams is one of many performers who have been described as the "new Bob Dylan." The old, actual Bob Dylan has never written a song called "New York, New York" — though he did, like Adams, release a record on 9/11: his thirty-first album, *Love and Theft*.

And he did come up with a couple of New York songs very early in his career. The first, "Talkin' New York," appeared on his first LP. It's a talking blues, heavily marked by the stylings of his mentor Woody Guthrie's "New York Town."

The second Dylan song about the city was "Hard Times in New York Town." Though unreleased till 1991 — officially, anyway — it was taped just before Christmas 1961, in the Minneapolis apartment of Bonnie Beecher. A good friend of Dylan's, Beecher was an actress whose best-known role was her TV debut in one of the last episodes of *The Twilight Zone*. She played a long-dead singer from whom "The Rock-a-Billy Kid" Floyd Burney learns the episode's title song, "Come Wander With Me." Burney has been described as the "first Bob Dylan-style folkie to appear on the small screen." Among the actresses Beecher beat out to get the part was an eighteen-year-old Liza Minnelli.

Dylan recorded "Hard Times in New York Town," in the year of his first trips to the big, big city. "I knew I had to get to New York," he said, in 1985. "I'd been dreaming about that for a long time." The song reflected — and, of course, this being the young Dylan, romanticized and mythologized — his own hard times in New York town. "New York City was cold, muffled and mysterious, the capital of the world," he wrote in *Chronicles Volume One*. "New York was a dream."

The deep, deep detail of archival pedantry shows that Dylan has officially released five other songs that name-check New York: three of his own and two covers. "I Shall Be Free No. 10" (1964) mentions the *New York Times*. "Joey" (1976) refers to the New York restaurant in which Joey Gallo, the gangster of the title, was shot to death. In "Just Like Tom Thumb's Blues" (1965), he sings about "going back to New York City." The two "New York" songs he has covered are Simon and Garfunkel's "The Boxer" (1970) and Woody Guthrie's "This Land Is Your Land" (1961).

And then there is "Visions of Johanna" (1966), a song written in the Chelsea Hotel on West 23rd Street. It doesn't namecheck New York. Its only reference to the city is a mention of the D train. Yet that was enough, when the *New York Daily News* ran a list, to put it at number seven in the tabloid's list of all-time greatest New York songs. What headed the list? A contemporary recording, LCD Soundsystem's "New York I Love You but You're Bringing Me Down" — a 2007 lament for the "filthy but fine" metropolis of Dylan's "Visions of Johanna." Sinatra's "New York, New York"? Sixth place.

**Thames and Hudson**

The LCD Soundsystem track is not the only 21st-century dystopic New York song. "The doctors don't know, but New York was killing me," sang Gil Scott-Heron on his last album, 2011's *I'm New Here* — recorded in London, produced by Jamie xx, a twenty-two-year-old Londoner, in the rear garage of Adele's label, XL, which is on Ladbroke Grove, a main thoroughfare of the Clash's hometown world. Scott-Heron died the following year, aged sixty-two, in New York.

Propping up the *Daily News* list at number-ten is the 2009 Jay-Z chart-topper that many think is called "New York, New York" — because that's the chorus. The song's actual title is "Empire State of Mind." It does, however, reference Sinatra and his song, if with welcomely predictable pop star narcissism. "I'm the new Sinatra…" When Jay-Z and Alicia Keys performed it at that year's *American Music Awards*, they started it off with a little bit of Kander-Ebb's "New York, New York."

It was, almost unbelievably, the first ever number-one hit to reference New York in its title. Now, wind back in time a little, to the moment when Jay-Z first handed the lyrics to Alicia Keys. His song, he told her, would become "the anthem of New York." Not *an* anthem for the city, but *the* anthem. And it did become a new city anthem of sorts — if never quite *the* one. It has been used in the TV show *Sex and the City*, at Yankees games, for a 2012 New York state ad campaign and to mark the end of Columbia University's commencement ceremony.

In May 2011, Jamie Cullum performed it at the opening ceremony of the *Cannes Film Festival*, to honor jury chairman Robert De Niro. The Essex boy jazz singer and pianist played it in a medley with the Kander-Ebb song, which was fitting for at least two reasons. One, Cullum was born in 1979, a month or so before Sinatra finished recording "New York, New York." Two, Jay-Z's song is yet another example of the North Atlantic passage between the Thames and the Hudson. Like Gerard Kenny's "New York, New York," it was born not in the Empire city but in London, where its first draft was written by two homesick Black women from Brooklyn, Angela Hunte and Janet Sewell-Ulepic.

Jay-Z (né Shawn Carter and also from Brooklyn) kept the London-based pair's piano hook and choruses but threw out the rest of the song. He then had five more writers work on it, including himself, a dead man (Bert Keyes) and a seventy-four-year-old woman who would herself be dead within two years (Sylvia Robinson).

Keyes, who died in 1987, was a New York music business veteran who started out in the 1940s. His name is all over 1960s soul and pop. By way of a substantive example, he produced the original version of "Let's Go Get Stoned," for the Coasters. Robinson was an Antillean Manhattanite high school dropout who had big hits in the 1950s ("Love Is Strange") and the 1970s ("Pillow Talk"), then started record labels (All Platinum and Sugar Hill), created "Rapper's Delight" with the Sugarhill Gang and was accordingly feted as the "Mother of Hip Hop." Together, Keyes and Robinson wrote "Love on a Two-Way Street," a 1970 hit for the Moments. And that's why their name is on the credits of "Empire State of Mind" — it's the tune which Jay-Z appropriated (with due acknowledgment and royalty checks) for his record.

The seventh, final and only white writer on the song was a Londoner in his mid-twenties, Al Shux (né Alexander Shuckburgh), who worked up the initial track with Hunte and Sewell-Ulepic. Born and raised in Shepherd's Bush — down the road from the Clash's cherished Westway — Shux did a BA in Commercial Music at the University of Westminster. His subsequent career in commercial music has included being Lily Allen's musical director, producing and making rap, grime and hip-hop, scoring Plan B's "Ill Manors" and winning awards for "Empire State of Mind." He was responsible for the enticingly odd-stepping beat of Jay-Z's record. "I wanted to create a gritty, urban sound," he has explained. "I wanted the feel of it to punch you around the face a little bit." So, the beating heart of New York's most modern anthem is a Londoner's vision of its rhythms.

(Shux is not the only member of his family to have a chart hit. His grandfather, who died in 2015, was Sir David Willcocks, who conducted the choir on the Rolling Stones' "You Can't Always Get What You Want." Sir David also directed the music at Prince Charles' (first) wedding and wrote the most familiar modern arrangements of many Christmas carols. What did he think of "Empire State of Mind"? It has, said Sir David, "a natural rhythmic energy and simple sense of harmony that is very attractive.")

Not everyone was so unambiguous. In 2010, *New Yorker* writer Malcolm Gladwell told *The Guardian* it was the song that reminded him most of New York, then added: "I'm kidding. But as excruciatingly self-referential and self-congratulatory as that song is, it is also perfect, because it's about the most excruciatingly self-referential and self-congratulatory city on Earth. At what point do you think New Yorkers will wake up to the fact that it is not 1950 anymore, and the center of the world has moved east?" (Gladwell is a Canadian with English and Afro-Caribbean ancestry.)

Jay-Z's track consciously echoed two earlier New York songs that played on the word "state": Nas's "N.Y. State of Mind," which appeared on the Queens rapper's 1994 debut, and Billy Joel's "New York State of Mind" from 1976. Joel's song is another by an exile — in this case, a Bronx-Jewish songwriter who had gone west to work but who has just, for the moment anyway, said goodbye to Hollywood.

It's an odd song, though. At first hearing, it's celebrating a return to New York, by train, on the Hudson River line. But it's as grounded in failure as success. The music undercuts the lyrics even as it underscores them. It's the song of a homecomer who knows that a celebration of hometown life can be close to an admission that the world will forever be beyond your reach. A realization that homecoming always involves a little defeat. A lament, a mourning even. (Which kind of makes it odd that it was for many years the song played at the end of New York Mets games, a "tradition" that stopped, without warning or explanation, in 2008. Then again, given that the Mets haven't won the World Series since 1986, maybe not so odd at all.)

It was the song Joel played, live, in Madison Square Garden on October 20, 2001, at *The Concert for New York City*, the immediately post-9/11 benefit for emergency workers. The show was pulled together not by a New Yorker but by a Liverpudlian, Paul McCartney. Strangely — or not unexpectedly, take your pick — there were almost as many Londoners as New Yorkers onstage that night. Even more strangely — *very* strangely, in retrospect — Joel's song was the only New York anthem played that night. David Bowie opened the show with Simon and Garfunkel's "America" — which gets no closer to the city than the New Jersey Turnpike. James Taylor played "Fire and Rain." And McCartney finished the night with "Let It Be" and "Freedom," a new song about the 9/11 attacks, which he'd seen from his seat on a plane waiting on a runway at Kennedy Airport.

Other than Joel's "Miami 2017 (Seen the Lights Go Out on Broadway)," there were no other New York songs. No "Sidewalks of New York." No "it's a helluva town." No Manhattan. Most strikingly, no "New York, New York." None of them. On that night of all nights, you'd think Kander-Ebb's "New York, New York" would have been on the bill. It was already the city anthem, after all. (Well, kind of.)

## Sidewalks of New York

According to *The Encyclopedia of New York City*, the first song with New York in its title was probably the "New York Patriotic Song" of 1799 or thenabouts. The city's first (unofficial) anthem was "The Sidewalks of New York," written a century later, sometime in the 1890s. A waltz that namechecks "London Bridge Is Falling Down," it was the tune that helped the growing metropolis through its straw-hat and ragtime piano years. It became and remained the theme song for Belmont Park racetrack until 1996 — when it was replaced by Kander-Ebb's "New York, New York," which was itself replaced in 2010 by Jay-Z's "Empire State of Mind." The sporting life crowd does, though, still sing the old tune as a kind of warm-up for a race.

The lyrics of "The Sidewalks of New York" were by James Blake, a salesman in a hatter's shop. The tune was by Charles Lawlor, a Dubliner, amateur composer and buck-and-wing dancer (loud tap dancing with an emphasis on single taps). It was an instant hit. The very first time it was sung in public the audience joined in the chorus. The performance was at — how suitably for this tale of transatlantic passages — the Old London Theater on the Bowery. The singer was Lottie Gilson — a Swiss-born vaudeville comedienne and (kind of) singer, age unknown then and now.

As well as becoming the city's first anthem, it was used as the theme song for Jimmy Walker's (successful) 1925 run for New York mayor. Al Smith also used it as the campaign song for his successive (and unsuccessful) tilts at the presidency. Not that Blake or Lawlor benefited from those outings. They had sold off their song back in its first heyday, splitting $5,000 for it. A lot of money back then, but not enough for life.

Lawlor died, blind and broke, the year his song helped Walker to the mayoralty. When the songwriting game went sour on him, Blake became a department store salesman, but that didn't work out either. In 1933, he was evicted from the apartment he shared with two siblings and was reduced to walking the very sidewalks he had made famous. Then the *New York Herald* heard about his fallen life and ran a campaign to help him out. With aid from Al Smith, the newspaper raised enough to pay Blake a pension of $25 a week. Two years later, a minimum weekly wage of $15 was introduced. That was the year the lyricist died. Roughly speaking, his pension income would have been a total of $2,500 — pretty much the same as his earnings from "Sidewalks."

Mayor Jimmy Walker knew about songs. He'd been a songwriter himself, even had a hit: "Will You Love Me in December (As You Do in May)." But his father made him give up songwriting and become a lawyer. He then turned to city politics. As mayor, he presided over New York's jazz years — in a manner, to the manor born. He left his wife for a showgirl, took bribes, gave the city a casino in Central Park, turned a blind eye to girlie mags on 42nd Street, let 32,000 speakeasies bloom and led an anti-prohibition march — 100,000 strong, united behind the slogan "Beer for Prosperity."

Along the way, he acquired the nickname Beau James — which became the title of a 1957 bio-pic, a colorfully bowdlerized life of an all-singing, all-dancing mayor, played by Bob Hope. There was a stage musical about Walker, too — *Jimmy*. It ran for a few months as 1969 turned into 1970. And before that, there was a song about him in *Fiorello!* the Pulitzer Prize-winning 1961 musical about his successor, the honest reformer Fiorello La Guardia.

As Walker's star rose in the jazz years, so it fell as the Great Depression dug in. New York governor Franklin Delano Roosevelt chased Walker's administration through the courts, in search of — amongst other things — an explanation for the large sums of money in Walker's personal bank account. Eventually, in 1932, Roosevelt allowed him to resign and head east, to exile in Europe. Three years later, Walker returned to New York, now married to his showgirl. The city's welcome was warm, but his casino had been torn down and replaced by a playground. He died in 1946.

In that last decade of downfall, Walker returned to his first love, the music business. He became president of the National Association of Performing Arts and of a record company, Majestic — whose A&R chief was the colorful Eli Oberstein, one of the most unethical early independent record men. Unethical? Oberstein passed off German opera recordings as his own. On the other hand, he was responsible for one of the first Black blues hits, Mamie Smith's "Crazy Blues," a 1920 recording in which the singer tells of her intention to "go and get some hop, get myself a gun and shoot myself a cop." (There's a path to be followed from those lyrics, isn't there, which is more likely to lead you to the Clash's "London Calling" — and on to gangsta rap — than to Sinatra's "New York, New York.") Oberstein also midwifed many of the first significant country music recordings, for the Bluebird label in the 1930s. And he had a son, Maurice — the man who signed the Clash to CBS and whose limousine was sleeping-producer-ed by Guy Stevens at the *London Calling* sessions. As one city breathes in, the other breathes out.

Maurice Oberstein died, of leukemia, on August 3, 2001. His ashes were scattered — within gobbing distance of the Westway — on the Loftus Road pitch of his football club, Queens Park Rangers. At every home game, QPR play "London Calling" before kickoff. (Every time I've been there for a game, Mick Jones has been there, too — quiet and discreet, generally in a long black coat, like the one he's wearing in the "London Calling" video. Imagine that — your team's eleven best men taking the pitch to the sound of your seven guitars. I wonder if Mick smiles a little secret smile of pride.)

**A girl, a boy, an isle of joy**
The second great New York anthem was Rodgers and Hart's "Manhattan" — which appeared just as Jimmy Walker was launching his bid to become mayor. It's the song in which the city is turned into an isle of joy. "'Manhattan' made an overnight success of Rodgers and Hart," wrote Philip Furia in *The Poets of Tin Pan Alley*. The song itself wasn't an overnight success, though. It was originally written for a 1922 show, *Winkle Town*. With as unprepossessing a name as that, it is little surprise that the show never so much as made it to the stage.

Three years later, Rodgers and Hart (both native New Yorkers) put their unused song into their first *Garrick Gaieties* show. It was a songs-and-gals affair with sketches, skits, a scarf dance and Lee Strasberg, who would become the great method acting guru and the cake-offering Hyman Roth in *The Godfather Part II*. I have seen the late Strasberg's beach house on Fire Island. It's tiny, homey, sandy and fabulous, looking out over the Atlantic Ocean, clear all the way south to Cuba and that terrible Havana New Year's Eve in *The Godfather Part II*.

Rodgers and Hart's *Gaieties* show opened, at the Garrick on West 35th Street, on June 8, 1925 — a year or so, that is, after Coward's *London Calling!* made its Broadway debut. "Manhattan" was sung, in front of a plain curtain, by June Cochrane, a leggy blonde, and Sterling Holloway — who, later, much later, would become the voice of Winnie the Pooh in the Disney movies. The audience loved "Manhattan" right away. That very first night, they demanded and got several encores. They understood somehow, instinctively and immediately, that here was a song that offered a new vision of New York and its place in the modern world.

Alexander Woollcott reviewed the show. *New Yorker* writer, son of a "ne'er do well" Londoner, life model for the deeply unpleasant central character in the 1939 play *The Man Who Came to Dinner*, Woollcott was also a drinking and lunching pal of Lorenz Hart and a bellwether for chic midtown opinion. He wrote that "Manhattan" was "bright with the brightness of something new minted." The adoration was general. The song's lyrics were reprinted in newspapers across America. By July, the *Atlanta Constitution* was telling its readers that it was the "most popular piece in New York, you hear it played wherever you go." New York's own *Morning Telegraph* said it brought the city "back into the limelight." Of the song and its lyricist, Irving Berlin said, many years later, "It's timeless because there's still a Manhattan. Larry [Hart] wrote about Manhattan the way other people are still trying to write about New York. They don't do it as well."

It's often said that the moment New York became the capital of the world — displacing the previous claimant, London — was September 18, 1929, the Wall Street Crash's Black Thursday. I'd suggest it came four years earlier and a few miles uptown, at that opening night in the Garrick. Rodgers and Hart's "Manhattan" offered a new set of thoughts and ideas: about cities and citizenship, about urban texture and metropolitan sensibilities, about the relationship between uptown language and downtown slang. It crystallized for the Garrick audience what they already felt about themselves and their city. It gave New York the chance to look at itself in the mirror and like what it saw. What New York saw was a democratic metropolis in which even the poor young lovers of the song could share its glories, if ironically. The idea that the subway ever emitted "balmy breezes" is a joke — an excellent one, at that. As is the evoking of the pleasure of Mott Street in July — in reality, it would have been hot and dirty and humid and smelly. And whatever Delancey Street was, it certainly wasn't fancy. It was the high street of the Jewish Lower East Side semi-shtetl world — lined not with trees or planters but barrels of pickles and smoked fish. A line and attitude that was echoed by Peruvian (well, he was born in Peru, Indiana) Cole Porter in his 1930 song "I Happen to Like New York": "I like … even the stink of it." Rodgers and Hart took a similarly tongue-in-cheek view in "Give It Back to the Indians" for the 1939 show *Too Many Girls*.

At the core of that mid-century democratic metropolis which Rodgers and Hart's "Manhattan" embodied — created, even — were Broadway and its dreams. In a special New York issue, *The New Yorker* editorialized: "The 20th century Broadway musical has been New York City's own PR department, extolling Manhattan in lyric after lyric and receiving top billing in the city's intoxicating mythology."

Nik Cohn (self-described as a "northern Irish Menshevik Jew — and typical of the sort") wrote the largely fictional article, for *New York* magazine, which inspired the movie *Saturday Night Fever* as well as the books which inspired the Who's rock opera *Tommy* and David Bowie's *Ziggy Stardust*. He also wrote a book about Broadway, and called it *The Heart of the World*, a clever, subtle, punning title. His Broadway — that is, all our Broadways — is the one that sat at the heart of the entertainment world. The Broadway, that is, which is evoked in "New York, New York" — the real but mythical place that captured, held and enraptured our hearts. This was the time of the city; New York was the city and Broadway its apotheosis.

Broadway merits its own entry in the New York songbook. "Numberless were the hymns of praise" for it, wrote Cohn. He catalogued the raw material for, and the creators of, those Broadway hymns: an ever-shifting (and often shifty) cast of "hoofers, chorines, sugar daddies and stage-door Johnnies (such as Mayor Walker, I'd cite by way of example), gangsters and their molls … lushes and hopheads … tunesmiths and rhymesmiths."

Songs of the Great White Way include — just to take the most successful and well-known tributes — Warren and Dubin's "Lullaby of Broadway," George M. Cohan's "Give My Regards to Broadway," Sondheim's "Broadway Baby," Mann-Weil's "On Broadway" (a hit for the Drifters and George Benson) and the Clash's "Broadway." (An atypically quiet, swinging, flute-led tune, it's on *Sandinista!*, the album that followed *London Calling*.) And "Broadway" by Hank Ballard, the man who gave the world the twist, well before Chubby Checker took the dance craze to the top of the world's charts. Ballard kicks off his hymn to the Great White Way by extolling its "bright lights, wine, women and song."

When Bob Dylan played that number in the New York episode of his *Theme Time* radio show, he introduced it as "the kind of song you call a flag-waver." When its piano-powered three minutes of 1950s rhythm and blues were over — if never done with — he added, both delicately and indelicately, "Just about made me drop my mustard-squirter."

"Lullaby of Broadway" was an Oscar-winner written for *Gold Diggers of 1935*. The music was by Harry Warren. "The most successful composer of songs for American films," according to the *Grove Dictionary of Music*. He had 42 Top 10 hits between 1932 and 1957. He was a real New Yorker, too, an Italian one, born Salvatore Guaragna in Brooklyn in 1893.

The song's lyricist, Al Dubin, wasn't from New York, but his life story could have been a Broadway musical. Born Swiss, in Zurich in 1891, to Jewish parents in flight from czarist Russia, he grew up American in Philadelphia. He was thrown out of high school for passing his days and nights in the manner to which he would dedicate his life: in the company of musicians, gamblers and drunks.

As a young, enlisted soldier, he was gassed in France. As a grown-up, he wrote the words to "42nd Street" (and all the other songs for the musical movie of 1933 about New York's Broadway fraternity, including "Shuffle Off to Buffalo"), "Chattanooga Choo Choo," "Tiptoe Through the Tulips," "You're Getting to Be a Habit With Me," "We're in the Money," "I Only Have Eyes for You," "Lulu's Back in Town" and "Boulevard of Broken Dreams." After a life in which "he indulged in excesses of eating, drinking, womanizing and drug-taking," he died in 1981. A real Broadway of a boy.

As there was a song called "Manhattan," so there was a movie called *Manhattan*, made by Woody Allen in 1979, the year of "London Calling" and Sinatra's "New York, New York." It became Allen's second most popular film, after *Annie Hall*. Its soundtrack was music closely associated with pre-WW II New York — though, oddly, Rodgers and Hart's "Manhattan" itself isn't in it.

But there's an even odder thing about the soundtrack, and there's an odd reason for that odder thing. The odder thing is that the soundtrack doesn't feature a single song that either has New York in its title or is directly about the city. And the odd reason for that odder thing is that the music is all by George Gershwin. Though almost umbilically associated with New York's mid-century apotheosis, Gershwin never actually got round to writing an anthem about the place in which he was born and raised and lived most of his life. He composed a couple of minor themes — "New York Serenade" (1928) and "New York Rhapsody" (1931) — but the closest he came to an anthem for his city was "135th Street Blues," with words by Buddy DeSylva, who produced Shirley Temple, co-founded Capitol Records and wrote "Button Up Your Overcoat" and "Birth of the Blues."

Gershwin — and his lyricist brother Ira — did, however, write an anthem of sorts for London, "A Foggy Day." First sung by Fred

Astaire in the 1937 movie *Damsel in Distress*, it has music which quotes the chimes of Big Ben and contains the wonderful line "the British Museum had lost its charm." That the Gershwins had rarely visited London only adds to the lyric's dreamy delight.

George Gershwin did, though, have a hand — if an oblique one — in "Autumn in New York." That song was written, in 1934, by a man called Vernon Duke. A refugee from the Russian Revolution, he was actually a classical composer, Vladimir Dukelsky. Gershwin's link to "Autumn in New York" was that he was the one who gave the Russian exile his Anglo pseudonym — which the composer used as an alter-ego for his ventures into popular song. As Dukelsky, he wrote for Diaghilev's Ballet Russes. As Duke, he wrote "Takin' a Chance on Love" and "April in Paris," with lyrics by Yip Harburg. (Yip was short for yipsel, Yiddish for squirrel.)

It's also true, as Tony Bennett testified, that Yip had never been closer to the city of light than the Staten Island ferry. Duke, by contrast, did know Paris. He had spent a good part of the 1920s there, becoming pals with Picasso, Cocteau and Coco (Chanel). He arrived in Manhattan in 1921, via Turkey, and sneered at the place, which he called "dirtier than Constantinople." He was, though, struck by the legs of New York women: "so many miniature skyscrapers." (A side point: why "autumn" in New York, rather than the more usual American English "fall"? Because two syllables were needed to fill the line?)

That Woody Allen chose to use inter-war music for his movie was part of a pattern, the same one which helped shape both Scorsese's *New York, New York* and Kander-Ebb's theme song. The 1970s was a period in which the city liked to think about itself through a prism of nostalgia. That prismatic vision was certainly better than the one out of the window.

Given the brutal reality of the late 1970s, it's understandable that nostalgia was a common New York emotion. A sense of what had been lost gave solace for the painful truths of the present — or at least some perspective on it. In my memory, New Yorkers' 1970s nostalgia for an old New York came in two basic flavors. Two backwards-looking views of two different cities that just happened to occupy the same physical space.

One view romanced the hugger-mugger of early 20th-century immigrant life. Handsome Dick Manitoba's lost Bronx was a variant on that. So was *The Wanderers*, his borough-mate Richard Price's fictionalized memoir of early 1960s teen ganghood, which was turned into a movie set in 1963 and released in 1979. "See the wonders of a forgotten world," boomed its trailer.

The other view was New Yorkers' ache for the romantic boulevards of middle-class life — of safety and Broadway melodies. The standard decor of many New York restaurants of those good old days was Tiffany-style table lamps and red-checked tablecloths — fashions that had been established before WW I and were mainstream in the 1940s of the Scorsese movie. They were still there in the 1970s. Possibly they'd never gone away. They looked relic-like and touristy but probably they weren't. Like the seafood-fronted brasseries of Paris and the luxuriantly mirrored pubs of London, New York's red-checked tablecloth restaurants offered both genuine continuity in a changing city and a slightly neurotic symbol of unchangingness. No matter that they were in a restaurant that may have only been open a couple of weeks. (I remember one such joint on Christopher Street, center of the city's loudly gay subworld. It was just down the street from the Pleasure Chest, a shop offering what was almost certainly the world's most extensive range of S&M leather and metal leisure wear.)

This nostalgic New York was rhapsodized by the Dutch architect Rem Koolhaas in his 1978 book *Delirious New York* — then barely known but subsequently a core document for the art-speak end of modern architecture. Rotterdam-born Koolhaas wrote about the Manhattan of the half-century between 1890 and 1940. For him, this city was "a laboratory: a mythical island where the invention and testing of a metropolitan lifestyle and its attendant architecture could be pursued as a collective experiment in which the entire city became a factory of man-made experience, where the real and the natural ceased to exist."

### John Lennon's New York

There were many 1970s songs about New York. In 1972, John Lennon, of Liverpool but by then resident at 105 Bank Street, in Manhattan's West Village, wrote "New York City" — number eight in that *Daily News* list of best-ever NYC songs. As Lorenz Hart once (ironically) evoked the joys of a pickle-lined boulevard, so the former Beatle (straight-facedly) hymned the delights of Harlem's Apollo Theater, the Staten Island Ferry and Andy Warhol's salon at Max's Kansas City.

At the start of the year, *New Yorker* magazine great Hendrik Hertzberg paid a visit to the Lennon and Ono proto-loft. He asked: Why New York? "We love it," said John. "And it's the center of our world. Everywhere's somewhere, and everywhere's the same, really, and wherever you are is where it's at. But it's more so in New York. It does have sugar on it, and I've got a sweet tooth." There was a jukebox in the loft, with just one "New York" single on it, Bob Dylan's "Positively 4th Street." (Fifteen years after Lennon's assassination, Yoko Ono wrote and recorded "New York Woman" for her 1995 album *Rising*. It was not a hit.)

Other New York songs of the era were dusted with the enchantment of distance. The 3,000 miles to England, for example.

In 1975, Marc Bolan of London (Stamford Hill, in particular) cut his own New York City song. His lyrics were not untypically gnomic, asking about women who come out of the city with a frog in their hands.

"New York Groove" also arrived in 1975. A UK Top 10 hit for the glam band Hello of Tottenham and Wood Green, it was written by Russ Ballard of Waltham Cross — five or six miles further north, just outside London. Ballard had been in the music business game since he was sixteen, and this was his biggest hit, a song that tells the story of an exile's return, with dollars in his pockets. It's the dream of millions, arriving in a Cadillac alongside "a wicked lady." The narrator gets the limo to drop them off at Third Avenue and East 43rd Street.

Three years later, a fairly slavish cover version of "New York

Groove" was a U.S. Top 20 hit, this time for a genuine New Yorker: Kiss guitarist Ace Frehley of the Bronx.

So, what exactly are the great attractions of the intersection of 43rd and Third? I've had a look, and there really are none. There's no plaque for either Ballard or Frehley. Walk west through Grand Central Station, however, and you'll reach the corner of Vanderbilt Avenue now known as David Ben Gurion Place. There used to be a hotel there, the Biltmore, which was torn down, more or less overnight and without warning, in 1981.

It was at the Biltmore, in 1942, that the Zionist movement finally decided its aim should be "that Palestine be established as a Jewish Commonwealth." (Ben Gurion was the first president of that Jewish commonwealth — hence the place name. I doubt that Ballard had any of that local history in mind when he wrote his New York dancefloor anthem.) The Biltmore's garage was celebrated for being the home of the oldest established floating crap game in New York, of course, by Sinatra's Nathan Detroit in the 1955 movie version of Frank Loesser's *Guys and Dolls*. The Biltmore had five underground levels and direct access to Grand Central platforms, making escape easy.

In 1976, the Ramones offered a rat's eye view of a junction that was then a gathering spot for male prostitutes, ten blocks north of the Biltmore, on 53rd and Third. Bassist Dee Dee Ramone, who had "worked" the junction, fictionalized himself into a Vietnam special forces veteran "tryin' to turn a trick." Things don't, needless to say, work out well for him. The same year, Rod Stewart had a big hit with "The Killing of Georgie (Part I and II)," based on the real-life story of a gay street murder in the area.

In 1977, the musical *Annie* opened on West 52nd Street, in the Alvin Theatre (renamed the Neil Simon in 1983). *Annie* was written by a pair of native New Yorkers (Charles Strouse and Martin Charnin), with a book by Thomas Meehan, an out-of-towner (but a long-term New York City resident) from Ossining, thirty-five miles up the Hudson River. The sixth song in the show was "N.Y.C.," a celebration of Daddy Warbucks and Annie's glorious night out in the big city. "No other town in the whole 48 can half compare to you." Manhattan cabaret singer Steve Ross thinks "N.Y.C." should be the city's official song. His reason? That it's sung by an actual New Yorker, while the singer of Kander-Ebb's "New York, New York" is merely a would-be New Yorker, on his way there with a head full of dreams and ambitions.

Also in 1977, there was Odyssey's "Native New Yorker" — still a dancehall evergreen decades later. A bigger hit in the UK than the U.S., it was sung by three non-native New Yorkers — the Lopez sisters, Lillian, Louise and Carmen, whose parents were from the Virgin Islands and who grew up in Stamford, Connecticut. But it was written by an actual New York native, Denny Randell, who'd made his name working with Jersey boys the Four Seasons — almost certainly the greatest group ever to be named after a bowling alley. "'Native New Yorker' was one of the most heartfelt, emotional songs I ever wrote," said Randell. When he wrote it, he was a prodigal son of the city, having just moved back to his hometown after years on the West Coast. One of those heartfelt, emotional lyrics proclaims that native New Yorkers don't have doors opened for them and another that love is merely a thought you have in a cab.

Two years previously — in London — Neil Sedaka (raised in Brighton Beach, graduate of his city's two great musical education institutions, Juilliard and the Brill Building) sang his "New York City Blues." He rhymes the title with "lose." There is also a rhyme of "U.S.A." and "okay." It's not one of his best.

There are at least four other songs called "New York City Blues," none of them exactly world-famous: a late-1940s misty, elegiac Gershwinesque meditation by Duke Ellington. From 1962, there is one sung by Peggy Lee, co-written by her and Quincy Jones. From 1966, there is one by English blues boomers the Yardbirds which involves "pretty little girls," a father and a "big black shiny shotgun." In the last years of the 20th century, the blues revival threw up a guitar-driven shuffle, in which "the Big Apple done gone rotten" for the singer. (Written by an Englishman, it was performed by a Texan,

Larry Dale, and the Houserockers.) From the second decade of the 21st century, there is one from New Orleans piano player, songwriter, singer and Grammy-winner Dr. John — recorded not long before his death in 2019, aged seventy-seven.

Another great New Orleans pianist, Jelly Roll Morton, made the rolling "London Blues." "I stood on the corner," he sang, "My feet was dripping wet." Now there's a finely hewn snapshot of the city's dangers — not an angry father but a day-long drizzle.

In the Queen's silver jubilee year of 1977, a transatlantic song fight kicked off between London and New York. In the east corner was West London band the Sex Pistols. The last-but-one track on their debut album, *Never Mind the Bollocks*, was "New York," an attack on the Heartbreakers, the downtown Manhattan band whose precursor, the New York Dolls, was briefly managed by Pistols handler Malcolm McLaren and who were now based in London, along with their hangers-on and addictions.

Once a true fan of the Dolls, Johnny Rotten taunted the Heartbreakers with the passion of a disappointed lover, calling the unnamed but unmistakable target of his scorn "just a pile of shit." Heartbreaker Johnny Thunders (born John Anthony Genzale Jr. in Queens) wrote a response song, "London Boys," telling the world that Rotten couldn't urinate without manual assistance. (Such was the coziness of the relationship between New York and London punk that the drummer and guitarist on Thunders' track were former Sex Pistols.)

Thunders' song was at least the third called "London Boys." In 1966, David Bowie released a Hogarthian tale of descent into drugs in contemporary Soho. "You hope you make friends with people you meet." The eternal hope of the big city newbie and a wretched lyric. It was not a hit; quality copies of the original Deram 45, on which the title is misspelled as "London Boy's," sell for anywhere between £700 and £2,000. A little later, Bowie wrote and recorded "London Bye Ta Ta." That was not a success either. In 1976, not a peak year in his career, Marc Bolan wrote his own "London Boys," a song about mods.

I looked hard for a transatlantic counterpart, a song called "New York Boys." I couldn't find one, but I did find "New York Girls." It's an old sea shanty sung by a sailor recovering from a night out on the city's Lower East Side — including Bleecker Street, future home of the punk club CBGB. Hungover, with an "aching head, robbed of all his cash and stark naked," he lies there bemoaning his fate. "You love us for our money" is the seaman's embittered judgment of the city's female population. Or at least that element of it open to a one-night stand with a drunken sailor.

The oldest version of the song I can find was recorded in London in the 1950s for the BBC by Bob Roberts, Britain's last commercial sailing ship captain (also a London *Daily Mail* reporter). The best-known version is now probably the one by Irish singer Finbar Furey for Martin Scorsese's 2004 film, *The Gangs of New York*, for which the Clash was originally slated to do the soundtrack.

In 1995, Stephen Duffy (a native of Birmingham, where he was an original, if short-term, member of Duran Duran) wrote and made "London Girls." His girls are the ones wearing "mama's pearls," hanging out in the Good Mixer — a pub, on the corner of Inverness Street and Arlington Road in Camden Town, which was Britpop's late-night romper-room. His song aches with hidden desire — or, at least, desires.

Long before the Duffy track, there was another "London Girls," by Chas and Dave. Once North London pub and rock group irregulars, Chas and Dave became true stars in the 1980s. Such was their appeal that one Christmas Day, they were simultaneously on both ITV and BBC television. "London Girls" was one of their last hits (a minor one, it peaked at number-63 in 1983).

It was revived in 1996 by, of all people, Tori Amos (born in North Carolina, now resident in Cornwall). Her "London Girls" is strange, strange as you can imagine, maybe stranger. It's also funny, touching even. As a piano triples along, Amos sings the backhanded litany of the terrifying qualities of the city's younger female population as if she's reading the lyrics for the first time. Which makes it sound as if she's actually discovering genuine truths about London girls. It is, believe or not, a genuinely sexy performance.

**Sinatra's other cities**

Despite the fact that Sinatra was almost a local, Kander-Ebb's "New York, New York" was far from his only (let alone his first) tribute to a city. Songs about other metropolises already figured large in his career. He included the archetypal London song, "A Foggy Day," on 1953's *For Young Lovers*. His 1957 album *Come Fly With Me* was a kind of "around the world in twelve songs" and is one of the founding documents of his particular jetset urbanity, whose illusions are epitomized by the title track's claims for Bombay as a source of exotic booze, a clear and lazy untruth driven by the demands of rhyme. The album also features "On the Road to Mandalay," one of the few pop songs — the only one, most likely — with words by Rudyard Kipling. And "London by Night," a song Sinatra had first recorded in 1950 as a fundraiser for the British Playing Fields Association, with a spoken introduction by the charity's main patron, the Duke of Edinburgh. It was written by Carroll Coates — no relation to Eric Coates, but also an Englishman, one who crossed the Atlantic, found his heart in San Francisco and wrote the lyrics for the theme song of *Sunday in New York*, a 1963 Jane Fonda rom-com. New York, London. As one breathes in, the other breathes out.

The same year that Sinatra cut "Come Fly With Me" he also recorded his first big-city tribute hit, "Chicago" ("that toddlin' town"). It wasn't a new song. It had been written more than thirty years earlier, back in the Windy City's gangster years, when Brooklyn boy Al Capone had just made the move west and the Toddle was a contemporary dance craze. The song was written by Fred Fisher, whose life beat even Sinatra's for dramatic parabola. Though a Chicagoan by aspiration, Fisher was actually German-Jewish, born Albert von Breitenbach in Cologne in 1875. He ran away from home at thirteen, joined the German navy, then the French Foreign Legion. Arriving in the U.S. in 1900, his first hit (as Fred Fischer) was "If the Man in the Moon Was a Coon." He followed up that racist ditty with "Under the Matzos Tree," then the still well-known "Peg o' My Heart" and "Blue Is the Night." So, in order: a blackface song, a Jewish ghetto-pleaser, an Irish charmer and a touch of the blues. Ah, pop music.

Almost immediately after coming up with "Chicago," Fisher abandoned his adopted city, leaving for Los Angeles and movie work. There, he wrote "Your Feet's Too Big" (popularized by Fats Waller) and "Whispering Grass," with music by his daughter Doris, a singer who went on to write "Put the Blame on Mame" and "Into Each Life Some Rain Must Fall." Two decades later, in January 1942, Fisher, an excitable, contentious, litigious man, hanged himself. (Hollywood turned his life into a tidied-up and cleaned-up 1949 bio-pic, *Oh, You Beautiful Doll*.)

Sinatra's updating of Fisher's "Chicago" started life quietly, slipping out almost unnoticed, but it quickly became the anthem of the singer's ring-a-ding-ding mobbed-up years. In the UK, it was eventually issued as the B-side of "All the Way," a number-three hit in 1969. Around the same time, its pivotal position in the Sinatra set was usurped by "My Way," originally a French song — Parisian, even. Written in 1967 by Claude François and Jacques Revaux, its English translation by Paul Anka turned a moving, clear-eyed song about a frozen marriage into something which had, in the words of film music composer Simon Boswell, "the pompous reverence of a hymn whose sole object of worship is the singer." Very Sinatra, then.

In turn, "My Way" was replaced by "New York, New York" as the hymn-anthem of his later years, taking the singer through the 1980s, with its triumphalism and greed, into the 1990s and so to death itself.

Not that Sinatra's reworking and reimagining of the Kander-Ebb song was much of a hit at first. It spent twelve weeks flopping around the bottom of the *Billboard* chart, rising no higher than number-32. In Britain, it topped out at 59, in 1980. Nominated for a Grammy, it lost out to Christopher Cross' "Sailing." It did pick up momentum, however, selling over a long period and eventually becoming his first million-seller since "My Way."

More significantly, it eased (greased, perhaps) its way into hearts and minds. Clawed its way, maybe. It was almost stupidly at home in the greed-is-good decade that Reagan's election ushered in, the one of Gordon Gekko's speech in *Wall Street*. "Greed, in all of its forms," announced the fictional, fraudulent financier played by Michael Douglas. "Greed for life, for money, for love, knowledge, has marked the upward surge of mankind." Or the one embodied by the career — and careering — of real-life fraudulent financier Michael Milken.

In 1985, the "junk bond king" opened the annual Drexel Burnham Lambert High Yield Bond conference, known as the Predators' Ball, with his usual flash. He said a few words, then drew back a curtain to reveal the performer who liked to call himself the Chairman of the Board. In all his seventy-year-old glory, Frank Sinatra was already singing the opening line of "New York, New York": "Start spreading the news…" That same year, Sinatra was awarded the Presidential Medal of Freedom by Ronald Reagan.

By the late 1980s, Milken's annual "compensation" from Drexel Burnham Lambert topped a billion dollars. Top of the hill, king of the heap. In 1990, the firm was forced into bankruptcy by the New York Federal Reserve and the Securities and Exchange Commission. Milken was convicted of insider trading, sentenced to ten years in prison and fined $600 million. The SEC permanently banned him from working in finance. His sentence was later cut to two years, in part for giving evidence against former colleagues. In 2020, he was pardoned by a fellow "New York, New York" fan, President Trump. (When Trump left the White House on January 20, 2021, his departure was soundtracked by the bombast of Sinatra's "My Way.")

**"It's Frank's world. We only live in it"**
In his 1995 biography, *Sinatra! The Song Is You*, Will Friedwald wrote: "As sung by Minnelli, 'New York, New York' is just your average show tune. In the hands, or tonsils rather, of Sinatra, it exemplifies the anger and the optimism, the ambition and the aggression, the

hostility and the energy, the excitement and the excrement that is New York. And that is also Sinatra."

Many stars talk about themselves in the third person, enabling them to worship at their own altar. There's that kind of self-adoration going on in Sinatra's "New York, New York." As there is in the aphorism "It's Frank's world, we only live in it" — big in its late-1950s genesis and bigger still in its mid-1980s revival. It's a powerful maxim, gleefully blasphemous, snappy as a Sammy Cahn lyric or a porkpie hat (if a little foxed by repetition). But only one person took it straight, without a heavy dusting of irony: Sinatra himself. He believed it, with an almost touchingly unrelieved narcissism. He was the apple of his mother's eye. He ate the Big Apple. In his own eyes at least, he *was* the Big Apple. According to the axiom, people confused him with God, albeit lightheartedly. He understood their problem. He got confused about that, too.

That's what we hear — and respond to — in his version of "New York, New York." A man who thought he was a city. A vision so grandiose, so extreme, so powerful that it sweeps us up like children. It's quite mad, of course, but we like that, too. Somewhere in all of us crouches a one-person church. The gross obviousness of Sinatra's narcissism makes us feel better about our own, perhaps less obvious, narcissism. Maybe less gross, too. Maybe.

## I♥NY

In 1977, New York State launched an ad campaign aimed at tourists. There were two main strands to it. First, there was a logo: a square of three (black) letters and one (red) symbol, in a thickened version of American Typewriter, an old-looking typeface created in 1974 by ITC, a New York company founded in 1970. The logo was designed by Milton Glaser (1929–2020), graphic artist and co-founder of *New York* magazine — which was sold, in 1976, to a quite different shaper of the city's future, Rupert Murdoch, back when he was still an Australian. Glaser, by contrast, was a native New Yorker — Hungarian-Jewish, born in the Bronx, Cooper Union graduate and a proud citizen, too. He was so pleased to help out his city (and his state) that he created the logo without taking a fee. Nor did he copyright it. His idea was that it would spread out into the wider culture. Which it did, rapidly.

Though the logo was created for New York State rather than NYC itself, it quickly became an emblem for the city. Soon, it was not just on the campaign ads but on T-shirts, coffee cups, hats and pretty much any surface that was white, didn't move and could be turned into, first, a tourist gewgaw and, second, profit. (After which, it was adapted — i.e., stolen — by cities, businesses and market stalls around the world.) Glaser's original arrangement lasted ten years, after which the state copyrighted it. By 2011, it was bringing in $30 million a year.

The other main strand of the New York State campaign was a song, "I Love New York" — the official competition to Kander-Ebb's song, if you like. It, too, was a freebie, donated by its writer, Steve Karmen. Another native New Yorker, Karmen, a Bronx High School of Science pal of Bobby Darin, was — maybe still is — the "king of jingles." His greatest hits include mini-songs for Wrigley's gum, Tic-Tacs, Michelin tires and the oil companies Exxon ("Energy for a strong America") and Sunoco ("I can be very friendly"). He also wrote one for Sunbeam Bread: "a sunwich is better than a sandwich." His New York song promised that "there isn't another like it" — no matter where you go. More nebbish than Fred Ebb-ish, but no matter. On July 1, 1980, Karmen's "I Love New York" was officially adopted as the state song — albeit by Governor Hugh Carey's declaration rather than by actual law.

Like "New York, New York," Karmen's "I Love New York" is not the only song with that title. Two are well-known. One is far superior, the other isn't. The first appeared in the same year as Sinatra's "New York, New York," with lyrics by Londoner Don Black — who started out in the same part of town as me and Sid Vicious, if a little earlier. His career bridged pre-Beatles East London Jewish music business (the generation of Lionel Bart, etc.) and the later worlds of James Bond themes and Andrew Lloyd Webber musicals. (He's still around, too — most recently heard DJing on Radio London.)

Black's catalogue of lyrics include one that could, I think, make a suitable North London anthem, the 1967 Oscar-winning "Born Free," as well as a likely anthem for dedicated followers of English football, "The Self Preservation Society." The latter was the closing theme of the 1969 film *The Italian Job*, with music by Quincy Jones, the American producer of Ray Charles, Michael Jackson and others.

Black's "I Love New York" was written for *Tell Me on a Sunday*, which premiered in September 1979 — right around the time of both "London Calling" and Sinatra's "New York, New York" — at, of all places, the Sydmonton Festival, Hampshire — in, of all venues, a deconsecrated 16th-century chapel. It's on the grounds of Lloyd Webber's country estate.

The show (which later became Act One of a 1982 production titled *Song and Dance*) tells the story of a young woman in New York, "a twenty-seven-year-old English girl from Muswell Hill," an exile on a hapless search for love. It is one of Black's smartest lyrics, making clever use of the New York State ad campaign's I♥NY logo, then fresh-ish and new-ish. It is the organizing metaphor of the song. The exiled Londoner sees ♥s all around her — on coffee cups, shirts, lollipops and baseball caps. But her own ♥ is empty.

The third "I Love New York" came a quarter of a century later, in 2005, and was by Madonna. It rhymes "New York" with "dork" and is regularly voted onto lists of the worst lyrics of all time.

**The rise and rise of Sinatra's "New York, New York"**

"New York, New York" became an anthem slowly. It made its way out into the world much as Sinatra's live version made its way from mere fragment in his shows to "king of the hill" set-closer.

It was baseball that first picked up "New York, New York" as the song of New York itself. At the start, it was played at both Yankees and Mets games. "Hearing it sung by 50,000 Yankees fans was the biggest thrill of my life," Fred Ebb told me.

The Yankees were then owned by George Steinbrenner, the shipping magnate who had led a group of investors to buy the team from CBS in 1973. The year after that, Steinbrenner was hit with fourteen counts of illegal contributions to President Nixon's re-election campaign — the Watergate one that brought Tricky Dick down.

Steinbrenner was an archetype of dictatorial management style. In the apposite words of a 2015 *New York Times* piece, "If Sinatra was the Chairman of the Board, Steinbrenner was the Boss." He fired more managers than you could imagine — one of them five times. He banned his players from having facial hair — beards, moustaches, even long sideburns. And he picked Sinatra's "New York, New York" as the Yankees' theme.

The team started using it at games in 1980, within months of its release. According to Marty Appel, former head of press for the Yankees, the song came to Steinbrenner via Le Club on East 55th Street, a "modish disco" which opened in 1960. (The "modish disco" phrase comes from a biography of Jacqueline Kennedy Onassis. Le Club was that kind of place.) It was members-only, with a billiard room, a handkerchief of a dance floor, a 17th-century Belgian tapestry on the wall and not so much as a sign on the street entrance. In 1978, Jackie Kennedy's two children, John Jr. and Caroline, held a joint birthday party — her twenty-first, his eighteenth — there. Le Club was that kind of place.

It was also a hangout for Donald Trump back when his hair was brown and his property business was being charged under the Fair Housing Act for declining tenants "because of race and color." In *The Art of the Deal*, Trump (or rather his ghostwriter, Tony Schwartz) described Le Club as "the sort of place where you were likely to see a wealthy 75-year-old guy walk in with three blondes from Sweden." Or perhaps you'd see Roy Cohn, the venal, closeted gay lawyer behind the McCarthy anti-Communist witch hunt and Hollywood blacklist, which pushed so many "red" and "pink" movie people to exile in London. Some of them took to eating Sunday lunch at my mother-in-law's house in the city's far western suburb of Wembley:

Nunnally Johnson (writer of *The Searchers*), for example, and *The Producers* star Zero Mostel (who made a determined pass at her).

Cohn and Trump met at Le Club in 1973. Cohn helped Trump "deal" with that Fair Housing case, advising the young property developer: "Tell them to go to hell and fight the thing in court." From that moment on, Cohn and Trump were inseparable. Cohn recalled that Trump would phone him more than a dozen times a day. By 1979, Cohn had become Trump's primary legal advisor and, in the delicate words of a contemporary piece in the *Village Voice*, "conduit to the upper reaches of power." That heft helped Trump push through the deal that allowed him to build his Trump Tower fifty-eight stories tall — twenty more than would usually be allowed. A couple of decades later, when Trump was launching an ad campaign for his East Side erection, the Trump World Tower, he did it with Sinatra's "New York, New York" as the soundtrack. When former New York mayor (1994–2001) Rudy Giuliani ran for the Republican Party's 2008 presidential nomination, his choice of campaign tune was the Clash's "Rudie Can't Fail," a spectacularly inappropriate pick from the *London Calling* album. It's the gleefully told tale of a Jamaican street criminal. Politics, huh. Pop music, eh.

Anyway, back to the Yankees. Steinbrenner was also a Cohn client, along with Anthony "Fat Tony" Salerno, boss of the Genovese crime family, and Paul "Big Paulie" Castellano, boss of the Gambino crime family, who owned the company that provided the ready-mix cement for Trump Tower — used to save money at the expense of strength. Steinbrenner was big friends with Le Club's manager, Patrick Shields, a 6'5" Boston Red Sox fan who would wear his Red Sox cap to Yankees games. Appel says Le Club's DJ regularly sent Steinbrenner tapes of music to use at Yankees games. Among the tunes was Sinatra's "New York, New York." Steinbrenner, it seems, really liked — really, *really* liked — two particular phrases in the track. King of the hill. Top of the heap. Steinbrenner kind of phrases.

Appel says he was the one who suggested to Steinbrenner that they should play "New York, New York" at the end of every home game. Unsure which version to use, they played both Sinatra's and Minnelli's over the loudspeakers to see how they would sound in the stadium. Mr. Steinbrenner — as Appel still refers to his late boss — decided that Minnelli's had "more of a Broadway feel." So, Sinatra's it was.

Then the Yankees fine-tuned their use of it. If the team won, the Frank Sinatra version swaggered out of the speakers. If they lost, it was Minnelli's. No one, it seems, remembers when this switch to bivalency happened — or if they do, they aren't saying. Which is understandable. When I first heard about the Sinatra-Minnelli switch-hitting, I was a bit shocked. I felt Minnelli's original had been somehow traduced. Then I thought again and decided it was fair, truthful even. Sinatra's version is about success, the heady, blind moment of victory — and the belief that that moment is forever. Minnelli's is about the striving towards that moment, knowing that — frankly — it ain't necessarily going to be so.

The Yankees stopped alternating the two versions in 2001. There are two stories about this. Version one: Kander-Ebb's musical administrator, Paul McKibbins, happened to mention this dual-track policy to a Yankees lawyer over lunch. The lawyer, according to McKibbins, "turned white." Soon, very soon, it was only ever Sinatra's version that got played at the end of games, win or lose.

Version two: this one puts Minnelli herself in charge. Understandably unhappy with being a siren of failure, she pretty much gave the Yankees an ultimatum: they should either play her version when they won or not play it at all. They called her bluff and took the second option. From then on, the Yankees played Sinatra's version (but, starting in 2025, only when they win).

In 2008, the Yankees tore down their old stadium and built a new one across the road. Marty Appel was, of course, there for the last game at the old place. And at the end of that last game, Sinatra's "New York, New York" rang out, again and again and again, then again. "They must have played it thirty times; people didn't want to leave."

### "New York, New York" as city anthem

In time, Kander-Ebb's "New York, New York" became city property — not officially (and certainly not in revenue terms) but effectively, by public acclamation. "The song is an anthem to the city and the hardworking people who live in it," said Yankees president Randy Levine.

It is played before the start (in Staten Island) of the New York City Marathon and at every New York Police Department Academy graduation ceremony. It's played every new year in Times Square. Liza Minnelli sang it on July 6, 1986, in New Jersey's Giants Stadium, at the closing ceremony of Liberty Weekend, celebrating the restoration of the Statue of Liberty. And she sang it live at the first professional sports game held in the city after the Twin Towers were hit, performing it in the middle of the seventh inning of a Mets game at Shea Stadium — the same year the Yankees stopped using her version of it.

Yet despite all that sporting and ceremonial recognition, it has never gained official metropolitan status. Thirteen years after Mayor Ed Koch proclaimed it the city's anthem (with no action ever following his words), legislation was introduced by the New York City Council, on May 21, 1998, to make Frank's version the city's official song — in honor of Sinatra's death the week before, in Los Angeles. City Council Speaker Peter Vallone said, "Every time we hear 'New York, New York,' we think of Frank Sinatra. He was our King of the Hill." But that was the last anyone ever heard about that apparently vital piece of legislation. Again, as with Koch's declaration, all words, no action. (It was played at Koch's 2013 funeral, though.)

In time, "New York, New York" made its way out into the wide, wide world. All kinds of people recorded it, some of them even singers. Mostly, they shouldn't have bothered. Between the two of them, Minnelli and Sinatra seem to have found all its possible meanings. That didn't stop people, of course. They just can't help themselves. Of the many, many failed attempts at it, I'll mention just one. Not just because it's awful, misguided, tasteless, thoughtless and inadvertently hilarious — all of which it is — but because, like nearly all of the bad, bad "New York, New York"s, its wrongheadedness is rooted in exactly the same kind of blind narcissism that is there (knowingly) in Ebb's original lyric and which powers (unknowingly or, at best, half-knowingly) both Minnelli and Sinatra's versions. This particularly terrible symbol of wrong-wrong-wrongness? Liberace clunkety-clunking it on piano, to the accompaniment of a tappity-tapping drum machine.

Regardless, the song's driving, impassioned symbolism gradually but inexorably matured it (rotted it?) into a song that non-professional singers loved to sing. "Big" Ron Atkinson was a Liverpool-born, West Midlands-raised football player and manager who became a TV pundit. "Big" Ron liked "New York, New York." He *really* liked it. As Aston Villa manager, he worked with Dwight Yorke, a striker from Canaan, Tobago. He never referred to the player as either Dwight or Yorke. Not ever. No, he always used the player's full name and, having always fancied himself something of a singer, he always sang it, to the tune of the Kander-Ebb song: "Dwight Yorke, Dwight Yorke." Soon, Villa fans made a terrace chant of it.

In the summer of 1994, "Big" Ron was in New York, working as a commentator on that year's World Cup — and in the hometown of his dream projections. On the late afternoon of Saturday, June 18, "Big" Ron found himself in Manhattan, in a limousine, in the always entertaining company of the *Mail on Sunday*'s lead sportswriter, Pat Collins, who shared this story with me. The sporting-life pair were on their way to the Italy-Ireland game at Giants Stadium in New Jersey, in a limousine heading down Fifth Avenue. "Big" Ron couldn't stop himself. He really couldn't. There was only one thing to do. He did it, too. He opened the limo roof. He stood up. His head and firkin of a torso poked out into the thick, smelly heat of a Manhattan summer. And he sang: "Start spreading the news…"

It's that kind of song, a container for people's fantasies about themselves, about ambition, fulfillment, success, destiny and, of course, their relationship to the physical New York, New York. It became a theme tune for a certain kind of person and set of values. Atkinson, Trump, Michael Milken, Jeffrey Archer … mogwais even. In *Gremlins 2*, as the furry little killers are about to invade the city, their leader puts on a trench coat and fedora and starts singing: "Start spreading the news…"

Sinatra's "New York, New York" was also a hymn to a particular kind of metropolitan life: affluent, aspirant, smart, suited and hatted, go-getting, forward-looking, optimistic. The world of a famous black-and-white photograph titled "New York, New York." Taken in 1959, it shows a couple running across the Brooklyn Bridge, with the Empire State Building in the background. It is surely the only exciting and sexy picture ever taken which features a man with a briefcase.

The photographer was Norman Parkinson, a Londoner who then had a house in New York. Nor were the people in the picture native New Yorkers. Both were English — they were Parkinson's Manhattan neighbors. The woman was Pippa Diggle, a medical secretary friend who soon moved back to London. The man-with-briefcase was a friend of hers, Robin Miller (1928–2010), a gay Old Etonian former Guards officer and actor — who went on to co-write the book and lyrics of *Dames at Sea*, an exceedingly camp musical in which a small-town girl makes it big on Broadway. Its first production, in 1966, was at Café Cino, an off-off-Broadway venue, and starred future Broadway diva Bernadette Peters.

Two years later, another photograph was made on the same bridge by another British pair, photographer David Bailey and his muse, model Jean Shrimpton. The tale of that photograph, the two Londoners and the two cities, was told, romantically, in a 2012 BBC film, *We'll Take Manhattan*, a title which filched the kickoff line in Rodgers and Hart's 1927 Broadway hit. In contrast to the film's rhetoric, Bailey's picture itself is scarcely revolutionary. If anything, Shrimpton looks a little antique, even by the standards of the day. In hat, gloves and knee-length coat, she leans, with one hand loose, on the bridge's parapet. The sky is grey — a true, thin grey over the East River.

## Frank turns 80

As for Sinatra himself, the last words he ever sang in public were the final "New York" of "New York, New York," at his eightieth birthday party in 1995. His real last words, I guess. It was a very public all-star celebration. Taped at the Shrine Auditorium in Los Angeles on November 19, it doubled as a fundraiser for the AIDS Project Los Angeles and the Barbara & Frank Sinatra Children's Center in Palm Springs. There was a parade of performers, each singing a song Sinatra had made famous. The show opened with Bruce Springsteen performing "Angel Eyes" (from the 1957 album *Frank Sinatra Sings for Only the Lonely*) and closed with Sinatra's own and final "New York, New York."

Between the Boss's opener and the Chairman of the Board's closer, there was — in the fine, mercenary tradition of music business tribute shows — a mix of old legends and chart newcomers. The bill of fare included a gender-fluid original rock and roller (Little Richard: "That Old Black Magic"), a blind soul legend (Ray Charles: "Ol' Man River"), a South Carolina pop-rock band (Hootie and the Blowfish: "The Lady Is a Tramp"), an Italian-American New Yorker (Tony Bennett: "I've Got the World on a String") and a sunglassed Irishman (Bono: "Two Shots of Happy, One Shot of Sad," written for Sinatra by Bono, but never actually recorded by Sinatra). Also — that music business hustle thing again — the New York rap duo Salt-n-Pepa, who delivered their biggest hit, "Whatta Man," as tribute to the evening's main man.

The last of the guests, the penultimate act, was Bob Dylan. Two decades later, Dylan would record not one Sinatra song but three entire albums of them. Yet it was a surprising choice at the time. Dylan's voice and songwriting had long cast him as a kind of anti-Sinatra — as did his jeans and hobo cap stage get-up.

The song Dylan sang was "Restless Farewell" — not a Sinatra song at all, but one of Dylan's own, an early one, based on a Scottish folk ballad which was generally sung as a goodbye song at gatherings of friends. Dylan had recorded it for his third album,

*The Times They Are a-Changin'*, back in 1963. He sang it at a concert in Berkeley, California shortly after the album's release and then twice more that year: on a U.S. TV show and in London, at the Albert Hall. After that, nothing until the Sinatra show. (He has only sung it live once since then, as a closer on May 21, 1998 — again in Los Angeles, this time at Pauley Pavilion, a basketball arena.)

It wasn't Dylan's idea to sing "Restless Farewell." It was Sinatra's choice, it's said. Why would Sinatra, of all people, pick something from the deep, deep recesses of Dylan's back pages? Because of its lyrics and tone. It has the barroom loquacity of a Sinatra ballad — a little maudlin, a little regretful, its worldly wisdom worn with slightly adolescent gravity. The final verse, though — that's different. Behind the mournful music, the words turn almost bileful. There is "disgrace" and "the dirt of gossip" and "the dust of rumors." Dylan wrote the song right after an interview in which he felt attacked by the journalist. So, with the rancor and entitlement of his youth, he got his revenge in song.

And there's more. Its final lines weep with the rage of wounded pride that was a stock-in-trade for late Sinatra. These are the words that must surely have drawn Sinatra — or, more likely, an adviser — to the Dylan obscurity. The singer declares his steadfast determination to be himself, to leave and "not give a damn." I Am What I Am. My Way or the highway. Bye-bye, ol' blue eyes.

Then Sinatra really did face his final curtain, in evening dress, with an orange handkerchief in his top pocket. He took center stage. The evening's cast gathered around and behind him. Together they sang "New York, New York." The last words, the very last words, were his, almost shouted out, a raging against the dying of the light.

Then all was silence. He died two years later, aged eighty-two.

### Around the world with New York, New York

By the time the Scorsese movie had flown into (and flopped out of) cinemas, the phrase "New York, New York" was already an established part of both English languages — most likely because of the

Comden-Green song. But it was in the late 1970s, in the wake of the movie — or, even more likely, the Kander-Ebb song — that it really became an emblem of metropolitan sophistication, a symbol used to sell stuff of all kinds. Stuff like burgers, for example.

The first New York, New York burger and steak restaurant opened in Miami in 1978. The decor was the same across the New York, New York chain: Americana on the walls and gingham cloths on the tables — classic restaurant design markers for a certain kind of non-threatening, family-ish urbanity. It was the same decor seen in the theatre-world Joe Allen's and in the pick-up joint (turned family celebration chain) TGI Fridays — both of which opened in 1965. At a time of high anxiety, both restaurant and bar were the actual New York, New York's nostalgia for its own past. (In time, the New York, New York chain went international. I once ate in the Tel Aviv branch. The bacon in the bacon double cheeseburger was substituted with acceptably kosher smoked goose breast.)

There is also the more recent chain of New York, New York restaurants that I mentioned earlier — the Asian hot dog and burger joints, headquartered in Singapore. In 2011, a branch opened in a most un-New York place, Ulaanbaatar, the capital of Mongolia, a country sitting on a cash pile of coal and copper. "High Growth, High Yield, Low Taxes" is a national slogan — so, maybe not so not-New York, after all. The restaurant is in the Naran Plaza, a six-story mall boasting BMW, Puma and L'Oreal outlets. One diner commented, online, about the table service at New York, New York: "Make sure you call out for the waiters clear and loud. Otherwise, they will NOT pay a bit of attention." A certain Manhattan authenticity then.

In Las Vegas, there's a New York, New York hotel–casino. Its facade and roofline feature mini versions of real Manhattan markers, including the Empire State Building, the United Nations, Grant's Tomb and the Statue of Liberty. Instead of a subway, it has the Manhattan Express, an indoor roller coaster. The Las Vegas construct likes to be called the Little Apple. "It is," wrote one critic, "the ultimate example of architect Robert Venturi's thesis of buildings as signs." Which is why the hotel has no "New York, New York" sign on it. The Manhattan skyline is its own sign.

There are also New York, New York nightclubs, most of them sticky-floored venues — not places to start spreading the news but places where dreams go to die. Occasionally, these small-city late-night fantasy providers appear on the inner pages of the tabloids. In one English New York, New York (Southampton branch), soccer player Rod Wallace became involved in a "1:40 a.m. fracas." In New York, New York (Rotherham version), actor Dean Gaffney (who played spotty loser Robbie Jackson in the long-running British soap opera *EastEnders*) was called "a Cockney bastard." Another "fracas" ensued. More enticingly, there is Manchester's New York, New York, the beating heart of the city's Gay Village. The bar is, according to its publicity material, "known for its hands-in-the-air nights." If you can't make it there, you really can't make it anywhere.

## "The city that never sleeps"

As well as its title, Kander-Ebb's song gave the language some new phrases. Or maybe it didn't. "The city that never sleeps" will forever be associated with Ebb's lyric but was, in fact, far from newly minted. Its long history has been charted, obsessively, by Barry Popik, New Yorker and semi-pro etymologist — in his own phrasing, "recognized expert on the origins of the terms Big Apple, Windy City, hot dog, hamburger and many others…"

Popik tells us that the first print reference to New York being the city that never sleeps was in 1907. It appeared not in a Manhattan publication but in the Macon, Georgia *Daily Telegraph*, in a piece about the New York mail — the Postmaster General had announced that an 8:00 p.m. delivery would be introduced in Manhattan's residential areas. A couple of decades later, there was a 1924 silent picture called *The City That Never Sleeps* — a proto-noir about a pre-prohibition Bowery bar owner. In 1953, it became the title of a real noir starring Gig Young — though the sleepless city in that movie was not New York but Chicago.

"King of the hill"? That's the children's game, of course — the American equivalent of the English King of the Castle. A contest of primal struggle for supremacy — how very Sinatra.

If I can make it there, I can make it anywhere? What about that linguistic snare for the unwarily ambitious? Well, that does seem to be Ebb's alone. And what a phrase to gift the language. Thirteen syllables long, turning on the sixth. Simple, easygoing rhyme. And it sounds, pleasingly, like something you've always known. Some clichés have a parent's name on their birth certificate.

**Kamikaze pilot**
In early 1980, Kosmo Vinyl happened to see a photograph of Martin Scorsese wearing a Clash T-shirt with a garish, pop art-ish image of a WW II Japanese kamikaze pilot preparing for his final flight. That kind of angry imagery, it seems, appealed as much to a New York film director who made gangster movies as it did to a London rock and roll band who screened war movies in the recording studio. The photograph — easily found online — was taken on the set of Scorsese's 1980 boxing movie *Raging Bull*. The director is blocking out a scene in the ring with a barechested Robert De Niro.

What Kosmo didn't know — but would soon learn — was just how much of a Clash fan Scorsese was. "On the set of *Raging Bull*," wrote Peter Biskind, "the director would retreat to his trailer, put on the Clash at top volume and sit there revved up by the music, pacing back and forth."

Kosmo decided he should meet this famous Clash fan, so he chased down a number for Scorsese, called him and met him. And thus began a relationship between the man who gave the world "New York, New York" and the band who gave it "London Calling." It was a close relationship, for a while at least. Joe Strummer nicknamed the director "Martin Maestro."

The whole band, plus Kosmo, appeared in Scorsese's bracingly sour *The King of Comedy* as "Street Scum," as per the movie's credits. (No one acclaimed them for having movie star potential. Or acting ability of any kind.) The Clash were asked to do the soundtrack for what was meant to be Scorsese's next movie, *Gangs of New York* — another Manhattan gangster film but set, long ago, even before Blake and Lawlor had written "The Sidewalks of New York." "But *Raging Bull* was a flop," said Kosmo. "The money fell out." (Scorsese finally made *Gangs of New York* in 2002. The music was by Howard Shore, who also did all three *Lord of the Rings* films.)

In the late spring of 1981, Scorsese invited the Clash to a private screening of his director's cut of *New York, New York*. The whole band plus entourage attended — the "London Calling" boys together with the "New York, New York" movie and its director, in a small Manhattan screening room. Kosmo found himself sitting next to Robert De Niro's first wife, New York actress/singer Diahnne Abbott. Sometimes big city and Hollywood dreams really do come true, even for a poor, big-mouthed but big-spirited boy from London's Bow.

Abbott and De Niro met, both cinematically and personally, on the set of *Taxi Driver*, in which she played the ticket-seller at a porno theater. She also appeared in *New York, New York*, singing Fats Waller's "Honeysuckle Rose" in a Harlem nightclub scene. And she was in Scorsese's next big flop, *The King of Comedy*.

The director's cut of *New York, New York* reinstated twenty-five minutes that the studio had insisted on taking out for the film's original release. The biggest and most significant reinsertion was a twelve-minute sequence called "Happy Endings." It was intended as a coda to the movie — Scorsese's footnote to his "no reality" Hollywood dreams creation. With that title, you'd expect it to fulfill George Lucas's suggestion that Scorsese would have a hit on his hands if only he could get Francine (Minnelli) and Jimmy (De Niro) together again at the end of the movie. But it's not like that. Not at all.

It's an old-style Hollywood march-of-time montage of what happened after Francine and Jimmy split up. Well, kind of. It's actually all a dream, dreamed by a movie usherette, Peggy Smith (Minnelli), with fantasies of stardom.

Essentially, it's something of a tribute to the glossy and glam directoring of Liza's father, Vincente. There are dancing girls, a sequence with spinning newspaper covers and a testimonial dinner at which Miss Smith is introduced as "the great lady of the American theatre" and "Broadway's dearest and most luminous light." (The uncredited dinner-jacketed man saying those words to the imaginary star was Minnelli's father-in-law, Jack Haley Sr. To put it another way, the Tin Man was paying tribute to Dorothy's daughter — in a movie that pays homage, obeisance even, to Dorothy's "real-life" husband. It was Haley's last screen appearance.)

That testimonial is not quite the end of the "Happy Endings" sequence. That comes when we see — or, as it turns out, seem to see — the "real-life" Jimmy (De Niro) in a cinema watching the end of it. And so we learn that the Peggy Smith onscreen fantasy is not "real-life" but a "real" movie starring Francine (Minnelli). We are seeing Jimmy — alone in a cinema, watching a version of the woman he once dreamed of major chords with. (Or, looked at from a more distant perspective, a movie fantasy of a movie star's life encased in a movie about a singing star played by a singing star on whose life both movie and movie-within-the-movie are, in good part, based.) A light smile plays across Jimmy's face as he watches the movie-within-the-movie. Who knows what he's thinking? It's certainly not of happy endings.

**A "New York, New York" Christmas in West London**
In the mid-'80s, the Clash and "New York, New York" came together again, this time on the other side of the Atlantic and in a quite different way. It happened on Christmas Eve in a West London pub, the Durham Castle on Alexander Street, just down from the former offices of Stiff Records (and Blackhill Enterprises). It was a home-away-from-home for all types and kinds — Stiff staff and artists, taxi drivers, fishmongers and Kosmo Vinyl (once of Stiff) who used it as his work headquarters.

"It was a great backstreet pub, with no passing trade whatsoever," Kosmo told me. "It had a jukebox, and you could get a drink after closing time. Joe loved it there." On this particular festive evening, Joe was there with Kosmo, the taxi drivers, the fishmongers et al. At "chucking out time," recalled Kosmo decades later, "Sinatra's 'New York, New York' came up on the jukebox. It played again and again and again, with the whole pub, Joe included, singing along, at the tops of our voices." London calling out happy Christmas to its transatlantic sibling, the two cities pulled together by song and their singers.

**Desert Island Discs**
Composer Eric Coates wrote two, maybe three, even more famous tunes than his "London Calling" theme for the BBC's World Service. One, England football fans' battle anthem, "The Dam Busters March." Two, the theme for Granada TV's *Forsyte Saga*. Three, "By the Sleepy Lagoon." That's the formal title of the theme tune to BBC radio's *Desert Island Discs*, first broadcast in 1942 and still running in the third decade of the following century. By asking the good, great and merely famous to nominate their eight favorite pieces of music, *DID* provides an intriguing barometer of taste. In 2011, the BBC did a tally of the show's most popular choices. The big hits of classical music were easily the top picks. Beethoven led the chart with his 9th Symphony and had three more entries in the top eight — though overall Mozart pipped him in the Most Popular Artist category.

"London Calling" and "New York, New York"? How have they fared on *Desert Island Discs*? I could only find two guests who picked "London Calling" as a *Desert Island* choice. Both were comics, writers and (ethnic) Londoners: Ben Elton (South London Jewish) and Sanjeev Bhaskar (West London Indian). West London Indian film director Gurinder Chadha (*Bend It Like Beckham*, *Blinded by the Light*) chose the Clash's "(White Man) in Hammersmith Palais" in November 2015.

By contrast, "New York, New York" has been a *Desert Island* pick nine times in all, with an even split of four choices each for Sinatra and Minnelli. The ninth choice, by movie critic Dilys Powell (from Bridgnorth, a small town on the River Severn, in Shropshire), is not the Kander-Ebb song at all but the earlier one, from the movie musical *On the Town* — which is, of course, sung by Sinatra.

Of the four guests who went for Sinatra's version of the Kander-Ebb song, none were actual New Yorkers. TV presenter Gloria Hunniford was from Portadown, Northern Ireland. Bill Cullen is a Dublin-born businessman, writer and host of the Irish version of *The Apprentice* TV show. American movie star Gregory Peck was raised in La Jolla, California, while British movie star Roger Moore was from Stockwell, South London. On the show, the Bond man said of Sinatra's "New York, New York," "That sentiment could apply to a Londoner."

For Peck, the link was personal. He had known Sinatra since "he was a skinny nightclub singer … and I was a brand-new actor in town." For him, the song had "all the energy and the gusto and the spirit of American popular music at its best."

Half of those who preferred the Minnelli version actually came from the New York area: chef Robert Carrier (Westchester County) and actor Stubby Kaye (Morningside Heights). "I would always keep this record with me forever," said Kaye. "It's home, you know." The pair of non-native New Yorkers were designer Nina Campbell (London, with a Viennese mother and a Scottish father) and actor Dirk Bogarde (West Hampstead, London) who chose it for its evocation of a "city of extraordinary glamour — and horror."

What of Frank's fans, what did they think of his "New York, New York"? Ted Nunn, who was president of the UK Sinatra fan club, says, "Actual fans preferred it to 'My Way' and 'Strangers in the Night.' But the original is not the best version. He always sang it better in concert. He'd make a joke of it, singing different words. Like many other songs he recorded, it was sung first by someone else and should really have been associated with them, not him. 'Lady Is a Tramp' should have been Lena Horne's, and 'New York, New York' should have been Liza Minnelli's. But it's not, it's Sinatra's."

And Fred Ebb, what did *he* think of Sinatra's version of his song? "The song achieved standard status very quickly and he hopped on the bandwagon. It's a wonderful arrangement but he sings the wrong lyrics. The bit about being A-number one — that never came out of my mouth. But, listen, I could do nothing but be grateful for his version." The song's greatest strength, Ebb told me, was not his lyrics but his writing partner's music. "There's such power in that melody and that vamp." That is, the phrase at the start. "It works even when Miss America sings it and hits the wrong note."

Those opening notes, Manhattan cabaret singer Steve Ross told the *New York Times* in 1998, are "probably the most famous vamp of any popular song in the world. The music primes the listener. It sets up this little buzz that all foreigners say happens when they hit the airport here."

## 5 London Calling New York New York

*"There's a kind of built-in pathos between reality and expectation."*
—NEIL TENNANT of PET SHOP BOYS on BIG CITIES

"London Calling" was adopted, pretty much immediately, by the rhetorically minded in search of some wider, deeper statement. Here's how Tom Carson greeted the U.S. release of *London Calling* in *Rolling Stone* in early 1980: "By now, our expectations of the Clash might seem to have become inflated beyond any possibility of fulfillment. It's not simply that they're the greatest rock & roll band in the world … Now, almost against their will, they're the only ones left."

At the end of the 1980s, *Rolling Stone* named *London Calling* its number-one album of the decade. When told he'd made the album of the 1980s, Joe Strummer asked the magazine, coolly and accurately, "But didn't it come out in 1979?" (Released in the UK that December, the album did not arrive in American shops until January 1980.) In its end-of-the-decade piece, *Rolling Stone* re-described the album as "an emergency broadcast from rock's Last Angry Band, serving notice that Armageddon was nigh, Western society was rotten at the core and rock & roll needed a good boot in the rear." The writer, David Fricke, added that it "singlehandedly set the agenda — musically, politically and emotionally — for the decade to come." Which, overblown as it is, does indicate a truth or so. Certainly, it was how a whole section of people felt about their resistance hymn — which, like so many resistance hymns, embraced defeat rather than promising victory.

It wasn't only *Rolling Stone* that got so excited, either. In 2004, *The New Yorker* — that is, *The New Yorker* magazine or, to come over all London for a moment, *The New* seriously fucking serious *Yorker* magazine — did, too. "Hyperbole cannot diminish this record," wrote Sasha Frere-Jones of *London Calling*. "Each of us is invincible when it's playing." He liked the title track, too. "If you can listen to it without getting a chilly burst of immortality, there is a layer between you and the world."

Yet, despite the praise lathered on "London Calling," the song has, by and large, remained pretty much the personal property of its originators. It has always been approached respectfully, as if it were the Clash's song and theirs alone. Strummer himself kept on singing it, first with the Pogues when he deputized for the band's sick singer Shane MacGowan, then with his final band, the Mescaleros. I saw Strummer lead the Pogues at the Town & Country Club in Kentish Town in 1988. As well as "London Calling," Strummer also sang the band's "Fairytale of New York" with Kirsty MacColl.

Years later, at the same venue — by then, it was the Forum, a reversion to its name in the hall's earlier incarnation as an Irish ballroom — I saw the final UK show by U.S. soul legend Bobby Womack. The packed and sweating Saturday night crowd was mostly middle-aged and fuller-figured, while still dressed like the soul boys and girls they once were. Many, like me, had brought along their grown children.

Womack started with his theme tune for the 1972 blaxploitation film *Across 110th Street* — that's the southern boundary of Harlem. The song has a long, slow groove of a beginning. Very long, very slow. Visibly unwell — he had diabetes, Alzheimer's and colon cancer — Womack sat center stage and let the band do his work for him. (Womack would be dead within two years.) After five, maybe ten minutes of that instrumental funk groove, it was time for the song's long-delayed opening line, which is its title. Womack did nothing, didn't even look at the audience, just in that general direction. But those aging soul boys and girls knew what to do, what life and love obliged them to do — sing out. Collectively, they took a deep breath, steadied their bodies and, when the moment eventually arrived, sang the line for Womack, shouting out, as one, "Across 110th Street." North London calling out to the northern part of Manhattan. A moment that put me in mind of another transatlantic conversation between inner-city areas — Motörhead's *No Sleep 'til Hammersmith* and the Beastie Boys' "No Sleep Till Brooklyn."

**Other "London Calling"s**
"London Calling" has been covered by others, but not often and rarely well — both indie rockers Yo Lo Tengo and bluegrass ironicizers Hayseed Dixie, for example, tried and failed. There are maybe five exceptions. There is "Londyn Dzwoni," a faithful version, in Polish, by Gdansk punk band Radio Bagdad. There was the performance of it at the 2003 *Grammy Awards* — just weeks after Strummer's death. Announced as being "for Joe," it was performed by a band that included Bruce Springsteen, Little Steven and Elvis Costello.

Even more notable, perhaps, was the version played by Bob Dylan in November 2005 in London. He encored with it in two of his five shows at the Brixton Academy — salutes to an old colleague, Strummer, and his city. Dylan later chose "London Calling" as one of 67 songs for his 2022 book, *The Philosophy of Modern Song*, writing, "This is probably the Clash at their best and their most relevant, their most desperate."

Springsteen also played a dynamic and faithful version to open his June 2009 Hyde Park show — so faithful, in fact, as if intimidated by fear of messing with the Clash's hometown shadow, only piano player Roy Bittan felt confident to break free from memories and punch his own skills into the song, then already thirty years old.

Fifthly (and finally, for now anyway) in March 2022, in response to the Russian invasion, Ukrainian band Beton ("concrete") recorded their adaptation of the Clash song as "Kyiv Calling." "The iron age is coming, the curtain's coming down." They had the English band's permission, of course. In writing, I should think. (War is one thing, but copyrights are another.) On the other hand, stories emerged online of Beton in T-shirts featuring Stepan Bandera (1909–1959), a nationalist politician and leader of pogroms who also, it is said, collaborated with the invading Nazis during WW II. Ah, pop music.

*"All great art is born of the metropolis."*
— EZRA POUND

Over time, "London Calling" has also become something of a brand. All kinds of people have used it as a name for their goods or services — before and after the Clash sent out their cry to faraway towns. When the band formed, in 1976, there was *London Calling: a Portfolio of the Performing Arts*, an avant-garde festival. On the cover of its program book, people lay, dead-looking, on a city street, as if nuclear Armageddon had just come to town.

Since then, many others have borrowed the punchiness of the song's title. There have been several *London Calling* publications: a Dutch-language historical guide to the city; a 2003 collection of essays subtitled *How Black and Asian Writers Imagined a City*; a 2003 report by left-leaning think tank Demos on how "mobile technologies will transform our capital city"; a countercultural history of London since 1945, written in 2010 by Barry Miles (who, as it happens, did know the Clash — though not as well as he knew Paul McCartney).

In more recent times, those who picked up "London Calling" as a brand identity were often aging Clash fans. That's certainly true of the London Calling arts-and-entertainment leaflet distribution company. For many years, if you wanted to promote your theatre or venue, London Calling would ensure that your fliers appeared in pubs and restaurants all over the city. The boss and founder of London Calling was a Clash fan. (I asked and checked.) *London*

*Calling* was also taken, in Amsterdam, as the name for the Paradiso club's annual festival of "up-and-coming" British bands. There was *London Calling* magazine, produced by Cable London TV — long since subsumed into Richard Branson's Virgin Media conglomerate. The cable network's *London Calling* even copied the L-shaped typography of the album cover.

There was a band called London Calling. Not in London — of course not — but in Evansville, Indiana. Shortly after Strummer died, Jamie Rowe of Popgun, a "hard pop" group, heard "London Calling" on the radio. "That's us," he decided and changed the band's name. "It's just a cool name." Not that Rowe and the former Popgun have much else in common with Joe Strummer or the Clash or even punk. The band's collective background is in CCM — Contemporary Christian Music. "Our personal spiritual mission as followers of Jesus is to be salt and light in a dark world." Not a claim you were likely to have ever heard from any of the Clash.

There have also been "London Calling" shorts and sunglasses — a handbag, too. And "London Calling" did successfully call out to the faraway towns. In Johannesburg, Tokyo, Helsinki and St. Louis, there were London Calling clubs. In Bogota, a restaurant. In Rome, a clothes shop. Yet "London Calling" has never become its home city's official anthem. It has acquired something of that status, but only informally.

Robert Elms — who has been around and about the city right back from its punk years — has hosted a morning show on BBC Radio London since 1994. "I love the idea of 'London Calling' from a faraway town," he has said. "It's incredibly evocative. Punk was very London." Julien Temple used the Clash song to open his 2012 film, *London: The Modern Babylon* — in fact, he even used a good bit of his old friend Don Letts' video.

*ES* magazine, the weekly color supplement of the London *Evening Standard*, once praised "London Calling": "For a blood-stirring, hair-raising, gutsy hymn to the capital, only one song does the job." Which, paradoxically, is not at all how film and TV makers tend to use it. Often, they don't seem to have listened to the lyrics at all. They just respond to the song's insistent rhythm and its title. For them, the Clash's song of dystopic rage and dread is simply shorthand for the city, like a red double-decker bus or Big Ben. In the French gangster bio-pic *Mesrine: Killer Instinct*, the track accompanies the arrival of the movie's "hero" in London, playing over an image of, yes, a red double-decker bus. The fact that the gangster moves to London a year before "London Calling" was written did not restrain the filmmaker's determination to use the song.

In the 2002 Bond movie *Die Another Day*, "London Calling" plays as his nemesis Gustav Graves parachutes into Buckingham Palace. In another film made that same year, *Billy Elliot*, the song is used in a manner far closer to Strummer's heart. It plays over the battle between police and striking miners in the imaginary pit town of Everington, a fictional version of a defining moment of early 1980s politics, the Battle of Orgreave. That was a battle waged far from the capital. Logically, structurally, "London Calling" makes no sense in the movie. But it does make emotional, thematic sense. The sound of marching feet. The ring of that truncheon thing.

In April 2006, up in northeast England but deep into post-London Tube bombings terrorism fears, a twenty-four-year-old man, Harraj Mann, was taken off a London-bound flight at Durham Tees Valley airport, by "anti-terrorism officials." The taxi driver who took Mann to the airport had heard him play "London Calling" and sing along to it. So, he called the police. Maybe he was worried by the bit about war being declared. Or perhaps the line about "London Calling" out to faraway towns.

**London calling out to the commercial world**
With its emotive, anthemic qualities, "London Calling" had obvious attractions for ad makers in search of foreboding, dread, violence or even just a play on its title. In 1999, British Telecommunications (BT) decided it would be just what they needed to dramatize a switch in the London phone code (from 0171 and 0181 to 020). The Clash rebuffed the company's approach, explaining: "Once a song gets

associated with something like that…" They also turned down two beer companies, Miller and Coors.

In 2000, the band uneasily agreed to it being used in a public-spirited way, in an ad urging people to vote in that inaugural London mayoral election — the one featuring "Maybe It's Because I'm a Londoner" and Jeffrey Archer, and which ended up with newt-loving Ken Livingstone beating closest rival Steve "Shagger" Norris by a clear fifteen points.

In 2004, there was an exhibition launch at City Hall, a brand-new grey glass building on the south bank of the Thames, just upstream from Tower Bridge. The DJ was the old Clash hand Barry "DJ Scratchy" Myers, born in the north of England but raised in North London. I talked to him in 2019, in a café just a few minutes' walk from where the Clash recorded "London Calling."

"Amongst my many memorable DJ moments was playing 'London Calling' that night," he told me. The party was on the second floor, and there were complaints from the fourth (top) floor where Ken — as the city's first mayor was universally known — was having a meeting with the police. "I was asked to turn it down because they could hear the music. At which point, I put on 'London Calling' and cranked it up. Fuck you, Ken." How very London — by an incomer from Salford, via Cockfosters, at the very northern end of the Piccadilly line. Myers called "London Calling" the Clash's zenith; he loved "that it is an anthem without being anthemic. It's not nationalistic. It's a song of defiance without being 'my city above all.'" Unlike, say, Sinatra's "New York, New York," it preserves the "right to be critical: which is essential for humanity to remain humane."

In 2019, the Museum of London marked the song's fortieth birthday with a small but cogent exhibition of significant artifacts, including Strummer's notebooks from 1979 and Simonon's smashed bass from that September night at New York's Palladium. (I was alternately over-busy and out of London at the time. So, embarrassingly, I missed the exhibition.)

Two years after that City Hall celebration and six months before

Strummer died, "London Calling" finally made its debut in a commercial. The decision to allow its use was a close-run thing in the band. Joe Strummer and Paul Simonon outvoted Mick Jones to allow its use in a U.S. ad for the Jaguar X-Type, the archetypally British company's first compact car (starting price $30,000). As the song played, the car moved down a London street. It was cobbled, naturally. (Forewarning for prospective tourists. Very, very few London streets are cobbled.) A young woman stared lovingly as a silver X-Type slid by. She was in a red phone box, of course.

The song was chosen for the Jaguar ad by someone at the Irvine, California office of Young & Rubicam. The agency decided that it fit their campaign, which focused on the "Britishness" of the Jaguar brand. Simon Sproule, Y&R's vice president of communications, explained the basic notion to the *Boston Globe*: that driving a Jaguar "makes you British." The ad — and the song — tested well in focus groups. "Actually, the people listening to things like this in the 1970s are older now," said Sproule. "And maybe they can afford a Jaguar." (Sproule is English, from Hampshire, but took his degree in geography in London. He would have been about ten when "London Calling" came out.)

Those lyrics, though? Nuclear meltdown and an entry-level luxury car, where's the link? Sproule again: "The lyrics are strong. But they're not offensive to anybody. They're strong and angry." (The ad only used an anodyne snippet of the lyrics.) Rob Walker, author of the *Boston Globe* piece: "From an ad-maker's point of view, even the most edgy rock and roll is just so much musical wallpaper."

What about Strummer, what did he think of his song being used to sell cars? His thoughts were posted online. "If you're in a group and you make it together, then everybody deserves something. Especially twenty-odd years after the fact. It just seems churlish for a writer to refuse to have their music used on an advert, and so I figured out, only advertise the things you think are cool. That's why we dissed Coors and Miller. We've turned down loads of money. Millions over the years. But sometimes you have to earn a bit, so everybody gets some." ("London Calling" was originally credited to Strummer/Jones but, at some point, the authorship was extended to all four band members. Share the credit. Share the cash.)

At the same time … *London Calling* was also used as the name of the newsletter of the capital city's branch of Class War, an anarchist grouplet with a flirtatious relationship to violence whose best-known slogan was "Bash the Rich." The newsletter was named in honor of Joe Strummer. Its obituary for him included these words: "A good song is probably worth a hundred books or pamphlets, and the Clash had some fucking good songs." That issue of Class War's periodical offered an "improved range of merchandise" — women's stretch tops, shorts and hooded tops, both summer and winter weight. All featured slogans: "Rob More Banks," "We Must Devastate the Avenues Where the Wealthy Live," that kind of thing. (Even anarchist grouplets need an income stream.) Naturally, the newsletter also contained the kind of members' news you find in any club's circulars. In this case, a thank you "to everyone who made the Xmas Social such a success. The video that was shown, *Incitement to Riot 3 — Insurrection*, should be available very soon." Irony has many graveyards.

And then again …

If our two songs were two sides in a war, it is one they are still fighting. "New York, New York" might have won the economics battle, but "London Calling" is still winning the cultural battle. In June 2019, Extinction Rebellion activists surrounded the Houses of Parliament protesting about the climate emergency. To make their point, the gathered crowd sang "London Calling" to — or, rather, at — the politicians. Somewhere inside the building was Boris Johnson — New York-born, formerly London's second mayor and at that moment maneuvering his way to becoming prime minister. Later that year, campaigning in a general election, he said, in a promotional video, that the Clash was one of his favorite bands. Oddly, they refrained from commenting on that. Even more oddly, it was probably true. It takes an angry man to love an angry band. (It was certainly an angry family. His father, who long lived around the corner from me, once launched an unprovoked and irrational attack on a local vicar at the door of his parish church.)

**City anthems**

So, how have the two songs done as anthems in "real life"? How did they do when times got tough? Have they, as "London Pride" did during WW II, helped carry their cities through life's vicissitudes? Here is an unmatched pair of tales, one for each song.

At the time of the 9/11 attacks, English journalist Zoë Heller was based in New York, writing a weekly column for the (London) *Sunday Times*. Before that, she had been a long-term neighbor of mine in London — though we never so much as nodded at each other in the street. She grew up just a few roads away, the daughter of an American screenwriter who was friends with a friend of mine. She went to the local school; her best-known book, *Notes on a Scandal*, is set in a lightly fictionalized version of it.

In the aftermath of 9/11, she wrote about seeing locals drawing solace and strength from "New York, New York" — in particular, the Big Apple Choir, in pink polo shirts, singing it "super-enunciated, barber-shop style" on the corner of Greenwich and Duane. The song played a similar role in the 2020 Covid pandemic.

And "London Calling," how did that fare on 7/7, when London's transport system was bombed, leaving fifty-six dead? Not at all on the scale of the New York attacks but still a big blow to the city and its citizens. I was in another country that day, but a good friend saw the 24 bus blow up in front of him — its route ends close to where I live. And a friend of a friend lost both legs in one of the three explosions on the Tube.

Was "London Calling" used as a rallying cry in that aftermath? Well, I never saw or heard anything myself, but how about this: On the night of the attacks, there was an event of immediate defiance in central London, with DJ Scratchy at the desks — the same man who DJed for the Clash and was there at that Chicago record store on that day in 1979 when Ray Lowry found and bought the Elvis album that he used as template for the *London Calling* cover. DJ Scratchy played "London Calling" that traumatized night in London. Of course he did. And the crowd — a diverse, mixed one of all ages — sang and danced, punching the ceiling and shouting out the line "I have no fear." A great story and an emblematic one. I've heard it many times, including on the radio. I've told it myself.

But it's not true. It's a myth, promoting Londoners' sense of collective self. How do I know that for sure? I asked DJ Scratchy himself. He'd never even heard the story before and had no recollection of taking part in anything that particular night. If he had, though, "London Calling" would have been right at the top of his list, he told me.

*"Without people you're nothing."*
— JOE STRUMMER

At the end of the final decade of the 20th century, the BBC's World Service launched *Joe Strummer's London Calling*. A half-hour radio show which ran for three years, it featured the singer's completely personal choice of music from all over the globe — from Elvis to Zaire, from Dust Junkies to Ibrahim Ferrer. And that was just the first few tracks in one show.

Each episode opened with an air-raid siren wailing away and Joe shouting out to the world: "All transmitters to full, all receivers to boost. This is London calling." The shows offered a world of music and a public view of his private charm — in part learned in those faraway towns of his diplobrat childhood.

The first show was broadcast on Monday, August 31, 1998 — the last day of that year's Notting Hill Carnival. By the time it aired, Joe would have been watching Carnival from a balcony with, as ever, a beer in one hand, a joint in the other.

His last *London Calling* was broadcast on July 15, 2001. It opened with one of his own songs, which he described as "a dubplate." It was the title track of the final album released in his lifetime, *Global a Go-Go*. The last song he played on that final *London Calling* show was "Beat on the Brat," a tribute to Joey Ramone, who had just died. Joe's last words on that last show were "See you next time."

But that future remained unwritten, to paraphrase one of Joe's most quotable statements, which later inspired the title of the posthumous film biography Julien Temple made about his friend and neighbor. (The nearest thing to Joe's show to be broadcast on BBC radio in the years following his death was knowingly, touchingly named *Culture Clash Radio Show* and presented by his old friend and colleague Don Letts.)

On October 21, 1999, Joe and his Mescaleros played the Astoria on London's Charing Cross Road, on the edge of Soho, whose nighttime streets Joe often patrolled. It was the last time I saw him perform. "London Calling" was the fourteenth song in a sixteen-song set, plus two encores. The crowded house was staggeringly enthusiastic, seemingly as warmly pleased and excited as I was that, after many years away from the main stage, Joe was back in the game. I was right. He would soon again be the big player he had been in his first flush — only he wouldn't be around to appreciate it.

**The final shows**

On November 15, 2002, Strummer played a show with his Mescaleros at Acton Town Hall in West London. It was a benefit for the Fire Brigades Union, whose members were on strike at the time. He was joined onstage by Mick Jones for the first time since the Clash had ended (in acrimony — that final show had been far from home, back in the U.S., at a festival in San Bernardino, California, and way back in time — May 1983. They opened with "London Calling," as ever, and the penultimate number was "Should I Stay or Should I Go?"). The encore at Acton was "London's Burning," of course.

Little more than a month later, Joe died of an undiagnosed heart defect — suddenly, far away from London and below sea level, in his new home in the Somerset Levels. The funeral was back in the city, just north of the Westway, at Kensal Green Cemetery — the same final home as London-loving cleric Sydney Smith and the Queen frontman, Zanzibar-born Freddie Mercury, whose coffin had been carried into the crematorium a decade earlier.

Joe's procession was led by a fire engine. An honor guard of a dozen firefighters stood sentry at the entrance to the chapel. I was there with former Sex Pistols bassist Glen Matlock, who had grown up not far from the cemetery. We had been friends since 1976, when Joe introduced us backstage at a Pistols gig. A few months after that, Joe tried to have me thrown off the *Anarchy* tour bus in Manchester — probably because I'd known him as a private schoolboy, long before he'd become a "punk rocker." Glen, pulling rank as a member of the headline act, countermanded Joe's order, and I was welcomed back on the bus. Now, more than two decades later, the three of us were together in the same room again. It was far from the first time that happened, but it was the last.

Joe's coffin had a guitar-shaped flower display. On it was the (flowery) message "Heaven Calling."

One other thing did stand out. Courtney Love was there, sun-glassed and dressed in full mafia widow's weeds — black and veiled. That much is true. She then threw herself, weeping and screaming, on Joe's coffin. But that isn't true. It's another story I have heard from many others. But it's just not true. I should know. I was in the room when it didn't happen. Sometimes memories are made of lies.

The wake, held right after the funeral, was at a pub called Paradise by Way of Kensal Green. Across the road from the cemetery, it takes its name from the final, deathly but life-affirming lines of G.K. Chesterton's 1913 poem, *The Rolling English Road*. The whole poem is inscribed across the bar front. Those last two lines are:

> *For there is good news yet to hear and fine things to be seen*
> *Before we go to Paradise by way of Kensal Green.*

Joe's final record, the Mescaleros' *Streetcore* album, was released a few weeks later. The last track on it is "Silver and Gold," Strummer's version of a 1960 Fats Domino recording, the final words of which stress that he has to hurry up before he grows too old.

**Ring Ring — "London Calling" here**
When my mobile phone rings, it's the sound of "London Calling" that plays. Those two opening guitar chords, again and again and again, till I answer. Whatever its disadvantages — noisiness and aggressiveness, essentially — it has its advantages, too. That noisiness and aggressiveness, most obviously. But also that no one ever picks it up by mistake, thinking it's their phone.

It wasn't my idea. My son did it without telling me. He fixed the ringtone and waited, patiently. Then he rang me himself, when he wasn't with me. He did a careful job. It is no thin digital hand-me-down. He had recorded it direct from the original vinyl via decent hi-fi speakers — mine, probably. Which means you can hear a "room" in it — not just the Wessex studio but the room my son had used to record it, live, kind of.

It was a real father-son thing. Still is. Every time I get a call, I hear E minor and F major, E minor and F major. E minor and F major, again, again, again. And, every time, I think of my son and my thirty-five-year friendship with the song's singer.

Yes, I have sometimes forgotten to put it on silent — too often, embarrassingly. Yes, it's interrupted a good few meetings and, early on, my son's school concert.

The whole track is on there, I think. But I've always answered it long before the song reaches its sad — tragic almost — ending: the morse code signal for S.O.S., played on guitar by Mick Jones, immediately followed by Joe singing the words "never felt more like…" He stops there, but the following phrase would have had him singing the blues. It's the refrain of Guy Mitchell's transatlantic 1956 hit, "Singing the Blues," which Joe would, I'm certain, have first heard as a young child, on the BBC World Service. "This is London Calling." With a London blues.

### Also available from Trouser Press Books:

**ZIP IT UP!**
The Best of Trouser Press Magazine 1974–1984

**THIS AIN'T NO DISCO:** The Story of CBGB

**MARQUEE:**
The Story of the World's Greatest Music Venue

**TIME HAS COME TODAY:**
Rock and Roll Diaries, 1967 – 2007

**SWEET, WILD AND VICIOUS:**
Listening to Lou Reed and the Velvet Underground

**LOOKING FOR THE MAGIC:**
New York City, the '70s and the Rise of Arista Records

**BACKSTAGE & BEYOND VOLUME 1:**
45 Years of Classic Rock Chats & Rants

**BACKSTAGE & BEYOND VOLUME 2:**
45 Years of Modern Rock Chats & Rants

**BACKSTAGE & BEYOND COMPLETE:**
45 Years of Rock Chats & Rants

**THE BLEECKER STREET TAPES:**
Echoes of Greenwich Village

**ROCK'S IN MY HEAD:**
Encounters With Phil Spector, John & Yoko, Brian Wilson
and a Host of Other People Who Should Be Just As Famous

**MUSIC IN A WORD VOLUMES 1, 2, 3:**
Fifty Years on a Rock and Roll Soapbox

**WANNABEAT:**
Hanging Out ... and Hanging on ... in Baby Beat San Francisco

**MARC BOLAN KILLED IN CRASH:**
A Musical Novel of the 1970s

**KICK IT TILL IT BREAKS:**
A Belated Novel of the 1960s

**KING CAL**

www.trouserpressbooks.com

www.ingramcontent.com/pod-product-compliance
Lightning Source LLC
Chambersburg PA
CBHW071159160426
43196CB00011B/2133